W9-BZL-671

Books by Theodore Solotaroff

The Red Hot Vacuum   1970
Writers and Issues (EDITOR)   1969
An Age of Enormity (EDITOR)   1962

The Red Hot Vacuum

Theodore Solotaroff

THE RED
HOT
VACUUM

and Other Pieces on the Writing of the Sixties

Atheneum   *New York*   1970

Thirteen of these articles originally appeared in BOOK WEEK
and are reprinted by permission of the copyright holder, The
Washington Post Company. The rest of the pieces, with the
exception of "The Red Hot Vacuum," appeared in
THE ATLANTIC MONTHLY, COMMENTARY, and THE NEW REPUBLIC

*In memory of my aunt, **Fanny Weiss Mann***

Acknowledgments

All of these articles, with the exception of "The Red Hot Vacuum," originally appeared in somewhat different form in *Commentary*, the *New York Herald Tribune Book Week*, the *World Journal Tribune Book Week*, the *New Republic*, or the *Atlantic Monthly*, and are reprinted by permission of their respective editors. I also wish to thank Norman Podhoretz, Richard Kluger, R. Z. Sheppard, Robert Evett, and Richard Gilman, who encouraged me to write them, and who bore with my doubts and delays. Finally, I have a special debt to Sherry Abel, Norman Maclean, and Hugh Hostetler.

Preface

The essays and reviews in this collection were all written during the past ten years. Throughout this period I was mainly employed as a magazine editor. (Someone who is in a position to make the suggestion has said that the most apt title for the book would be "Moonlighting Through the Sixties.") Like most literary journalism that I know about, these pieces were written under the gun of a deadline by a tired and more or less desperate man who was putting the words down and hoping for the best. The last thought he had in his mind was that they would some day have to stand together in a book.

Before I became an editor I was a graduate student and an English teacher. Just as I applied, *faute de mieux*, what I had learned from correcting freshman themes to editing magazine articles, so I learned best how to talk about books and writers through teaching students whose passion for literature and faith in its relevance could hardly be assumed. This need to say something interesting as a teacher helped to alleviate the narrowness that graduate students acquire along with their expertise and provided a kind of model for addressing the so-called "common reader" or "general audience." Perhaps the main thing I learned from teaching was to look for what might be a common ground of experience and then use the book to illuminate it. At the same time, I was also getting a pretty rigorous training in close reading at the University of Chicago, the main point of which was that a book was an individual whole and that you could not say much about it until you understood its structure—its principle of being what it was and not something else. In teaching, and then in journalism, I tried to fit these two lines of inquiry together, with the one guarding against the excesses of the other. Occasionally, too, I was to put my rusting research tools to work, as in the studies of the reception of Harry Golden and of Katherine Anne Porter's *Ship of Fools*.

All of which is partly responsible for the tone of most of these pieces: a certain didacticism aspiring to liveliness. This tone was probably further reinforced by my work as an editor. Being a magazine editor, as I soon found out, was not unlike being a teacher, though perhaps for one of those courses that are given on TV. You were trying to reach a large, vague, heterogeneous audience and to establish a particular direction and level of awareness. Moreover, being an editor provided a general subject to explore in my own writing. Because I worked on literary/intellectual journals—whether *Commentary* or the former *Book Week* or *New American Review*—I was concerned in an almost daily way with the new initiatives and options, the new problems and perplexities that marked the writing and thought of the Sixties. Generally speaking, it was a period in which the literary consensus, like the political and social ones, broke apart and began to fly off in various directions. The great modern writers were no longer quite like some rich and powerful father who went on ruling the family from the grave. Their departure as strongly felt presences, along with the decline of the literary journals that preserved their hegemony and maintained a community of writing around it, left the literary scene both much more open and much more uncertain. The characteristic work that began to emerge no longer had Hemingway or Eliot or Kafka in its bones, but rather a kind of feverish present-mindedness and self-absorption. Similarly, the market for serious writing cracked open in the Sixties and soon became a kind of howling forum where all manners of ideas, styles and standards contended for attention. As the literary climate altered radically, there was a distinct shift among writers and editors from a preoccupation with values as the ground of experience to a preoccupation with experience as the ground of values— a shift that was, of course, to be felt everywhere in America as the decade of opposition and revision careened along. For those, like myself, who entered the Sixties wedded to their values, the more or less standard ones of academic liberalism and humanism, but quite out of touch with their own experience, this breaking of the ice was alternately exhilarating and dismaying: one felt stirred but also swamped.

As an editor, I could have avoided involvement in these matters only by refusing to open my mail and by soliciting material from the dwindling group of writers who still remained firmly plugged into the past. At the same time, being an editor meant acting as a kind of middleman for other men's transactions with the age. This could be extremely instructive at times, but it could also become personally burdensome and disorienting, a kind of overload of perspectives. Also, by the kind of psychic economy that editors adopt to function within the policies and image of the journal they work for, my daily duties tended in time to depersonalize and dull my own awareness, impeding the development of new convictions as well as springing the tensions of those I still held.

So my own literary journalism became a way of responding somewhat more directly and individually to the altered environment of letters and, inevitably, to the political, social and cultural developments that related to it. More importantly, these articles, along with several non-literary ones that I have not included in this book, became a way of letting into my work some of the impact of the drastic changes that took place in my private life, some of the truths that had come with the blows. Twice during the past decade my pat-

tern of living and feeling foundered, and the consciousness
that broke through pressed for expression. I lodged most of it
elsewhere, but still it inevitably conditioned my interests and
ways as a reader. And since I was trying to become as faithful
as I could in my reviewing to the responses of the man who
had read the book, I was pushed to indicate something of
their changing personal ground. This was hard to do because,
as I said earlier, I felt a responsibility to the book or author;
also, I had habits of diffidence and evasiveness to break; also,
I was wary of the cult of ego that seemed to be springing up
everywhere. Often enough I didn't succeed very well, but near
the end I began to get a firmer grip on this conflict of approach, and to come a little cleaner, a little clearer, I think,
in learning how to use that most difficult word in the writer's
vocabulary, according to Gide—the word "I." Moreover, I
continued to find writers who were facing the same "strangeness of discontinuity," in Saul Bellow's haunting phrase, that
I felt in myself and who were attempting to wrest from it a
freer and more accurate attitude toward their own experience.
As such, they helped me to take this feeling seriously and
provided a sense of direction through the mixed conditions
of activity and emptiness that I encountered amid the changes
of the Sixties.

T.S.

March 1970

Contents

xii

The Red Hot Vacuum

The Spirit of Isaac Rosenfeld

That which dies acquires a life of its own." The statement, made by Isaac Rosenfeld himself in one of his stories, describes what has happened since the evening of July 12, 1956, when he died suddenly of a heart attack at the age of thirty-eight. The image of him that survives today has all but detached itself from his gifts and significance as a writer of criticism and fiction and embodies instead his uniquely affecting presence: the wise and tender, the charming and fated "Isaac." In those circles—mainly in New York and Chicago and Minneapolis—where he is still intensely remembered as the Greenwich Village seer, or the academic bohemian, or the quintessential American Jewish intellectual, his character and life have taken on the aura of a legend. One talks to people who knew him and they speak his name in a special way, as though the word "Isaac" were precious and had incantatory power—a way of recalling not only the man but something valuable in themselves.

Nor did one have to know Rosenfeld to be affected in this way. Reading his criticism, as I began to do after leaving college, was almost always an experience—a lesson in what it meant to be personal as well as educated, straight as well as sophisticated. As one does in such cases, I invented a figure to fit the voice and the name: a tall, powerful, inward Russian Jew. Some of my details turned out to be pretty wide of the

mark, for behind that warm, masculine tone was in fact a
pale, chubby *luftmensch* gazing quizzically over the top of his
glasses like a figure out of the Yiddish renaissance. However,
the substance of my image was accurate, deriving as it did
from the signature of his character on each page he wrote, a
strength of heart and mind that communicated itself even
when the level of the discussion was somewhat over my
head. Responding to his charisma and adopting him as
my special mentor, I was behaving no differently from the
group of his students at the University of Minnesota who, I
am told, used to trail him around the campus.

I begin with these matters because they seem to me important. Rosenfeld's appeal, particularly as a critic, comes in
good part from the ability, rare in modern criticism, to make
one *listen* by expressing himself directly. This ability was the
result of personality as well as of precept, an open, vulnerable
engagement of his nature that differed little from his way of
relating to people and that he was no more able to avoid than
to fake. However, he was also acting on a principle—that a
judgment of a book or a writer, like that of a life, was an
individual act: to be impersonal was to be evasive. He did not
believe for a moment in T. S. Eliot's influential notion that
literature was an "escape from personality"; his writing was
rather a test of it, a way of putting his reactions, and ultimately his values, through the fire of honesty and clarity. The
quality he most admired was what he called *Innerlichkeit*,
or inwardness—the imaginative self-awareness that formed
the true relation between subject and object and between
the experience of the man and the identity of the writer.
From the acknowledgment—rather than the evasion—of personality he drew his detachment.

Passage from Home, Rosenfeld's first novel, is a study in
the development of his inwardness—the story of a boy-
philosopher, "sensitive as a burn," whose moral intuitions are
the more remarkably sophisticated as his actual experience of
life is limited, even relatively retarded. A child of the tidy and

solemn and self-enclosed life of a petit-bourgeois family on Chicago's Jewish West Side, Bernard describes himself at the age of fifteen as a "fervent but rigid little boy, nervous, fastidious, plagued by a sense of order and propriety." But his imagination is that of a rebel, and not very far from the drab streets of home is the Near North Side where his Aunt Minna lives in splendid bohemian isolation from the family.

In time, Bernard runs away from home to live with Minna and her lover. However, he discovers that his aunt's sacred "freedom" contains little more than bitterness, and in her tense and sloppy relations with life he eventually detects more misery and waste than there is in the depressive, cautionary moralism of his father's world to which he returns in the end. His "actual longing," he finds, "looked neither to home nor exile, but to a life foreign to both in which some beauty and freedom prevailed." Bernard has at least one glimpse of the quality of this life when he goes to the home of a Hasidic Rebbe with his grandfather and sees the face of the cranky, ineffectual old man grow radiant with joy and dignity in sharing the wisdom of Reb Feldman and the ecstatic dancing of his followers. Later Bernard realizes that it is for these transcendent moments of true understanding and true connection that one must live. In a remarkable passage toward the end of the novel, he sees the alternative spelled out as he sits in a conservatory in which tropical plants are kept. He senses that these plants have a "much stronger and more ponderous grasp of life" than he does, and that beside them his own existence seems "ailing and cold . . . a form of death." At the same time, whatever little life he has in himself is also merely part of their blind, unconscious cycle of growth and decay, and subject to the same process of "meaningless non-being, counting for nothing."

The autobiographical ground of *Passage from Home* is particularly apparent at the points of emphasis where character and theme intersect. Rosenfeld, like his young hero, felt that values must derive from nature as well as transcend its blind and indifferent course. Like Bernard's encounter with the plants, this was a matter of experience rather than theory; as Rosenfeld later wrote: "The natural derivation of value must be experienced directly, the dependence of everything on nature must be felt concretely within one's own life, before naturalism can be anything more than an attitude and a superficial one at that." Similarly, Bernard's early grasp of his "homelessness" in the world, his glimpses of the "divided and alien aspect" of life—"that empty space which . . . stretched between person and person, between ignorance and knowledge, between one hand and the other"—were, for Rosenfeld, some of the primary facts of his own identity. From them came his abiding preoccupation with the problems of human ties and self-integration. Bernard also shares his creator's efforts to feel more directly and deeply, to define his life and its quality by his emotional attachments. Or again, the boy's notion of a freedom beyond self-indulgence, one that must be fought for against inner fluidity, inhibition, and compromise, underlies Rosenfeld's prolonged struggle toward the same end.

Finally, there are the terms of Bernard's passage from home, which stand as a paradigm of Rosenfeld's own journey —that is, from the restraints of the parochial Jewish culture and the "essential sadness" of its life, to the "freedom of the world without God against which we shut our doors," and the effort to find in this world a measure of both natural and spiritual satisfaction. But what gives this journey its special character is precisely the fact that it never ended. Just as Bernard's "passage" involves a telling experience of Jewish mysticism and the realization that he resembles more than anything else the father he has fled, so Rosenfeld's character and writing involve a to-fro relationship between what he called "Jewish intellectualism" and a type of Reichian bohemianism.

In 1941 Rosenfeld left Chicago and came to New York. He was twenty-three, recently married, and starting on a fellowship in philosophy at N.Y.U. Within a year he gave up school to become an editor at the *New Republic*. By the end of 1943 he had established himself as a literary journalist of the first rank, a fiction writer of unusual promise, and one of the key representatives of the post-Marxist, post-Depression temperament.

Rosenfeld's response to his fortune was to leave the *New Republic* after a year and take a job on a barge in the East River. After that, he lived in the Village and went his own way. The self-image that he sought to preserve and assert was that of the marginal man who stands at a necessary remove from all entanglements foreign to his nature, of the uprooted intellectual who comes to rest at a position only to move on again. Like many writers of his period, he described his condition as one of alienation. He would have preferred a time and a culture when a writer was able to speak for his people, to identify his consciousness with theirs. He had had a taste of some such solidarity during the late Thirties and had seen it operating in the fiction of a folk-artist like Sholem Aleichem on which he had been raised. However, the dehumanizing society he saw himself living in during and after the war offered no role to the writer which he did not think was disastrous, and he saw no other resource for the writer in an "age of enormity" than his own humanity. This he kept alive and concrete by being "the man whom one encounters when there is no longer any uniform to wear . . . the man who is naked, who is alone, and the man who pretty much of the time is afraid: the man who sees himself as he really is in this flesh and in these bones and in these feelings, in these impulses, in these emotions. . . ." Such a man had no social role, only a positive commitment to being alive—that is, to the perspective of his own experience, to the satisfaction of his natural desires, and to the consciousness and truth that could be found even in our artificial and fearful times. The commitment to this image of himself shaped his daily life— that of a steadfast and eventually irreversible non-conformity

—and also his symbolic life—that of a free seeker whose fate would be "either an adventure or a crack-up of the spirit." It proved to be both.

From the start, he thought of himself as primarily a writer of fiction, but his strongest and most original writing was generally to be found in his criticism. Most of his stories, like *Passage from Home*, were analytic rather than descriptive and dramatic—intricate, well lighted, but rather colorless. His fictional imagination was introspective and symbolic, and it was best at producing an air of reality when it was freed from representing the daily world. His two best stories—"The Hand That Fed Me" and "King Solomon," the one at the start of his career, the other at the end—were freely imagined and powerfully felt studies in self-characterization. Naturally drawn to Kafka and his philosophical parables of alienation, he also tried to develop the intuitive and manifold grasp of life that he admired in Tolstoy, and his career in fiction, like his character, involved a prolonged conflict between his predisposition for and skill at dialectic and his insistence upon the primacy of feeling. At the back of his fiction was often a series of luminous ideas about his experience that were struggling unsuccessfully to become an intuitive feeling.

Even in his earliest book reviews there was seldom any sense of this struggle. Given a book, he quickly saw its salient characteristics, the general point to be developed from them, and the precise emotional tone that his judgment should carry. This was true whether he was discussing the technique of Nancy Hale or Kenneth Patchen, the world of Jean Malaquais or Sholem Aleichem, the aesthetics of Kenneth Burke or the problems of philosophical naturalism. As a literary critic he was noticeably freer of preconception and influence than he was in his fiction, and his sensibility operated usually in a more truly personal and vivid way. His aim was to restore the "confidence, within our right, to take a simply human measure of literature," and so his own humanity was always at stake, the source of his attitudes and tone. While the discipline of letters after the war was everywhere becoming concerned with the detection of subtlety and order, and the influential critics were busy with the canons of explication that released in a jet of analysis those meanings that our age still loves to constantly rediscover and re-encapsulate, Rosenfeld's abiding concern was for "the plain fact, the plain reality of human life," as it was captured or missed or compromised by a writer. His method, if he can be said to have had one, was Sainte-Beuve's principle that criticism is "justness of characterization." He tended to work from a close description of the writer's image of experience, and mainly by "taking a good look," as he liked to say, at the literary and moral values that shaped this image, he usually made his way to the center of the book under discussion and of the writer's *oeuvre*, often within 1,000 words. How much of inner or social actuality was a Henry Miller or a Henry Green or a John O'Hara able to grasp by means of the attitudes with which each approached and represented experience; how deep did they go in their judgments of it? These were the typical questions Rosenfeld asked and answered. In his explication and judgment of the character—the moral-aesthetic core—of a book, he was aided by a classical critical style—simple, limpid, but with great power of definition and concentration. Into this style flowed much of his nature—his directness and subtlety, his wit and earnestness, his taste for dialectic and concreteness, his irony and his love.

For all of his individuality, though, Rosenfeld's critical imagination was broadly typical of the literary temperament that he found in New York: the firm, terse, intellectually ambitious prose, the fluent, sophisticated breadth of reference, the concreteness of idea—political to the core—the taste for epigram. It was a style, as Seymour Krim has recently pointed out, that young Jewish writers in particular aspired to control, and during the 1940's a good number of them succeeded. Besides Rosenfeld there were Saul Bellow, Delmore Schwartz, Alfred Kazin, Irving Howe, Leslie Fiedler, Robert Warshow, to name only some of the more prominent ones. Their backgrounds in lower- or middle-class Jewish life gave them certain similarities in attitude and ambition that have come to be discussed a good deal in recent years; but perhaps more crucial to their work was the legacy of political and social awareness that they had brought from the 1930's, and their common search for direction in the dark and lonely years of the early 1940's.

Like many of these young writers who came out of the Depression, Rosenfeld had learned, as he says, "through political activity, to admire the vigor which a social orientation will impart to thought," and from the start his criticism was given urgency and point by his consciousness of what a given book was saying—implicitly and unconsciously as well as explicitly—about the times. He took positions, committed himself; his mind was most political in the sense that he distrusted "wisdom without thesis—the inexpensive kind." But if the young Rosenfeld's experience as a Trotskyite had made him aware of the traction and thrust of radical ideas, it had also made him aware of the ironies of accepting them. As he put it in his early story, "The Party":

> To us has been willed also a fortune; as yet it has no
> value except in our own circle. . . . But what a fortune
> —the whole world!—Some day the world may actually
> fall into our hands! Then where would we run?

The thought and the tone were typical. Where to go now? What to live for? These became the leading questions as the "economic crisis" of the Thirties faded into the "moral crisis" of the Forties and "the alienation of the masses" was changed by the war psychology and the war economy into the "alienation of the individual." This is the period of *Partisan Review's* series on "The New Failure of Nerve," of Bellow's *Dangling Man*, of Rosenfeld's story "The Hand That Fed Me." The last is a complex evocation of the new underground man. It is made up of a series of unanswered letters from a young Jewish intellectual—whom the end of the Writers' Project and the coming of the war have made "irrelevant"—to a working-class girl from a Russian family who had flirted with him a few years before at a WPA office and then suddenly dropped him, as he believes, for a dull but successful white-collar man. The political parable here is fused with a social one—the Jewish boy who goes on carrying a torch for a Gentile girl, hurling at her indifference his protests and solicitations, now proud and then humble, now demanding that attention be paid to his injuries, then offering himself all over again. The third theme of the story is the unfolding of Feigenbaum's present desolation as one of the "bare, pared, essential" men, desperately in need of some sense of personal meaning and hope, who says near the end, on a note of rock-bottom existentialist awareness: "For that is happiness: The conviction that something is necessary." In all of the irony and sadness of his situation, Feigenbaum concludes:

> Be gentle to the unfulfilled, be good to it. We are accustomed to sing the joys of the happy and fulfilled men. Let us also learn to sing of the desolate, the empty men. Theirs is the necessity without the fulfillment, but it is possible that even to them—who knows—some joy may come.

In the tone of the story, Jewish sensibility fuses with the new existentialist one: for example, the little question "who knows" tucked into Feigenbaum's bitter analysis of his aloneness and freedom. In the early 1940's the situation of the contemporary Jew adrift in a Gentile society could be felt as a parallel to the aloneness of the artist and the radical in a prosperous mass society. "As a member of an internationally insecure group," Rosenfeld wrote of the Jew in 1944, "he has grown personally acquainted with some of the fundamental themes of insecurity that run through modern literature. He is a specialist in alienation (the one international banking system the Jews actually control)." But Feigenbaum's position on the extreme also provides a "comfort" that as a Jew he knows in his veins. His wacky little "who knows" comes like a murmur from the past, a remnant of a long tradition of hope in misery, of the shrug between adversities, that characterized a people who accepted suffering rather than anything short of complete deliverance. Similarly, Feigenbaum's final statement to the girl ("But God, if you only knew, if you only knew how willing I am—always—to take the risk of my happiness!") is another ground-note of a religious culture which, as Rosenfeld wrote of Sholem Aleichem's comedy of endurance, had never learned in its unremitting hunger for *Eretz Yisroel* "to rationalize adaptation to the world." To the extent that he holds out, delivers himself up to the fantasy of his desires, insists on receiving nothing short of full gratification and transcendence, Feigenbaum is a true son of East European Jewry, among his other roles. And he resembles his creator in nothing so much as his faithfulness to the saving image of his expectations and what he was willing to endure for it.

Like his unsuccessful alter-ego, Feignenbaum, Rosenfeld was obsessed for many years by the familiar Jewish theme of salvation—or what Harold Rosenberg, in a brilliant reading of Jewish character, once called "the Jewish vertigo." Naturalist that he was, Rosenfeld saw the way out of the underground not through Jewish faith in another, redemptive place but through the satisfaction of his sexual desires. But he was a mystic for all that—and a Jewish one. He tried to bridge the gap between alienation and connection, depression and joy, secularism and transcendence, through the flesh rather than through religious experience, and he found his mentor in Wilhelm Reich. However, Rosenfeld's Reichianism, under the inevitable conditioning of his character, often reads as much like Hasidism. "To love all love," he writes at one point in his journal, "even the beloved partner's love for another. For then we see the world spelled out in letters of flame."

In the meantime he wrote his criticism from the point of view of man trying to remain level with his generation's experience and casting about for signs of life, awareness, moral initiative in the cultural doldrums that had followed, in William Phillips' words, "the utter breakdown of values and distinctions and a failure of the will to independent radical expression." Rosenfeld believed that philosophical naturalism offered the best ground for the reconstruction of values, but that it would first have to go beyond the finicky and narrow rationalism in which it was bogged down. In the contribution of Hook, Nagel, and Dewey to the "Failure of Nerve" symposium, he saw the failure of naturalism to confront the motives for the growing allegiance to the obscurantism and consolations of religion by dealing with the contemporary yearning for belief "as an illegitimate form of inference." He believed that naturalism "must be liberated, broadened, and extended over the regions in which the dominant anxieties of our time have grown." Further, it must attend to, not simply deplore, the irrational in man as a dominant factor in human personality. Finally, he noted that orthodox naturalism in its adherence to the methods of science had missed "the richness, the variety, pleasure, tragedy, the sheer possibility of existence," and that in its increasing commitment to the analysis rather than the assertion of values there lay its own failure of nerve, or, as he put it, "failure of verve."

Besides its methodology, then, naturalism required what he called "the full moral temperament" to provide the motive and imagination for its doctrines. In the fiction he was sent to review he saw much the same problem: a preoccupation with literary method or style, if not merely with the writer's own ego, a narrowed range of moral awareness and judgment. Again, what was needed was the inwardness and comprehensiveness of temperament that would allow the writer to grasp and respond to the daily losses that all defensible values were suffering, and a renewed vitality that came from the struggle for affirmation. The artist's primary task as he wrote in 1944, was "to bring together the human and animal in man, to make an imaginative synthesis of what society has dismembered." In the work of Nancy Hale or Irwin Shaw or John O'Hara, on the one hand, and of Henry Miller or Kenneth Patchen, on the other, he saw little of this synthesis, or little chance of it. In the first case the human animal was reduced to his behavior, in the second to his fantasies and sensations. In general, the problem of the fiction writer could be summed up as follows:

> You have a story to tell and you sit down to write it, and you might as well be wood for all the place there is in modern fiction for the fact that you are human. You are either hard-boiled or hysterical; you are either a grim little behaviorist, as objective as a sack of nails, or a natural gusher with a wild mouth or snakes in your hair. . . . Choose either pose and say nothing. Or choose surrealism and go to sleep.

In fictional terms, the problem was the reconstruction of character. "Character"—whether in the conventional literary sense or as the writer's self-portrayal—was for Rosenfeld not only the essential element of fiction but also the most telling test of the writer's intelligence and passion, of his capacity for understanding and judging the world. Thus the trouble with Irwin Shaw was that his characters were constructed from a false sophistication, a tissue of Freudian and liberal platitudes in the service of the "guts and dry Martini" attitudes to life, and from an affirmation that begins by accepting "nearly everything as it is." In a British novelist like Charles Williams the characters were weak because they were made up completely of writing or "sensibility" in the service of a fastidious piety. "Gross distinctions [such as that between life and death] did not concern him," Rosenfeld writes of Williams. "His was too fine a sensibility to be impressed by anything obvious."

Rosenfeld's own attitudes about alienation and freedom led him to the example of Kafka, whose alienated men were cast whole, despite their creator's full recognition of the modern forces of fragmentation that operated outside and within them. What also drew Rosenfeld to Kafka was the comprehensiveness of his art and the singleness of his purpose: his struggle to arrive at a "purely human freedom," wrested from all the obstacles of the external world and of the self. By his genius for combining and unifying disparate traits of experience, Kafka had created characters of such thick and complex texture that a figure like K. could stand for theological, moral, psychological, social, and even political man; but even so, Kafka's description of human nature was seen to be complete only when one grasped that its "final cause" was the assertion of man's irreducible freedom.

Such an affirmation appealed deeply to Rosenfeld. So, too, did Kafka's method in its marriage of storytelling and a philosophical order of thought. And there must also have been an equally deep attachment to this lonely, transcendent art produced by another uprooted Jew, who had been able to sublimate his own and his people's needs and terrors into an absolute statement of the human crisis; here Rosenfeld found the ghetto sensibility, which he himself loved, with all its hallucinations and ironies both intact and transformed, reaching outward in Kafka's parables to comprehend and redeem the broken moral order of Europe.

During the later Forties, Kafka became a particularly relevant figure in this last respect. In 1943 Rosenfeld had written that the recent sufferings of the Jews would lead their writers "to make certain inevitable moral discoveries. These discoveries, enough to indict the world, may also be crucial to its salvation." In the ensuing five years, as the first reports of the Nazi death camps mounted and later the memoirs and studies began to be published, Rosenfeld himself was making the discoveries he had predicted. In 1948 he published a review of Jacob Pat's *Ashes and Fire* in which he argued that our "numbness" when confronted by reports of the screams of the dying Jews made us "no different from the murderers who went ahead and did their business and paid no attention to the screams." His point was that to acknowledge the facts in full, both of the screaming and of the numbness, was to realize that the fundamental reality of Western culture was now one of terror. All the rest was the blindness of wishful thinking, the comforts of complacence—especially the liberal assumption that the slaughter lay "within the realm of the explainable, the workable, the preventable"—that is, of the old morality of good and evil. Another book he reviewed, on the Soviet labor camps, provided but another text for the moral.

In an essay of the following year titled "The Meaning of Terror," Rosenfeld developed his proposition that terror had become the main reality by examining the current state of culture. One recognizes today in his moments of truth that a civilization which killed six million innocent Jews yesterday, or used the atom bomb on the civilian population of a defeated enemy, may very well allow sixty million on each side to die tomorrow—and that no traditional culture survives the abrogation of its canons of good and evil. To Rosenfeld this truth was already perfectly clear in 1949:

> War is the model enterprise and the model form of communality. These are abstract propositions, but even so they are obvious; when we fill them in with experience, they are overwhelming. Unfortunately, there is nothing else into which we can fit our experience—traditions are broken and culture is unavailable. Our culture is an empty form, standing for a continuity of experience which is now discontinued, for the reality and inviolability of human values that are everywhere violated and denied. . . . Today the cultured man is isolated . . . the cultural form that conveyed humanity and assured the transaction from one man to the next has been destroyed.

To bear witness to these facts was essential, if our sense of humanity was to remain concrete and a culture be initiated that conformed again to men's experience. But with this knowledge of terror beyond evil, one was led to give up the old and equally compromised and useless notions of good and to realize that the only basis of renewal lay in a "joy beyond good." The ground of this joy was a radical humanism nurtured by the development of "a new capacity, proof against terror, to experience our natural life to the full."

During the latter part of the Forties, Rosenfeld worked on a novel that incorporated his Reichian analysis of terror and joy in a Kafkaesque method and perspective. *The Enemy* (of which three sections have been published*) begins in a setting of prolonged and indefinite war; its hero, a pleasant intellectual named Brigadier, has been given the task of determining the nature of the enemy. When conventional methods—observation and interrogation, then torture and murder—are found to be unavailing, Brigadier disguises himself and under the name of Pathfinder travels into the country of the enemy to acquire definitive information. But the nature of the enemy remains obscure depite his best efforts; the intelligence he collects is mainly about himself, derived in good part from his experiences with asceticism and sex along the way. In time the landscapes of repression—stockade and monastery—give way to those of liberation—peaceful towns, green woods, and running water, and Pathfinder enters the kingdom of his desires.

The Enemy was completed in 1951. The three published sections are deeply conceived and beautifully written, but the novel was rejected by Rosenfeld's publisher, and then by others. Whatever the publishers' reasons for rejecting it, by 1951 it was no longer a very "topical" book. The Kafka vogue had run its course; Reichianism was taking on an increasingly crackpot aura; and, more importantly, the sense of the age had turned. *Commentary*, which in its beginnings, in 1946, published a symposium on the crisis and alienation of the

---

* "The Brigadier," *Partisan Review* (March-April 1947); "In the Monastery," *Kenyon Review* (Summer 1951); "In the Holy City," *New World Writing 20* (Lippincott).

individual, was by 1949 asking its writers if the anti-Semitic tradition in English and American literature blocked their "full participation and integration in the tradition." The next year *Partisan Review* was asking its contributors if they felt that culture could exist without a positive religion (a far cry from the tenor of the "Failure of Nerve" series of 1944). And in 1952 came its famous symposium "Our Country and Our Culture," whose keynote was the reaffirmation and rediscovery of America. What all of this, and more, bespoke was a new political and social orientation on the part of the old radical intellectuals which, in 1946, Rosenfeld had described as the shift from Marx to Freud, from "change the world" to "adjust yourself to it." He saw it as an orientation that "blesses the bourgeois in all of us" by shifting the perspective from a radical and historical understanding of contemporary society to one of accommodation and apologetics and by trading in the lonely sense of differences for the "ecstasy of belonging."

This was not the way out of the "terror," and Rosenfeld resisted it. If indeed the end of alienation had arrived, why this was simply because society had fulfilled the intellectuals' worst fears and expectations, thereby ending their sense of being outside of it. He did not worry about the problems of integrating and participating as a Jewish writer ("So they won't name any streets after me"). He held out against the refuge of religion and took the risks of the margin of freedom he guarded against the encroachment of an increasingly mass-minded age. In 1952 he left Greenwich Village and went away to teach at a university, but he did not confuse its quiet atmosphere, its orderly intellectual interests, its highly developed manners with the different tone of American life and culture outside the academy. The new interest in social codes and manners that had gone hand-in-hand with the embourgeoisement of the old radicalism seemed to him largely beside the point, whether of fiction or of contemporary society. Responding to Lionel Trilling's idea that manners were indis-

pensable to the novelist for the "hum and buzz of implication" they gave to character, Rosenfeld described this argument as a "variant of the old claim for the necessity of
traditional society" which was becoming popular again in the
academy. "Within its shelter," he wrote, "the hum and buzz
of implication can still be made out. Off-campus an age of
enormity is in full riot and the roaring in the ears is bloody
murder."

In such an age the only way forward, Rosenfeld insisted,
more forcefully than ever, was through the exploration of the
self and its potential for autonomy and growth. One sees in
the later criticsim—of Hemingway, Faulkner, Orwell, Henry
Green, Gandhi, Cahan, Simone Weil, Stendhal, Sartre, and
others—a deepening of both the natural and moral perspective of inwardness, a more patient and radical effort to
analyze literature, politics, and religion in terms of their life-
giving or life-denying possibilities for the individual. In his
literary criticism Rosenfeld continued to rely a good deal on
the analysis of character—both of the personages and of the
writer himself—as it reveals the writer's grasp of experience,
but this too was carried on at a deeper level and with a more
explicit attempt to explore the relationships that linked instinctual drives, strength of feeling, and force of values.

His main interest came to center in such figures as Gandhi
and Tolstoy who had succeeded in transcending their limits
by a sustained action of will, imagination, and feeling that
carried them beyond the habits of their personalities into a
new domain of personal freedom and power. In the achievement of "self-realization beyond the ego" he found the
sources of Gandhi's triumph over politics along with his capacity for love and joy that had survived what seemed to be a
crippling inner life. Judging by the opening section of a book
on Tolstoy that he began writing in the early 1950's, Rosenfeld was embarking on a similar investigation of Tolstoy's
style. He felt that the sources of the great Russian novelist's
power over life and art derived from the continual enounters

of a strong sexual nature and a no less strong religious one, which drove Tolstoy to fuse nature with morality in his work and, by-passing the struggles of the ego, to give himself up to his grasp of the great themes of existence. Similarly, he saw that Orwell's approaching death had had the effect of forcing the writer of 1984 to surrender his "life-long image, the character and style and habits of reason and restraint," and by the force of his passion and imagination to "express the totalitarian agony out of his own."

To acknowledge one's instinctual life, to educate the feelings, to be thoroughly on to one's self; to understand the moral "fall-out" of recent history—the small steady doses of heartlessness and untruth—and oppose its poisoning of the spirit by the force of one's desires and intelligence and hope —so Rosenfeld continued to live and to write. He found a positive example in Stendhal; a negative one in Hemingway; a mixed one in Faulkner, Sartre, Simone Weil. In his own fiction he was trying to break away from the large, symbolic design of Kafka and write about his own experience in the world in more immediately concrete ways. However, after 1952 his fiction, like his criticism, went slowly and fitfully. The rejection of *The Enemy* was a serious as well as bewildering setback and he was a long time recovering. He had not used his early success to armor himself against the possibilities of failure, and he remained an indifferent caretaker of his career. Also these were the years of "the fat gods," in Saul Bellow's phrase. It was not a period that Rosenfeld felt at home in, and he fought against it, as Bellow saw, trying to maintain his faith in "health, naturalism, the joy of love, the preservation of secular culture." According to Bellow, he paid the price in "boredom and deadness, despair, even madness."

Bellow believes that he won in the end, and there is some indication of that in his writing. In the last year of his life he wrote his best piece of fiction—a story about a king, a rather nondescript and homely Jew, to whom both love and wisdom came easily. In his Solomon, Rosenfeld was able to create a character who embodied Feigenbaum's anguished assertion of ten years before—that "some men are capable of rising out of their own lives. . . . Their only secret is a tremendous willingness—they do not struggle with themselves." I suspect that the creator of both characters was approaching this much peace after the long passage that had lain between them. Similarly, his last few reviews and articles have a simpler touch, an even more direct sense of the man who wished to write "so truthfully that only I, as I actually am, will appear on the page." However, Rosenfeld was an individual who, to use a phrase of Silone's he liked to quote, "was coming from far and going far," and there is little point in trying to determine which path he was on when he died.

He had left Minnesota after two years and was teaching adult education in Chicago when his life ended where it had begun: a death that came abruptly and found him alone. Otherwise, he died as he had lived—amid the disorder of provisional arrangements, manuscripts, and fresh plans. At the end of a piece on Chicago which he was just completing at the time, he advised the reader to look "for the everlasting in the ephemeral things":

> not in iron, stone, brick, concrete, steel, and chrome, but in paper, ink, pigment, sound, voice, gesture, and graceful leaping, for it is of such things that the ultimate realities, of the mind and heart, are made.

(1962)

"All That Cellar-Deep Jazz":
Henry Miller and Seymour Krim

The times seem to have caught up with Henry Miller, not only in the sexual sophistication that permits the recent publication of *Tropic of Cancer*, but in the further respect of often seeming as disordered and disposable as he was claiming modern life to be in the early 1930's. If in 1934, the year of *Cancer's* publication, it was histrionic to call for and accept the imminent destruction of civilization, Miller has lived on to see his political and social maledictions gain in plausibility, so that he now appears on the scene as a prophet with a certain grisly honor. Moreover, the literary extremism of *Cancer* ties in with the recent revival of the romantic impulse, particularly the more unrestrained attempts to respond to—or swing with—the times. Karl Shapiro's rather frantic introduction to the Grove Press edition of the book suggests some of the reasons why Miller has not only been serving as one of the father figures of the Beat writers but also as a Vergil to more sophisticated writers, like Shapiro himself, who, having been brought to an impasse by the modern literary sin of intellectual pride, are following Miller's lead to liberate their creative selves by a journey into their own tropics of cancer.

In *The World of Sex*, Miller describes the central concern of *Cancer* as being "not with sex, nor with religion, but with the problem of self-liberation." A son of the German-

American middle class ("They were painfully clean," he writes in *Tropic of Capricorn*. "Never once had they opened the door which leads to the soul. . . ."), Miller was an employment manager at Western Union until one day when he walked out, determined to alter his life once and for all. A few years later, at the age of thirty-nine, he settled—if that's the word—in Paris, where the expatriate colony, following the Crash of 1929, had dwindled away to a hard core made up (as George Orwell put it) "partly of genuine artists and partly of scoundrels."

Tropic of Cancer records by a mixed method of narrative and spontaneous notation Miller's more characteristic experiences and meditations during the next two years of liberating himself in the dingy twilight zone of the Montmartre slums. Some of his friends feed him; others put him up if the other half of their bed happens to be vacant. Now and then he stumbles on a good thing—a period of steady work as a proofreader, an affair with a wealthy woman, a few months of living with an open-handed young American. But for the most part he drifts on an empty stomach, his eyes attracted by the "sinister splendor . . . [of] certain leprous streets," his nose lifted resolutely to the rancid odors of poverty, his ears tuned to the gurgling of the urinals, and his mind reeling with the impressions of a Brooklyn bohemian amid the ruins of Europe. The assault on Miller's moral sense is no less formidable: one of his jobs involves working for a Hindu who takes particular pleasure in having Henry assist him in the lavatory; he models for lewd pictures; he has a turn living with a homosexual ("I could have forgiven him everything if only he had handed me a decent breakfast!"). To keep a few francs in his pocket, Miller comes to lie, fawn, cheat, steal, pimp, taking it all in an easygoing *ça m'est égal* way.

His discovery that he has a stomach for everything except hunger is accompanied, not unexpectedly, by his discovery that he is an artist, the two being aspects of the same process of freeing the inner man by a complete abandonment of con-

ventional moral norms and social values. As he says in setting
forth to describe his situation: "I have no money, no resources, no hopes. I am the happiest man alive. A year ago,
six months ago, I thought that I was an artist. I no longer
think about it, I *am*."

The two main elements of *Cancer* follow from the development of these two images—Miller the asocial man and
Miller the artist—though they are a good deal less integrated
than this opening statement presumes. The first results in the
scenes from low life, the anecdotes of sordidness and disorder, usually presented in a spare, impassive prose, touched
infrequently with joy, but almost invariably with comedy.
These are by far the best moments in the book, for Miller is a
fine natural writer and storyteller in the deadpan manner, a
kind of Left Bank Mark Twain. The few pages in which Miller describes moving his shiftless friend Van Norden from
one scurvy roominghouse to another, and the narrative of
young Fillmore's liaison with a dizzy Russian princess who
has been to the well once too often, are classic evocations of
the makeshift, conning life of the international flotsam that
was being washed up in Paris during the 1930's.

However, there is also Miller the "artist," and a good half
of *Cancer* is occupied by his ingenuous mannerisms and ful-
minations. If Miller came to Paris too late to cadge a living in
the free-spending Paris of the 1920's, he came in plenty of
time to be caught up in the foaming aestheticism of surrealism, with its techniques of "unconscious writing," its often
facile tilting of psychological and moral norms, and its underlying attitudes, as one critic sums them up, of "an under-
standable disgust with world conditions, boredom, and the
desire of individuals for self-advertisement." From such surrealists as Lautréamont, an early predecessor, and Blaise Cen-
drars, Miller seems to have found much of his apocalyptic
nihilism and primitivism (he describes *Cancer* as not a book
but "a prolonged insult, a gob of spit in the face of Art, a kick
in the pants to God, Man, Destiny, Time, Love, Beauty"), as

well as the vehicle for his prolonged bouts of manic self-entrancement ("I know that I spring from the mythological founders of the race," and so on). The surrealists also aspired to create an immediate, uninhibited avowal of emotion by capturing those charged images that are released during extreme states of psychic pressure. (As Miller puts it: "My idea briefly has been to present a resurrection of the emotions, to depict the conduct of a human being in the stratosphere of ideas, that is, in the grip of delirium.") Like all extreme romantics, the surrealists were preoccupied with instinctual forms of behavior, and this led them to prize those precincts of the social Id, the slums, of which Miller comes to be so enamored. Finally, the surrealists believed that the conventional literary forms were as artifical and deforming as the social and moral codes that fostered them; this belief, combined with their taste for self-expression in its most exhibitionist and esoteric modes, produced as their characteristic form a sort of fictional-poetic personal tract. This, too, Miller took over; when, in his pioneering review of *Cancer*, Edmund Wilson wrote of it as a novel, Miller protested to him in a letter: "I don't use 'heroes' . . . nor do I write novels. I am the hero, and the book is myself."

The surrealist influence on Miller leads him to a number of remarkable images, but it leads more often to passages of quasi-spontaneous hokum. Many of Miller's friends in Paris were Jews, and he has some very shrewd observations about them. But the "artist" in Miller typically produces the literary baloney of the following passage:

> For the Jew the world is a cage filled with wild beasts. The door is locked and he is there without whip or revolver. His courage is so great that he does not even smell the dung in the corner. . . . Standing there . . . he finds that the lions do not understand his language. Not one lion has ever heard of Spinoza. Spinoza? Why they can't even get their teeth into him. "Give us meat!"

they roar, while he stands there petrified, his ideas frozen, his *Weltanschauung* a trapeze out of reach. A single
blow of the lion's paw and his cosmogony is smashed.

Under the surrealist influence, even Miller's sharp little
comedies of émigrés hanging on to their fantasies by their
fingertips often are weakened by the writer's fantasies about
his artistic originality and power. Thus the brilliant description of Van Norden sitting blankly amid the little bundle of
junk he carries from one flat to the next, and cheering himself up by complaining of his limitless sex life, suddenly fades
into a surrealistic trance, a number of trite Freudian symbols
having entered Miller's mind. Similarly, the faces of other
characters, along with certain street scenes, the interiors of
bars and houses, are portentously blown up or spitefully contracted into soulful epiphanies or vicious caricatures. Just as
Miller's inflamed "cosmological eye" can see in the "dark un-
stitched wound" of a prostitute's body a whole liturgy of
meanings—from the matrix of all mathematical systems to
the crumbling of the modern world—so it can as easily reduce
other of his people to a leaking bladder or an insect.

This split in vision between the actualities of Miller's life
in Paris and his artificial reveries has two implications that I
want to spell out a bit. The first leads back to the split in
Miller himself between the rather simple, hardheaded American, with his coarse but honest voice, who is involved in
these liberating experiences, and the avant-garde thinker and
writer who feasts on the lusts and cruelties of his heart as well
as the splendors and miseries of his imagination. Now, this
split is no accident, for Miller's celebrated powers of acceptance often seem to rest on the tactic of his withdrawing,
under a smokescreen of apocalyptic projections and rationali-
zations, from the nastier realities that he dredges up about
himself. When, for example, he and Van Norden degrade a
prostitute (their wills being usually more horny than their
bodies), Miller soon turns his back, in effect, on the crime

against life taking place in the bed—their making a human being into a thing—to generalize instead about the coldness and cynicism of modern war. Similarly, a great deal of his literary, like his moral, exhibitionism, parading under the attempt to forge an idiom that will allow him "to translate all that is in his heart," works to aggrandize his powers of passion and to evade his coldness—even deadness—of feeling.

In effect, this process of "self-liberation" in Miller's first book (and it becomes progressively more devious in *Black Spring, Tropic of Capricorn,* and the later autobiography) demonstrates that using writing in this way can easily lead the writer to the magic of a rhetoric rather than to the resistances of the ego, to his guises of liberation rather than to the self. The truth is that the ego is far less interested in "self-liberation" than it is in protecting its own images and interests; and it has a distinct preference for fantasies, projections, and highly metaphorical styles when the self is being exposed. It's hard to take a candid camera shot of yourself without mugging. This is a problem that writers who, like Miller, are bent on "going all the way" frequently succumb to rather than confront, and it is why both the content and the style of *Cancer* often function to evade the self in the process of asserting it. George Orwell's chaste and impersonally honest chronicle of being down and out in Paris seems to me a more truly personal account of experience than does Miller's posturing self-revelation.

The other general point that arises from this split in *Cancer* is that in straining to get literature, as Miller says he was, "off the gold standard," it is fatally easy to substitute merely a tin one. The need to rebel and the need for company led him directly into the form of romanticism *in extremis* that was available. And more particularly, they led him to those surrealists who offered him a set of attitudes—indeed, a primitivist subject matter—that was disencumbered of the discipline and lucidity essential to the surrealism of Breton, the early Aragon, and Henri Michaux. These writers carefully distorted objective realities to evoke the atmosphere and some of the imagery of reverie, but their main interest was in criticizing life in terms of the fantasies that dominated an individual or a society. In so doing they developed a mode of satiric vision that is strongly marked in the work of the other American surrealist of note, Nathanael West.

However, it is Miller's example rather than West's that seems most characteristically American and that also characterizes the more extreme attempts by writers in recent years both to reassert the role of the self in literature and to engage it with the fantastic tenor of the times. Seymour Krim, who wishes now to "gun out some leveller messages about reality" than he was able to do in his years of writing criticism for *Commentary, Commonweal, Partisan Review,* and *Hudson Review,* states the aim of the "unbugged" writer as follows: "Nothing can speak for itself like what is. . . . The writing I want to do now is inspired by the pertinent, the immediate, the actual of this very minute; that would be sufficient greatness for me if I can give it full voice." And just as Miller's efforts to make "use of those elements in the air which give direction and motivation to our lives" led him to focus much of the time on his own drives and fantasies, so Krim's essays make use of the same touchstone—that of "extreme consciousness of Self." For, as he writes, "so complex and in many ways unprecedented has urbanized modern life become for the individual that the writer just by owning an 'I' can find more of the traditional stuff of fiction (Dostoevskian drama, Melvillian speculation, Verne-ish fantasy) in personal reality itself than in deliberate invention." Krim's idiom is different from Miller's but it places just as high a premium on rapid metaphorical invention or "spontaneity" in looking for "new colors, new sounds, new equivalents for the extremity to which the Self has been pushed." And, finally, he has become preoccupied with the lower depths, which in times of affluence means mainly Negroes, deviants, and mass culture. It is not surprising, then, that Krim should find Miller to be one of his four exemplars of "real personal honesty," "actual American experience," of "the imaginative emancipation of life based on this same ruthless love for what is."

Much of what I have been saying in objection to Miller seems to me even more thoroughly relevant to Krim. However, it is a touchier argument to carry to *Views of a Near-Sighted Cannoneer*, for while *Cancer* leaves me with a certain amount of objective disappointment, Krim's book leaves me stimulated, annoyed, and perplexed. This means, purely literary judgment to one side, that Krim speaks more to me than Miller does. Partly this is a matter of the subjects he writes about: the New York intellectual scene, particularly as it involves the problem of writing for certain intellectual magazines; the realities of Negro community life, to which both "white Negroes" and white liberals tend to be equally blinded, though in different ways; the attitudes today in America toward mental breakdown and suicide; the dismay of writing fiction about a world whose daily life can seem as unstable and portentous as a dream. These all happen to be matters that touch me. More generally, Krim's essay on "making it"—the new nihilism of our affluent times—his dialogue on the growing confidence of the homosexual revolt in America, his essay on the teasing sexuality of the mass media: all these involve subjects that relevantly characterize the atmosphere in which one lives and breathes today.

Along with being drawn out by Krim because he writes about these things, I also share his point of view in almost every essay: the fact that his manner of thinking and writing is "beat" or "hip" and mine is, as he would probably say, "square" dissolves partly at least in the deeper similarities of background and development, which inevitably confer similarities in attitude. That we both grew up as wayward sons of the Jewish middle class and came of intellectual age in the 1940's is a large point to have in common. Also crucial is the fact that we both tried to become writers during a period when the conditions of the higher literary apprenticeship were as grueling and distorting as Krim says they were (though this was hardly confined to the New York journals). Until fairly recently only a few models seemed open to "serious" young writers, and all involved pretending that one was at least forty-five years old in his politics and in his erudition, and fifty-five in his "tragic sense of life." This made it very hard for someone twenty-five to stay in touch with himself and hence with his times. In the last few years, however, it has become clear that there are certain advantages for one to have come fresh into the postwar world and to rely on his independent sense of it. This, in turn, means trusting that margin of individual, *lived* experience that one shares with his contemporaries and must look to in good part for his point of view and his voice.

So I couldn't agree more with Krim when he tells my generation of writers that we "face the same problems" and that we "need each other." The main problem, of course, is that to acknowledge that one belongs as an individual and writer to postwar America is mainly to realize that the pounding tensions and amorphousness of its social life and the low emotional pressures and formalism of its literary norms are primary facts of one's experience and training. This realization is useful to disabuse one of the notions that our social and moral arrangements are still largely stable and satisfactory ones, and that a settled social vision and self-restraint and arch-subtlety are likely to produce pertinent literature. But in the end, the same realization also leaves one alone with the truth that in questioning the ideological assurances and literary standards of our cultural fathers as increasingly beside the point of contemporary American reality, one has little else besides a massive sense of fluidity. *The Liberal Imagination* or *The Waste Land* or *The Portrait of a Lady* are of little help after the candors of the newsstand or a Sunday evening of watching TV, but what else *is* of help? This is the America one has lived with more intimately and formatively than he has with any ideology—but what then? How to confront, and let into one's writing, the suspicion that the society we have been led to take for granted is more like the inner life of a sociopath than that of a rational community of men? How, on the other hand, to take into account that countervailing influences operate as well, that one's life is probably less of a grind than his parents' was, less culture-bound, less inhibited, less closed of mind? For only by recognizing this does the particular problem of the modern "educated" self come into view: the teasing possibility of liberation which both makes us so jumpy and keeps us in place, like the audience at a burlesque show.

Now, as I indicated earlier, what partly redeems Miller and also what makes him an interesting and useful writer today is his ability to stand still, sturdy as a peasant, at the extremes of poverty and crudity and disorder, and accept what is happening long enough to get it down as it is, before he takes off on another of his evasive flights of imaginings. Since I agree completely with Krim that our best and most truthful writing today must involve "the extreme to which the Self has been pushed by contemporary reality," I am that much more impressed by Miller's ability to often confront "the extreme" in a cool and steady way. For all his fantasy and pretension, there is a hard center to Miller which remains, in good part, detached from his egomania and from the pressure of events, and which allows him to capture a solid feeling of reality. Krim, on the other hand, for all his courageous candor and assertiveness, keeps reveling in a self and a sense of the world that are shaky to the core.

Here, for example, Krim is talking about the most important event he finds in his own life, his break from the confinements of the New York intellectual scene:

> It wasn't until I was 33 . . . not until I spewed up every hunk of undigestible matter in my psyche and bloodily broke through to my own raw meat via the whistling rocket-ride of what is called insanity—that I

began to think for myself because I had to. Man, this wasn't any bullshit about beautiful words and dream-masterpieces anymore—this was life and death and all that cellar-deep jazz!

Here he is talking about non-conformist thought in America:

There is much reason to think that America has reached such a point of ultimate no-return in making its world-play, that ununionized free-thinkers could easily be sacrificed today to the national destiny; our head-on position in history blushes steel and warships to permit embarrassingly free beatnik snooping into every uneasy pocket of existence; we are in the spotlight of the globe and no finks are wanted to spoil the picture.

The obvious trouble in both cases is that Krim is less concerned with exploring an insight into himself or the society that impinges on him, than he is in exhibiting himself as a very hip, very imaginative, very candid writer, one who writes directly from the guts and the nerve-ends. As such his efforts and mistakes are largely Miller's, only weaker and more complete: the notion that one arrives at personal and social truth by applying a pressure pump to one's feelings, which creates false emphasis; the idea that self-discovery is merely the willingness to lay one's personality on the line, which creates evasions; and the notion that the *Zeitgeist* requires an entirely new set of liberated attitudes and modes of expression, which means merely dressing up in one of the new styles of extreme romanticism—in Krim's case, that of the Beats.

As in Miller, the exhibitionism often functions as a cover-up—a way of writing about ego-threatening matters by a rhetoric that detaches them from a full range of inner response, and buries uncertainty under a discharge of worked-up feeling. For beneath what Norman Mailer chooses to call Krim's "odd honest garish sober [*sic*] grim surface" one senses the fluidity of a writer who is unable to allow the truth of what has happened to him to speak for itself, who can possess his insights only by doing violence to them, either by word or idea, who believes in his own voice only when he is posturing with it. The writer who speaks of a "life and death" confrontation as so much "cellar-deep jazz" is not merely practicing what Krim calls a "swinging" style; the rhetoric throughout the first passage quoted is also a way of sliding past any serious engagement with that world of the self that Krim tells us he has given up everything to write about. This is also true of the essay itself, "The Insanity Bit," which is much less about what it means to have an emotional break-down than it is about experiencing "the sheer ecstasy of 100 per cent uninhibitedness" and then having to pay for it at the hands of a repressive society.

Similarly, when he formulates the very real and very subtle problem of dissent in America by announcing that the beat-niks are in danger of being liquidated in the interest of our foreign relations, I begin to see much the same necessary flashiness of formulation and much the same desperate pathos of uncertainty driven to total assertion. Similarly, when Krim tells me that the mass media have released a stream of sexuality "which has eaten into all American life . . . which has savaged through my tiny literary life and your Plymouth-hustling life. . . ." And similarly, when he has to attack the New York literary pundits for their impossibly high and false standards by suggesting that these led to his own crack-up and to the premature deaths of Isaac Rosenfeld, Robert Warshow, James Agee, Weldon Kees, and William Poster.

The fact is that behind each of these compulsively extreme, compulsively souped-up characterizations of himself or of his world one detects a baffled but adaptable figure of our times, now looking for a home in the Village among the Jewish intellectuals, now for one in Harlem, finally for one among the Beats; forcing the underlying tractability to flow this year into the channels of *Commentary*, next year of

Hudson Review, and eventually, and with no less forcing, into the brassy pipes of the new demi-underground that run from the *Village Voice* to *Swank.* Having made all the literary scenes, as they say, of the past twenty years, Krim seems now to be compressing his protean ambition and intelligence into a new take-off after the *Zeitgeist: "Survival at its highest conception means making it! To live you must conquer if you're normal enough to hate being stuck with your futile being and smart enough to know you must trade it for success!"*

So perhaps, then, Krim is finally breaking through to bedrock, to the naked ego drives he spends most of the other essays evading by half-confessions, half-excuses: "my innocence was raped (willingly)"; "as a man I was self-deceptive, self-indulgent. . . . Ah, the extraordinary mismating of thoughts in the mind of the modern American literary romantic . . ." and so on. But the point remains that Krim is still writing as much for his "ego's bread" as he ever did in writing fancy criticism and is mainly using the very real need for more self-awareness and less academicism to put himself under a new spell.

As Harold Rosenberg has noted, the world of the convert changes, not his character. At present, in the vestments of the hip, self-liberated writer, Krim lives in a world where suicides are "stubborn amateur Hamlets and Ophelias" who "unconsciously reclaim their humanity and even ours"; where "fiction [is] much less relevant to today's actuality than the more universal story of sheer being"; where "change only occurs . . . when we stand against the ultimate wall and realize that there is no place else to go except in a totally opposite direction"; where the "pioneering 'psychotic' is the human poet of the future"; and where *"Baby, there is no significance today but YOU."* As I have said, there's a sector of one's awareness of life today in which these assumptions make a certain amount of perverse sense. But in the total ambiance of *Views* they also mark the end of the line in the opposite direction from the restraints of "objectivity" and "impersonality": they emerge less as ideas than as symptoms of the recklessness, self-righteousness, flatulence, panic, and compulsiveness of a writer who in freeing himself of inhibition has also left himself with practically no conception of "otherness" with which to correct and connect with his self-preoccupations.

The pity of it is that Krim is in a first-rate position and has the perceptiveness and zeal to become one of the underground historians of the past twenty years. One essay stands out in this collection, in which Krim argues that many whites who take and imitate Negro life in terms of its jazz have "literally no idea of the conditions of life that lie behind this music." Here Krim avoids trafficking in his self-apologetics, inside dopesterism, and facile lingo, and writes with the clarity and sincerity of a man whose point is too meaningful to risk misunderstanding or require false emphasis.

So too are his points about the narrowing and unnerving literary standards of the past fifteen years; about the mixed reactions of a white in Harlem; about the cult of genius in the American mentality; about the causes behind the new wave of personalism and irrationalism in the novel. But in each case one is left not with a truth but with the same overflowing Eighth Street cocktail, one part bile, one part blood, and one part corn.

Coming back to my original point, what *Views* finally dramatizes is, in Krim's own words, that "increasing chasm which separates intelligent people from understanding each other." This polarization of attitudes is very real today and my criticism of Krim is part of it; for in the end I am driven back by reading him in the direction of those genteel, authoritarian souls who write patronizing essays about the Beats. But is the soft, indulgent, hysterical element in Henry Miller an answer to the common problems of our generation of writers? And, in effect, isn't Krim himself failing this generation by confusing it with a coterie, by falsifying its consciousness with frantic and whining exaggerations, and by adding his watery extremism to the general fluidity that threatens to swamp us all?

(1961)

The Fallout of the Age

Georhe P. Elliott's *David Knudsen* is a deeply topical novel that deserves more attention than the perfunctory or hostile reviews it has received. It is concerned, in a remarkably concrete and sensitive way, with the contemporary problem that impinges upon one's consciousness like an unsolved murder in the next building and that makes most other topical subjects seem dated or peripheral. The subject of Elliott's novel is what it means, specifically, to live in the nuclear age—the problems of morale and morality which we face as we sit tight in the valley of the shadow of death, depending upon the mercy of science and the goodness of the state.

To read *David Knudsen* is to realize how little has been done with this subject until now. There has been, of course, a good deal of muttering about "The Bomb" in contemporary fiction, but it seldom goes beyond that to define its influence upon thought and feeling. As part of the nihilistic melodrama that we've been getting so much of recently, "The Bomb" serves as a key device to darken at one stroke the sense of the times or to provide a kind of instant comment on the hysterical behavior of the characters. The characters—that is to say, the author—think no more to the point about the specific import of the "deterrent"—both public and private—than do our theologians, sociologists, or ourselves, and the sense of evil it produces fades into the anxiety about Russian intentions or child-rearing or sex. Perhaps this is why *David Knudsen* was either ignored or reviewed as though it were mainly another novel about modern marriage or "the quest for values." When it comes to the Bomb, it's easier to pass on to other, more graspable questions. Except that we don't—not quite. This is the point of Elliott's novel. What he has tried to show is how the "deterrent" has disturbed the normal relations of one young man to society, has undermined and debased rational thought, and has fostered our permissive and brutal gods.

David Knudsen, an articulate young photographer who tells his own story, is the son of an important physicist who happens to have been one of the men that designed the atomic bomb. The central event in David's life occurs one morning in the Pacific when a hydrogen test bomb is detonated and an unexpected shift in the wind carries the fallout to the island where he and some other soldiers have been stationed to collect meteorological data. Elliott uses David's radiation sickness and the coincidence of his father's responsibility to get hold of his subject in a direct way, to engage his issues on the immediate personal level where they are lived and take effect as feelings. He is not concerned with the physical horror of radiation, which is not yet our main problem, but with the social and moral fallout from our politics and military technology, which is. Thus David's illness, after the first effects have passed, is not a very palpable one. He resembles less the hideous victims of Hiroshima than he does a personable young American who learns that there is a dangerous congenital disease in his family. One of David's friends who was with him at Paraklulei eventually develops and dies of cancer, but the effect of his own illness is mainly to make his relations to American society and modern technology somewhat more hostile, his future somewhat more uncertain, his sense of purpose and responsibility somewhat more shaky, his normal capacity for self-destruction somewhat more formidable than they all would otherwise have been. In other words, Elliott uses David's illness much like the chemical in a developing solution that brings out the dark and obscure imprint that already exists on the film.

Like many of the characters in Elliott's stories and in *Parktilden Village*, David comes from one of those talented and well-bred San Francisco Bay area families whose spirit in the present generation has either run thin or gone violently awry. His oldest sister, Anna, is a hard-working conformist—a "shmug"; his sister Julia is a tough, passionate radical turned sour. In temperament, David lies somewhere between—wary both of the insulation of Anna's life and the sloppiness of Julia's—the son of his rational, civilized, emotionally diffident father, but without James Knudsen's underlying firmness and delicacy. Seen against the background of the San Francisco locale, with its genial surfaces and turbulent center that make it so evocative of the modern American scene, David emerges as a typical member of the postwar generation, a young intellectual, as he says, "with a void" that facilitates his taking the imprint of the age.

As he says, "I had not acquired, by the one way that matters most, social osmosis, a strong, clear image of what it meant to be a man, but I had acquired by osmosis the strong dread that attaining maturity was as difficult and rare as it was ill-defined." Like many of his contemporaries, he begins his quest for personal identity by trying to declass himself and to recover the radicalism of the Thirties in its twilight during the Henry Wallace campaign. However, as David soon realizes, he is merely camping; the real ground of social responsibility lies elsewhere and in the present; just where, he still doesn't know—except that to become a responsible member of society after Hiroshima can mean nothing less than accepting its guilt. Yet such acknowledgment is precisely what is most absent from the scene. With the beginning of the cold war and the rising fear of nuclear espionage, he finds that the demand for loyalty offers new scope for the mentality of power and repression. As political initiative passes into the hands of demagogues of expediency and vindictiveness, David falls into a soft, nihilistic malaise, having encountered in the society a void that answers to his own sense of hollowness. Or, as he puts it, "some mutual enemies within me were taking heart from the confusion and violence of the world around me." He drifts into marriage with a social worker who is moderately unconventional, moderately decent, moderately empty like himself, then finally into the Army. Long before the fateful morning in the Pacific, he has become familiar with the feeling that the life he leads is not his own, that he belongs to a society whose channels of rebellion and adjustment are equally suspect, whose spirit (like his own) is as narrowly functional as its technology.

Viewed in this background, David's radiation sickness becomes mainly an intensification of the disabilities he has already suffered. He returns home and slides into various new roles—Catholic convert, commercial photographer, conventional "young married," dedicated family man—that are mainly expressions of his own vindictiveness and evasiveness. Before he is finished turning himself into the type of person —"the shmug"—that he has most despised, he has forced his wife to abort their baby for fear of producing a monster, wrecked his marriage, and eventually led his father to suicide by a series of devious attacks that culminate in a letter he is unable to remember writing which accuses physics of allowing itself to be contemptuously seduced by politics—a copulation of irresponsible rationalism with power that has produced "a thing which is wholly and only bad." He is talking of course about the Bomb, but he is also talking to some extent about himself, about the self-destructive connivance between his facile intellectuality and his whining but sedulous attempts to sign on with society. He has "adjusted" to his illness far better than he knows by internalizing the brutal pragmatism of the society that inflicted it upon him. However, the strain of this adjustment is more intolerable for

David than it is for most of us, and eventually he cracks up. Through his relations in a sanitarium with a vital young nurse and his ex-boss Mr. McKee—a rugged old sensualist whose life had also been torn apart by a bomb—David's powers of desire and forgiveness are awakened and he begins finally to recover from his past. In the end he has gained enough inwardness to live with himself, if not with anyone else, enough faith that the world still coheres to practice his art, if not his citizenship.

Over much of the novel broods the vision of a Godless culture—whose jet bombers and factories, campuses and highways reiterate the theme "made by man" but have "little to do with the modes of love or choice or human suffering," and whose scientific cosmology, as James Knudsen writes just before he takes his life, ends in chaos—"the ultimate disorder behind all the facts and constructs." However, threaded through David's story of his encounter with an age and a self that support secular humanism no better than religious belief is a persistent evocation of the saving moments and modes of what men once called grace: the awesome rose window at Chartres, and the pathos of a fifteenth-century crucifix hanging in a nuns' sanctuary; a little girl's inarticulate hymn to love, and a blues refrain floating above the steam of a laundry; an overpowering intuition of oneness with the early-morning miscellany of a back street in Oakland, and the candid, joyous nubility of a girl. These and other assertions of value not only temper the tone of David's vision and bring it into relation with the common, conscious life as such, but also serve to define the influence by which David is led in the end to his liberating moment of self-recognition, when the statement made by the religious man from the soul can be made by the neurotic from the ego: "I am weak, and I want."

The religious element has always been strong in Elliott's fiction, and if *Parktilden Village* is finally a book about original sin, *David Knudsen* is a close study of the doctrine of *charity.* "The sons of physicists find it hard to forgive," as David notes. His own rationalism, thin and pretentious, effectively holds him within the circular pattern of his resentment and guilt when it does not give way to a fatuous piety. The behavior of an Army nurse and a Catholic priest give him glimpses of what Christian charity is, and the grave skepticism of his friend Martin, a fellow victim and an apostate who accepts the tragedy in the Lutheran vision without its reasoning, forces him to see what charity is not. However, it is characteristic of Elliott's handling of the doctrine that the closest David comes to an awareness of what his father is suffering, to charity toward him—and hence toward himself —should be brought about by his flaccid sister Anna. In the course of revealing to her brother why she gave up driving a car, Anna instances a more profound and independent response to the daily assault of modern life upon the self than he is capable of, a more candid recognition of her weakness and resources than he has allowed himself to make.

In the end, David's long obscure struggle to live with himself and his fate leaves him with perhaps no greater capacity for living in this world than Anna has. He has withdrawn into the shelter of his art, just as Anna huddles within the cocoon of her imperfect marriage to a specialist in biological warfare. But the moral strength of the novel lies just here—in the cogency of the qualified but real spiritual autonomy that he has erected against an age whose physical and moral encroachment takes the form of little, impalpable doses of poison. Few members of David's generation have experienced his physical illness, but most of those who possess even his limited moral consciousness are no strangers to the erosion of feeling and the canker of negation that comes, in part, from the steady exposure to the modern void, whose ultimate epiphany is the Bomb. Thus David's experiences with education, with politics, with art, with marriage, with military service, with religion are all deeply typical, if in some cases more miserable. It is only when he stops colluding with the age by blaming it for his life and hence accepting its power to rule him that he becomes a man. The truth that emerges from this tersely understated story of a young man who has suffered "an illness peculiar to our time" is that one leads only his own life, not the age's. After a certain point and short of the apocalypse there is no general fate—postwar or otherwise. There is only "charity" or "adjustment"—inwardness or the various kinds of rays that men use now to destroy themselves.

(1962)

The Wages of Maturity

Judging from all one reads and hears, there seem to be as many writers tramping around the suburbs these days as there are postmen: for every man carrying in the news, another is sending it out. Since *Revolutionary Road* is one of the more interesting American novels that have appeared in some time, one might expect it to contain some arresting new disclosures. But the truth is that its major figure, Frank Wheeler, is still another bright young man who has lost the way and ended up in a New York corporation, where, limp with boredom, he pushes sales correspondence around on his desk. He spends his weekends attempting to build a stone walk or trying to hold his troubled marriage together or lapsing into a mild alcoholic haze. His wife April is still another sensitive, frustrated housewife—an ex-drama student who is beginning to lose her hold. Their two young children are equally familiar; so are almost all of the minor characters, the nondescript house in Connecticut, the office tedium, the suburban anomie. The dust jacket tells us that Richard Yates spent five years working on this, his first, novel, and since he is a writer of intelligence and imagination, I suspect that he spent a good part of the time asking himself if he could really bring off a book burdened by so much banal typicality. That he has been able to do so is a tribute not only to his talent but to his feeling for the material, to his power—

at times, almost obsessive—of identifying with the world of Frank Wheeler.

What makes *Revolutionary Road* as good as it is is mainly Yates's ability to tell the truth—both about the little, summary moments of work and marriage today and—though less clearly—about the larger social issues which the behavior and fate of the Wheelers express. Passage after passage has the ring of authenticity: Frank's sinking feeling as he returns to his desk on Monday morning, his writhing with self-irony as he nods deferentially at an important executive's vulgarities, his different poses in order to look masculine or "interesting." Yates has the superior novelist's instinct for the nuances by which people give themselves away; he can render Frank's glib denunciations of the illusions and the sentimentalities of American life as unerringly as he catches Frank demonstrating them. The fights between Frank and April, the long earnest "talks" in which nothing of their real feelings is communicated, the network of dependency and egotism, guilt and self-righteousness, supportiveness and betrayal, in which the young couple is trapped—all of this Yates catches with remarkable aptness.

The broader ramifications have much the same immediate truth. Early in the novel, the Wheelers are driving home from an amateur theatrical in which April, along with the rest of the cast, has flopped dismally. Frank consoles himself with the thought: "It simply wasn't worth feeling bad about. Intelligent, thinking people could take things like this in their stride, just as they took the larger absurdities of deadly dull jobs in the city and deadly dull homes in the suburbs . . . the important thing was to keep from being contaminated. The important thing, always, was to remember who you were."

Much of the story that follows is patient documentation of the contradiction here that Frank tries to live by—one of his characteristics that make him representative. A nagging concern with one's "identity" lands most young "thinking" people today in the same boat, just as it has become one of the leading themes of postwar fiction: the critical need to locate a self that is independent of one's daily circumstances. But once one subtracts the effects on the personality of an unsatisfying job and home life—subtracts, that is, all but a few hours of life out of each week—the identity that remains becomes painfully abstract and volatile. So Frank and April both learn—and with disastrous consequences. Frank is also typical of many members of his generation in having to go back seven years to his student days at Columbia to remember who he is, for it was there that he had his last, as well as his first, chance to develop.

The leading fact about Frank is, in a sense, his typicality, for he is made of the promising but unstable human stuff that the culture shapes according to its dominant values. At Columbia he rebels against his middle-class family; he is the World War II veteran, still wound up from his experience, alertly stalking ideas and girls in the streets of Greenwich Village. However, all the while he is merely enacting the vague tribute the educated middle class pays to intellect and independence; for all real purposes, his rebellion is over by the time he is twenty-three. After graduation, he has married and his wife has gotten pregnant; now bent on behaving "maturely," so that she will carry the baby, he takes a job at Knox Business Machines. The important thing about the job is that it is dull and undemanding; in that way he can preserve his "own identity" until he has enough money to go to Europe.

Seven years later he is still with Knox, still doing "the mature thing" by owning a home in the suburbs, and still trying to preserve his identity as one of the thinking, intelligent people. But there is "a faint, chronic fever of bewilderment in his eyes," his "thinking" is confined largely to self-projections about the sickness and emptiness of American life, and his intelligence is employed mainly in analyzing and manipulating his wife. Now and then he looks sadly at his

impressive collection of books "which were supposed to have
made all the difference but hadn't." When his wife offers
him the chance to "find himself" while she supports them in
Europe, he discovers that he is more threatened than pleased;
the years at Knox have taken their toll and he sees himself in
Paris "hunched in an egg-stained bathrobe, on an unmade
bed, picking his nose." What he has really come to want is
the more prestigious job that is offered at Knox.

Over the whole novel broods this sense of incompleteness
and attrition, of rural landscape that has become commercial-
ized without losing its rawness, of young couples whose best
possibilities are already years behind them, who have had to
rely too much on their marriages, who work at life—as April
sees in her moment of truth near the very end—in a way that
is "earnest and sloppy and full of pretensions and all wrong."
"Maturity," "love," "morality," "self-identity"—these are the
catchwords of the Wheelers, and of their World War II generation. But, as the novel argues convincingly, these words
stand less for viable values than they do for excuses and evasions of failure. With each of these words as a justification,
Frank manipulates April to give up the idea of Europe and
carry their third child, and then uses the same slogans to de-
tach himself from her predicament in order to concentrate on
his new role as a rising executive. Eventually he makes it to
shore as a successful, if hollowed-out, huckster of the Madison Avenue vintage. Meanwhile April has given up, has tried
too late to abort the baby, and died.

Who is to blame—Frank? April? the failure of both their
parents to raise them adequately? the *Zeitgeist?* middle-class
American life? All of these are implicated in the disaster of
the Wheelers, and there is at first glance a satisfying complexity in the moral vision with which Yates distributes the
blame. However, it is just here that the novel betrays a certain equivocation and patness of conception that blurs its
meaning and dissipates its power. The commentary on the
times, both implicitly and explicitly, tries to go beyond the

Wheelers' smug criticism of America's "drugged and dying culture." Every so often the local renegade emerges from the state mental hospital to tell the truth about everyone and everything; but his comments on the "hopeless emptiness" of the times are hardly more substantial or illuminating than what we have been hearing from Frank. Most of the explicit social criticism explains too much or too little: its indictment is amorphous and merely irritable, and compromises the powerful commentary implicit in the details.

At the same time, the psychology of the novel has a way of letting the air out of whatever large social protest is being made. Embedded in the narrative are a number of flashbacks that explain why Frank and April behave as they do—why he has problems with masculinity and why she is crippled as a wife and mother. The stress on their supposedly determinative childhoods undercuts the other issues being raised, for in making his tragedy neatly probable, Yates is saying in effect that the Wheelers probably would have failed under the best of circumstances. To write a more meaningful novel about the deadening effects of modern work and marriage, Yates needed characters who could have put up considerably more resistance. As is, Frank and April retain their social significance only to the extent that their early deprivations are typical. And the larger cultural point is obscured: the white-collar man today has a tough time with the problem of masculinity whether or not his father was as overbearingly virile as Frank Wheeler's; nor do the April Wheelers need to grow up without their parents in order to have serious trouble relating their lives to the demands of their husbands and children. Further, the neat consistency with which the Wheelers' behavior is shown to betray their emotional problems, the ease with which they are seen through, weakens the impact of their failure. Psychology, as Raskolnikov discovered, is a two-edged knife: depended upon too schematically in a novel, it leads the reader to begin to play the same game as the novelist, and it is easy to end up thinking: if only April had found a good psychiatrist in time.

In the end, *Revolutionary Road* is too obsessive and portentous a novel, too laden with personal meanings of all sorts placed on the frame of a slender and overly simplified story. But it is also an extremely *conscious* book, and Yates's ability to see so much in his material, to bring out so much of the truth that lies behind the clichés about suburbia and the organization man is more important finally than his partial failure to dramatize his characters and ideas effectively. One of his ideas seems particularly interesting. Frank Wheeler is a son of sturdy hard-working middle-class stock; for all his joking about it, he follows his father's example of working for Knox and eventually becomes an attenuated and slick version of him. April is a daughter of the reckless "golden people" of the 1920's, cherishing the memory of their glamour and freedom, and, in her way, she becomes a coarsened, joyless version of the former aristocracy. In other words, the attrition that marks their life together lies along a greater curve of decline in American life—a thinning out of class vitalities from generation to generation, an ever-diminishing legacy from the national dream of combining hardiness and grace. The revolution invoked by the title has several possible references, but the main point is that its spirit in America is nearing the end of the road.

(1961)

Harry Golden and the American Audience

Ln October 1958 the Delphian Club of Forrest City, Arkansas, met for one of its literary teas. The "theme" of the program was "Americanism," which was illustrated by the floral arrangements and refreshments, and by the book that had been chosen for discussion—Harry Golden's *Only in America*. Since a considerable portion of Golden's book was occupied by his stand in favor of integration, it might seem curious that it should have been so honored by the ladies of a state which only a year before, at Little Rock, had threatened to oppose the desegregation of its schools by force of arms. No less curious, perhaps, was the fact that the recollections, attitudes, and tone of an unregenerate Lower-East-Side Jew should have been taken by these small-town Southern Protestant women as an exemplary expression of Americanism.

But the enthusiasm in the Delphian Club for Golden's liberal wit and Jewish wisdom was hardly exceptional and, by this time, hardly surprising. Published three months before, *Only in America*—a risky publishing venture at the start— had been the spectacular hit of the summer season. And the rush to the bookstores for this collection of snippets from the *Carolina Israelite*, Golden's one-man newspaper, seems to have been matched by the rush of the reviewers into print to praise it. Stamped across the cover of the 1,750,000 copies of the paperback edition sold in the first year (the sales of the trade edition ran to 250,000) was the legend: the "best seller which has taken all America by storm and which all America has taken to its heart"—and for once these time-worn claims appear to have been perfectly true.

Out of some several hundred reviews this writer has examined of *Only in America*, exactly two declined to participate in the love feast between Golden and his audience. This "miracle . . . of receptivity"—as Nathan Ziprin, a syndicated Jewish columnist, called it—transcended not only regional prejudices but political, social, and intellectual ones as well. On the far left, the Communist *Worker* rejoiced in Golden's "lusty" way of "ridiculing Jim Crow hypocrisy and know-nothingism," while on the far right, the Chicago *Tribune* was delighted by the "sympathy and humor" with which Golden handled minority-group problems as well as the "approval," "tolerance," and "tart wisdom" with which he surveyed the American scene generally. He was praised as fulsomely by the *Nation* as by Hearst's Chicago *American*, just as he later charmed the skeptics both of *Time* and of the *New Yorker*. In the middle of a food column in the New York *Town and Village* (a solid, middle-class paper from Stuyvesant Town), the writer interrupted describing an experience with Italian sausages at the home of a friend to marvel at Golden's "warm and loving and thought-provoking philosophy"; meanwhile, across town in Greenwich Village's off-beat *Voice*, a writer applauded the acid satire with which Golden put down the hypocrisy of Brotherhood Week in the South. The Springfield (Massachusetts) *Republican* observed, that "there's still a lot of us who are neither eggheads nor beatniks, and Harry Golden says right out in print what we've been thinking." At the same time, intellectuals elsewhere were claiming this "urbane," "erudite" journalist as their own, in their own terms. Writing in the *Saturday Review*, Joseph Wood Krutch spoke of Golden's "amiable Rabelaisian streak," and wound up saying that "as a debunker

. . . Mr. Golden is closer to Montaigne than to Mencken."
Gerald Johnson found Golden to be less sentimental than
Dickens, before running him through a battery of flattering
comparisons with Socrates, Montaigne, and Anatole France.

And so it has gone with *For 2¢ Plain* and *Enjoy, Enjoy!*,
Golden's next two collections of miscellaneous pieces from
the *Carolina Israelite* and from the widely syndicated newspaper columns he began to write following the success of
Only in America. Today, some two years after his rise to national fame, the tide of affection and approval may be falling
slightly, but Golden's prestige is still such that *Life* selected
him from among all the Jewish intellectuals and leaders in
the country to stamp its publication of the Eichmann confession as kosher. It is still worth asking, then, why Golden
looms as the most widely attractive writer to emerge in recent
years.

Before looking into the more immediate sources of
Golden's success, one ought to note that it probably owes
something to the traditions of native American humor. From
the *Farmer's Almanac* to Will Rogers, from Finley Peter
Dunne to Sam Levenson, there has been a stream of humorists who, both in their kinds of wit and popularity, anticipate
this "Yenkee Tarheel." American humor has, until fairly recently, been largely a marginal-group humor. During the
nineteenth century such humorists mainly exploited the
idiom and folkways of the Yankee farmer, the Southwest
hunter or adventurer, the Far West prospector and gambler.
The practice of out-group humor was so strongly entrenched
that highly literate New Englanders like James Russell
Lowell and Harriet Beecher Stowe and a host of bookish
Southern lawyers like Augustus Longstreet, Joseph Baldwin,
and Johnson J. Hooper usually turned to it when they were
trying to be satirical or just funny.

Toward the end of the nineteenth century, a parallel tradition developed as the European immigrants settled in and
began to produce their own comic spokesmen, who cast upon

the American mind the exotic, incongruous images of the new form of marginal life. Relying upon ethnic rather than regional coloring, and creating a city rather than a rural humor, the Irish and Jewish comedians followed their native American prototypes in bringing their Gallaghers and Sheans, Potashes and Perlmutters into some sort of problematic relation with American society, and using the immunity of the clown to make some telling hits on its political, social, or moral follies. Also, they continued the traditional role of native humorists in keeping alive the sense of individuality and diversity, of a common touch and an uncorrupted shrewdness, all regarded as particularly American. Thus the redneck and the greenhorn provided America not only with most of its laughs but also with a considerable amount of self-criticism and even of self-definition.

These two parallel traditions of humorists have remained alive through the past five decades, becoming modified, to be sure, as regional and ethnic differences weaken and blur through their rapid assimilation by the cultural blender of the middle class. However, many of the major characteristics have continued to be fairly distinct and to maintain their appeal. For example, in the 1920's a champion long-run hit, *Abie's Irish Rose,* was manufactured by bringing together the two leading strains of immigrant life; and Milt Gross, Arthur Kober, Leo Rosten, Sam Levenson, among others, have gone on amusing a large audience by their comic presentations of the Jewish corner of the American scene. And now there has emerged the humorist who—if one is to accept the common description of Harry Golden as "the Jewish Will Rogers"— seems to have combined the native and immigrant traditions.

Anyone who is at all familiar with the history of American humor will not be surprised at the delight Golden calls forth by his demotic readings of history and literature (Cleopatra was the greatest call-girl in history, the Roman Empire fell because the women were left home with the "Senators and the 4-F's"); or by his whimsical nostrums for social ills (ending school segregation by removing the chairs from Southern classrooms or destroying anti-Semitism by having the Jews threaten to convert); or by his good-natured inventory of the oddities and odd-balls of the ghetto and of the quirks and foibles of American society generally; or by the relish he takes in pointing out the chicaneries of politicians and in deflating a stuffed shirt; or, finally, by a homey touch which manages to merge Jewish "understanding" and American horse sense.

But to say there is a historical background for Golden's role hardly explains the magnitude of his popularity or covers its significance. Clearly, he speaks to and reflects a present-day state of mind. Since the reviewers of his three books have been largely preoccupied with the question of why they and their constituencies find him so pleasing and useful, a number of clues can readily be picked up from them.

Of the several areas of consensus, the leading one, perhaps, has to do with the reviewers' interest in and respect for Golden as an American Jew and as a raconteur of the delightful, instructive world of the erstwhile Lower-East-Side ghetto. In his introduction to *Only in America*, Carl Sandburg remarks that it is an outstandingly "pro-Semitic book," a point that was echoed repeatedly in the newspaper reviews. The Chicago *Tribune* suggested that Golden's "tart wisdom" is "rooted in the mores of an Old Testament society." A writer for a Baptist Sunday-school book service in the South attributed not only Golden's delicious nostalgia but also his wisdom and penetration to his "Yiddishe heart." And his "lovely Jewish slant on the world" was related by a host of reviewers to his grasp of history, to his compassionate understanding of the modern problem of Negroes and other minority groups, as well as of "the proud, embattled, defensive Presbyterians of Charlotte" because (according to Harry Ashmore) Golden himself is "the unapologetic product of a close-knit embattled defensive community." Other connections were made between his Jewishness and his reverence for family relations, his faith in the brotherhood of man, his optimism, his whim-

sical humor, his sense of paradox, his humility, his individuality, his perseverance, his erudition, his righteousness, his
politics, and his appreciation of good food.

Telling its Jewish readers that *Only in America* "will make
you proud to be a Jew," the Worcester (Mass.) *Sunday Tele-
gram* left its other readers with the thought that Golden's
pieces "increase your respect for the folk who have been with
us since approximately the landing of the *Mayflower.*" Here,
as elsewhere, Golden's unabashed Jewishness was taken as
the leading sign of his most widely celebrated quality—his
"sincerity." A writer in the *Village Voice* summed up the
over-all reaction, saying that "Golden's most important asset
is that he presents his Jewish heritage in a manner that
arouses admiration, amusement, and even envy."

Even envy? Well, the attitude reflected by Golden's reviewers is further evidence, perhaps the strongest yet, that for
a writer to be recognizably Jewish in America today is an asset, that "the Jewish slant" is decidedly in vogue—whether
the bourgeois pieties warmed over by Herman Wouk, or the
tough, brooding moral imagination of Bernard Malamud, or
the inspirational theology of Buber, or the folksy simplicity of
Leo Rosten and Sam Levenson, or the sophisticated wit and
candor of Saul Bellow and Philip Roth. It is significant that
the attraction Golden exerts even touches, here and there,
the prose of his reviewers: the Baptist woman in the South
who uses the phrase "yiddishe heart" is not just characterizing
Golden; in a small and subtle way, she is reaching out toward
what she believes he possesses. To be sure, there is a hint here
and there of the old condescension, as in *Time's* faintly patronizing puns about Golden as a "leprecohen" who is
waging a "blintzkrieg." But the "Yiddishe heart" phrase is far
more typical. One finds a four-square critic like Leslie Hans-
com of the New York *World-Telegram*, among many others,
straining after expressions that not only emulate Golden's
prose but suggest the same kind of quasi-identification with
the Jewish mentality.

None of this seems to have come as a surprise to Golden. In one of his more expansive interviews, for the *Jewish Post*, he remarks: "I knew the Jews would be lukewarm but that the goyim of America would go nuts over it." And he continues: "The names of the Americans who are pleading with me to accept them as Jews would amaze you." In the same interview he attributed the fascination of his Gentile readers as being partly

> due to the fact that I have eliminated the "Jewish joke" of Sam Levenson and the dialect of Mr. Kober. These fellows are anachronisms. They will thrive for a little longer but basically they are on the way out. . . . The "Jewish" humor on the American scene is part of the humor involved in the entire American middle-class. I have eliminated the ghetto for good, I hope.

Golden's view of his work is quite accurate. His prose has only a flavoring touch left of the pungent Yiddish influence and is pretty much the English spoken by the second-generation businessman. Similarly, Golden's humor tends to be a middle-class type that strains for effects and softens the edge, in contrast to the older Jewish humor with its abundant supply of natural, resonant incongruities. Golden will describe in detail the long, involved process by which a family finally bought a suit for their son, but it isn't really very funny because he is much more interested in explaining the Jews to the Gentiles than he is in portraying the special comedy and pathos of the ghetto for their own sake.

As for the ghetto itself, whether or not he has managed to "eliminate" it, he certainly has bent the shape and feeling of its life to his special uses. If his treatment of the Lower-East Side has been one of the great selling points of his books, one reason seems to be that he has taken care to make the ghetto easily comprehensible to his Gentile readers—less ghetto, in fact, than a kind of incipient suburb where a steady stream of immigrants settled down to live family-centered, healthy, and responsible lives for the sake of their children. A review in the Columbus (Ohio) *Dispatch* offers a representative reaction:

> Most of his subjects make delicate but jolly humor of the heavy duty to Jewish family life that has been the subject of tragedy by so many other writers. And best of all, most of them carry a wonderfully gay and well-remembered picture of the immigrant Jewish family life in lower East Side New York.

There are, to be sure, occasional references in Golden to the overcrowding and the poverty, the sweatshops and the tuberculosis, but in his benign and invigorating Rivington Street, Golden portrays a satisfying way of life that both Gentiles and Jews today find to be instructive and—again judging by the reviews—inspiring.

The *New Yorker* reviewer was stretching it a bit when he said that Golden "recalls a romantic, vanished world full of drama and gallantry, something like the mythical Dixie. . . ." But what distinguishes Golden's Rivington Street from the so-called suburban "picture-window ghettoes" of today is not so much the noise, the grinding penury, the wear and tear on the nerves, but rather the vividness, energy, aspiration, discipline, and finally the warmth of its life—that is, precisely those qualities which are said to be declining in the modern middle-class family and suburb. The most frequently noted passage from *For 2¢ Plain* was the one in which Golden describes how as a boy he came home after staying away all day because he had lost five dollars on an errand; instead of punishing him, his mother kissed him and said, "It's better than giving it to a doctor." The fact that in Golden's childhood the title phrase *Enjoy, Enjoy!* meant "tomorrow" has also had a highly appreciative press. A writer for the Chicago *Tribune*, for example, commented that such sentiments and ideas illustrate "a character pattern prevalent in the 1900's that gave these groups [of Jews] the stamina to rise above poverty and discrimination." And, as Golden frequently re-

minds us, that kind of "character pattern" is seriously wanting today.

Other reviewers have found that the value of Golden's recollections is simply that they let us look briefly at "a world
we might not otherwise know." As a writer for the ILGWU
Justice puts it: "No place else but in Harry Golden's wonderful book can the reader find essays on boiled-beef flanken
. . . two cents plain and secondhand pants." Golden's
anecdotes are crammed with the little details of what the
Lower-East-Side Jews ate and slept on and took for medicine,
of how they courted, voted, and shopped. His strong sense of
detail, in fact, is one of the best things about him, and with
its help he has been able to satisfy both Jewish nostalgia and
Gentile curiosity. But what also sells his product, it is clear, is
the packaging—the inspiriting morals drawn from Jewish experience in which he manages to wrap even such sordid happenings as the famous Triangle Shirtwaist fire. After describing how 146 girls perished and how the owners were then
exonerated, Golden ends in a typical surge of upbeat moraliz-
ing by claiming that the disaster produced "fire-prevention
legislation, factory-building inspection, workmen's compensa-
tion, liability insurance, and the International Ladies Gar-
ment Workers' Union."

Another leading motif that runs through the reception of
Golden is the lament for the decline of ethnic variety, and
the related loss of individualism, in America. A good many
writers quoted Golden's statement that "we are heading for a
ghastly sameness in our country, in which the magnificent
Latins from the Mediterranean, the wonderful Swedes from
Scandinavia, the brilliant Jews from Eastern Europe, and the
effervescent Irish from the Auld Sod, will soon be indistin-
guishable from the Cape Cod Yankees. This is good?"

The reviewers didn't think it was and they jumped at the
chance to corroborate this and other of Golden's criticisms of
American sameness and conformity and to celebrate him as a
notable exception. Martin Levin, writing in the *Saturday Re-*

view, explained the appeal of *Only in America* as "offering an individual point of view . . . a refreshing phenomenon in a decade that has been thirsting for the humor of ideas and finds instead squibs on such yeasty themes as the rigors of commuting." In papers across the country, from the New York *Times* to the Detroit *News* to the Sacramento *Bee*, Golden's reviewers hailed him (in the words of William Du Bois) as a striking asset "in an era when the urge to conform is taking on the aspects of an epidemic." Taking their cue from Carl Sandburg's introduction to the book, in which he quotes Emerson's remark that "Whoso would be a man must first be a non-conformist" in order to praise Golden for being both, the reviewers made Golden's non-conformity their prevailing reason for touting *Only in America*.

It goes without saying that Golden's popularity was at the same time held to be an encouraging sign of life. William Hogan of the San Francisco *Chronicle* summed up this side of the reaction by suggesting that

> the most interesting point about the popularity . . . is that in the ambitious, selfish, increasingly uninteresting middle-class society we inhabit today so many people should turn to Harry Golden's simple honesty and warmth for some relief. Not since Will Rogers has there been such a people's philosopher.

In other words, Golden's "unorthodox" opinions—as several reviewers characterized them—such as his attacks upon the "platitudes and shibboleths" of American conformity have not apparently deprived him of being "the voice of unassuming millions." As the Springfield (Mass.) *Republican* went on to say, Golden's great following had been drawn by his "reassurances that there still were plain, sensible, kindly citizens . . . [who] wanted to be told that quiet, loving, family life wasn't out of style, but actually was rather well thought of in some circles." Heavily mixed in with the clippings that applauded Golden for the originality and independence of his thinking were those which, like one from the Evansville (Indiana) *Press*, asserted that "what Harry Golden thinks usually you think too, only you've been a bit shy about coming right out and saying it."

But how, then, does an outspoken non-conformist in a highly conforming society become the voice of its "unassuming millions"? Part of the answer lies in the ambivalences of the American audience that so many reviewers reflect: the desire to live freshly in the strangeness of the present but with the assurances of the past, and with this the development of a state of mind that seeks both criticism and approval. Just recently we saw how the psychic appeal of Kennedy's campaign was directed to one side of this ambivalence, that of Nixon to the other; the relatively small distance between the actual politics of the candidates themselves, and the virtual fifty-fifty split in the vote bear out the drift of the American psyche toward a misty equivocal blend of self-images and needs.

Harry Golden's success derives quite clearly from the successful way he confronts and bridges the two images. Just as his version of the Jewish East Side both stimulates and soothes his middle-class audience, so does he soothe and stimulate by his musings upon the state of America. Here he tells us that our society is in trouble—it is bored, materialistic, frivolous, apathetic; there he tells us that this or that sturdy accomplishment of democracy or social progress could happen only in America. His collections are a handbook of contemporary bourgeois confusions; except for an occasional piece of direct and *meant* protest, his unorthodoxy, on examination, is seen to reside largely in the Jewish and the plain-truth-from-honest-James colorations of his tone. He speaks of America as being on "a huge breast binge," and says the "whole thing is psycho"—"the instinct to seek the safety and comfort of a 'mother.'" This, of course, is nothing new—even to readers of *Coronet* now. But a few pages later Golden imperturbably defends Mother and America against the denigrations and warnings of Phillip Wylie: "As long as the American boy continues to be dreamy-eyed every time he thinks of mother, just so long will our American freedom be safe." Here he talks about the sexual *angst* that gnaws away at the bourgeoisie; there he tells us that "if it were strictly a matter of virile, normal sex, all the pin-ups combined are not equal to one spinster school teacher with eyeglasses." If he is not forthrightly damning Governor Faubus and Senator East-land, he is likely to be praising the "warm-hearted people of the South" who vote for them; if he is not telling us that popular culture today is corny and commercial, he is likely to be recording his "deep admiration and respect" for the "wonderful" way Robert Montgomery and Batten, Barton, Durs-tine and Osborne televised President Eisenhower's birthday party: the family sitting around the President while from off-stage came his favorite song, "Down Among the Sheltering Palms."

And so it goes. The American public, he says, is forever trying to escape from the realities that impinge upon it, but it is right and proper that the most important event of the next decade for most families will be getting the kids off to school. For the human story, as he tells us, is "a man and a woman and the love of a home." "The 'Big Story' is about people who struggle to pay the rent and get up the tuition for a girl in college . . . about people who lose jobs and find better ones." Also it is about the home town, and Golden draws a bead on the *New Yorker* for failing to realize that home means "father, mother, sweetheart, past, present, future, and PARNOSSEH." The use of the Yiddish term for livelihood is fairly typical of Golden's approach and appeal: garnished with a little Manischewitz horseradish, the perplexed banal-ities of the middle class come back to them as the wisdom of the ages.

That Golden's own "platitudes and shibboleths" should be as immensely popular as they are is not too startling, then, for they occur on both sides of practically every issue that worries Americans today, without ever disturbing the desperately held notions that our society is fundamentally fine and the future, in any case, will somehow deliver us from our dilemmas. Yet Golden and his reviewers cannot help but reveal, all the same, anxieties endemic in our culture today —the loss of national energy and imagination, the conformity, soft-headedness, and even the joylessness of the people —before managing to gloss them over. The reviewers' glossing over is in their pointing to how many people read and swear by Golden; his is in applying the varnish of his much-admired "optimism."

It is perhaps to be expected that so many members of the American middle class—feeling that they have somehow lost the way despite what they tell themselves—should turn for pointers to the minority groups who they believe still possess some special vitality and individuality, some esoteric wisdom about how to live. For one group—the restless young—the supposedly "cool" self-contained style and highly instinctual behavior of the Negro have become the objects of envy and emulation, just as the Jews—to judge by the success of Wouk's *Marjorie Morningstar* and of Golden's essays—are currently thought to have the secret of why and how to lead the good, American family life, whether on Rivington Street or in Mamaroneck. So Golden says himself in the introduction to his latest book. Pointing to the thousand letters a week he receives these days, he tells us of the loneliness they testify to, the "unhappiness in a rootless society"; the most important meaning they disclose, he says, is that "the strongest memory of life is the *family*" (his italics). Thus his anecdotes of a family-centered childhood are a sedative, and offer hope as well, for, as he put it in a previous introduction, "I know with all my heart that whether you look down a path leading from a farmhouse near Fountain Run, Kentucky, or out of one of the magnificent residences in the Myers Park section of Charlotte . . . these pleasures and joys await you, too—'for 2¢ plain.'"

Yet another source of Golden's appeal as a commentator on American manners is his emphasis on success as natural, healthy, and self-justifying. For Golden's Jewish immigrant story is also the American Dream writ small and concrete. As the prose-poet of upward mobility, Golden once again translates the values of the older, parochial Jewish culture into terms that his affluent audience can find satisfying. Though he speaks now and then of the penalties of success, he nonetheless worships it about as uncritically as the first Jewish immigrants did. His essays are studded with accounts of how this lawyer and that doctor, this comedian and that song writer climbed to fame and fortune from the ghetto—accounts which are redolent of his persistent confusing of celebrity with merit. Within this compulsion for touting winners, virtually all distinctions collapse: "The New York *Times* . . . is one of the finest American institutions, along with Harvard, the New York Yankees, and the Supreme Court." When Golden tells us about an East Side boy who is now a lawyer whom "the oldest families in his city make . . . the administrator of their estates," there is nothing further to add. To be on top is to be on top, which is a wonderful place to be.

This is a dose of the good old soothing syrup in the America of today, where the problem of getting ahead has begun to make everyone nervous. Whether or not one wishes to relate this to some final assertion of American Puritanism, to the frequency with which success in America is revealed to have begun or ended in some form of fraud, or to the mass frustration of a people who at a vast cost to their pockets and their souls are constantly buying the symbols of success but never achieve its substance—the fact remains, as Leslie Fiedler has been telling us, that nothing fails in America like success. But by his examples and by his tone, Golden reaffirms the unsophisticated, guiltless ideal of success which has been characteristic of immigrant groups; and he does so most effectively, perhaps, when he prefaces his point that we were hap-

pier when we had iceboxes instead of status symbols in the
kitchen, by saying that he learned this from all "the people
who wrote me after they saw me on Ed Murrow's *Person to
Person*, and on the programs of Dave Garroway, Jack Parr,
and Arthur Godfrey."

What also makes Golden's presentation of success attractive, of course, is that—true to form—he occasionally de-
bunks its more outrageous manifestations, poking fun, for
example, at Elvis Presley; once he even downgrades Albert
Schweitzer for not having been "on the firing line during the
past two or three decades." But what he generally concen-
trates on is the more superficial problem of status, which, in
most cases, can be handled as a humorous consequence of
the magic American carpet of upward mobility, or as a less
noxious and alarming by-product of the frustration, tension,
and apathy that result when the possibilities for meaningful
achievement are reduced or compromised.

In his critique of status-seeking, Golden depends as much
on present-day Jewish life to make his points as he does upon
the vanished ghetto to provide him with his morality and
sample of success. "I use Jews as examples and rely upon
Gentiles to get the point," he told one interviewer. Thus
every ten pages or so there is some mention of bobbed noses
or Ivy League *yarmulkes* or the quest for a blond rabbi. This
is all very amusing to Golden: "They're worrying about a
country club when Abe Ribicoff has gotten to be Governor
of Connecticut." In general, the eager-beaver foibles and pretensions of the Jewish middle class provide him with another
safe way of giving himself a critical voice. Golden's reviewers
in the Jewish press do not appear to take offense over his
gibes, and the Gentiles can examine their own silly search for
status through an innocuous analogy. Also in this way,
Golden emerges as a Jew who is not above criticizing his own
people—another reason for the reviewers to praise him for his
"fearless honesty."

But what is, finally, most interesting about all this is the success with which Golden has made the Jew seem entirely representative of the middle-class American—representative of a pattern that holds for the multitudes of Americans who in the course of their life have traveled from the lower to the middle class, from the closely knit enclave of the slum or the farm or the small town to the thinner, more mannered life of the suburb.

Here, as elsewhere, Golden reinforces the cultural situation he describes by the example of his own personality and career: the big-city boy who has settled in the provinces, the Jew who has had to make his way in the Protestant culture of the South, the son of the slums confronted by a highly organized pattern of middle-class life. Now, while he points to the Jews of today to evoke everybody's anxieties, he uses his frequently conveyed relish for the disparities and incongruities of his own position to allay the same anxieties. What makes the rest of the Jews nervous about their marginal status merely makes him rock with laughter; they wrestle foolishly and gloomily with the problem of identity, he stands fast in his happy acceptance of what he was and is; they trade their "marvelous" heritage for the dubious consolations of pseudo-Gentile attitudes and interests, he uses his heritage to make himself a respected, if off-beat, member of the community.

Moreover, in his "ease and naturalness in accepting joyously the fact that he is a Jew," Golden is able to exploit the traditional opportunities and immunities of the American humorist as the wise "original" whose very marginality arms him with the sensible, unvarnished truth. At the same time, as the "Yenkee Tarheel," Golden revives and flatters the declining notion of American variety and of a free society that is invigorated and kept on the beam by its robust minorities. (When Golden asked in his North Carolina newspaper whether he was a "Tarheel," he was answered by editorials all over the state which hastened to assure him that he most certainly was. And when Golden asked Governor Luther

Hodges at a press conference how it "felt to be governor of a state where one-third of the population is embittered," Hodges turned to the other reporters and said, "Gentlemen, I think Harry Golden is one of the most valuable citizens of this state.")

As the freedom-loving Yankee in rigidly hierarchical Dixie, Golden is, in fact, as useful and appealing in his way as Mark Twain's energetic, ingenious, progress-minded émigré was to the tradition-ridden court of King Arthur. Unlike the hero of Twain's satire, Golden does not bring to his new home the industrial know-how and its social benefits that came to Camelot, but he does his part by celebrating the South's "day-to-day industrialization without parellel in the history of our country." In his role as a kind of one-man Chamber of Commerce reporting on Dixie's progress, Golden is also reminiscent of Twain's Connecticut Yankee in having to rely on some "stretchers" here and there. While one is willing to concede that "Tobacco Road today is full of TV antennas, with electric washing machines on every back porch," he may have trouble swallowing Golden's further claim that "Mrs. Jeeter Lester is getting dressed up for the Tuesday afternoon Garden Club or the League of Women Voters." This happy ambience of an up-and-coming South arises repeatedly from Golden's portraits of enterprising Southern manufacturers who are doing "more to end segregation than the NAACP" and of the states which are "spending fortunes to bring in new industry." Meanwhile the Southern Negro, according to Golden, no longer tips his hat as he walks "briskly along the street on his way to pick up his little girl at the dancing school, that is, if he's not arguing a new writ before a Federal judge."

It is within the context of a healthy, liberalizing society that Golden places the Negro question, a context that flatters the South while criticizing or lightly lampooning its intransigence on the matter of integration. There is also the good-natured blandness that operates along with the widely praised trenchancy of his satire. If Golden's famous plan for "vertical integration" was reprinted, as John Barkham claims, "in virtually every paper and magazine south of the Mason-Dixon line," it was surely not because the proposal to take the chairs out of Southern classrooms was—in the words of a Southern reviewer—"as mordant as, if slightly less savage than, Dean Swift's modest proposal for a solution to the Irish problem." Swift proposed that the Irish kill their starving children and sell them as delicacies to the English who kept the land in poverty; Golden's satire is a fairy tale by comparison. When the Greenville (North Carolina) *Daily Reflector* reflects a dozen Southern newspapers by speaking of this plan as "one of the best solutions to the segregation problem we have heard yet," it seems clear that Golden's value to the South lies largely in permitting a tolerance for the integrationists that comes easily because it costs nothing and endangers nothing. "If we were as impossible as we are often told we are," writes the Asheville (North Carolina) *Citizen Times*, "we wouldn't put up with this outsider coming here and poking fun at us."

Of course, Golden repays tolerance with more tolerance, constantly assuring the Southerners that he "understands" and respects their viewpoint. He understands, for example, how a young Southern engineer cannot reconcile himself to his children's attending an integrated school, though once he had driven a school bus and had had " 'a very bad time of it' " whenever a Negro mother had to train her child to sit in the back: " 'She would mount the bus again and again and lead it to the back again and again, until it understood.' " "Somehow I felt very close to that man," Golden concludes, "but I was anxious to see him go before we both started to bawl." His schmaltz along with his humorous ribbing of the incongruities of the segregationist position both end by leaving the nastier roots of Southern attitudes undisturbed (such as the one implied by the engineer's use of the neuter pronoun in speaking of a Negro child). "His barbed pen," according to the New York *World-Telegram*, always has "a soothing ointment as well"; the total effect is that of satire with the stinger removed—somewhere between a bite and a kiss.

Then there is the unction of his famous Jewish "under-standing." "The segregationist needs your respect more, per-haps, because what he believes is less deserving," wrote Golden in *Pageant*. This trait is seen by Northern liberals and reactionaries and Southern traditionalists alike as a great virtue—the virtue of tolerance, concern, and "open-mindedness." "Golden has an open mind about practically everything except treason and dishonesty. He doesn't wait for the egghead butcher paper weeklies to make it up for him," writes the Chicago *American*. "Golden keeps his oppo-sition off-balance by practicing the respect for others' racial, religious, and national heritage that he preaches," writes the New York *Post*. "You know he is concerned. Never does he stand outside and accuse," states the Greensboro (North Carolina) *Record*. But what this comes to in the pages of Golden's books is a tolerance that is so soft that any strong conviction is unable to stand upon it for more than a para-graph, and a mind that is usually so far open that it is unable to close decisively on the realities of racism. As one of Golden's rare critics put it, "with equal equanimity, he singes Klansmen's sheets and sings the praises of Southern White Protestants, liberals and otherwise." He is at his best in making a clear, convincing case of what segregation costs the South economically and morally; but otherwise one tends to find him explaining the South just as he explained the Jews.

All of which is not to say that Golden's approach is craven or that his opposition to segregation is ineffective. Because he lives in the South he has to measure the tone of his criticism carefully. And I am told by Southern friends that liberals such as Edward P. Morgan are right in saying that Golden's genial satire helps "to loosen the preposterous rigidity of the segregationists' stand." But it is hard to see that the "truth" he speaks, as the Kalamazoo *Gazette* puts it, is "the hurting, troubling kind." On the contrary: the truths he speaks about segregation, like those he speaks about America today, nei-ther hurt nor disturb. Instead they flatter and tranquilize by making the reader think that he has come to grips with social problems when all he has done is to watch the issue of segregation or conformity or apathy being nudged lightly before he is hurried on to a joke about chocolate-covered matzos or to a plug for Shakespeare or for the Jewish authors of songs about Dixie, or to another rousing affirmation that Nixon's adoption of proposals which once landed their Socialist backers in jail is something that "could happen only in America."

Going through the bundles of enthusiastic reviews of Golden's books, one comes upon an occasional lonely voice, usually in an obscure newspaper, raised in dissent. Aaron Epstein, writing in the Santa Rosa (California) *Press Democrat*, points to the "specious wrestling match between the author and his subject" in which Golden relaxes his grip whenever there is any chance of a fall. Meier Ronnen, a visiting Israeli journalist, turns up in a Louisville newspaper to smile at Golden's knack for presenting "the obvious as philosophy," and adds that "as a philosopher, his sharp stylus does little more than scratch the surface of his schmaltz-covered tablet." Mortimer J. Cohen in the *Jewish Exponent* notes the "sameness" of Golden's three collections which he convincingly argues comes from "the relatively narrow range of his emotions." Cohen also finds that Golden is a little "too full of love for people," that, for all his highly touted "sweetness and light," there is "an obsequiousness in his voice." And a young man in Park Forest, Illinois, begins a review: "This is tantamount to being un-American or something" and goes on to say that Golden "is to prose all that Edgar Guest is to poetry."

Much else might be added. There are the glib or sometimes idiotic discussions of history and literature: Brutus was "a neurotic who spent his entire life worrying about whether Caesar was his father"; *The Merchant of Venice* is, in reality, a philo-Semitic play; modern poetry is so untopical that only Benét and Sandburg have given us "a sense of time and place" to match Longfellow's "Listen my children and you shall hear,/ Of the midnight ride of Paul Revere." There is also the forcing of relationships that allows Golden to relate Jewish history or "ideas" to almost anything under the sun. Jews and Gentiles alike have hailed the goodwill toward the Jews that Golden has elicited, but a more extended treatment would want to show how he has accomplished this by presenting the Jewish mind in an advanced stage of vulgarization, which probably explains why his stiffest critics have been Jews.

But what is most disheartening about the Golden case is not the books themselves nor the mindless praise of them but rather the malaise of American consciousness which these books and their success reflect. "The wonderful progress of science has brought no improvements in the hearts of men," says Golden. Where do we seem to have heard that platitude before, that special quality of affable flatulence? Golden has been described by several reviewers as "the court jester of American democracy," but I would be more specific and call him the court jester of the Eisenhower Age. He is very much a phenomenon of a period in which great national success came to bland, homey Americans who could best soothe anxieties, provide a confident if vague sense of direction, and preside over the evasion of issues. For all the supposed vitality and alertness in Golden's writing, there is a softness in his prose and in his thought, a steady veering away from complexity and controversy to the safe banality or the nice sentiment, and a power of accommodation that eventually occupies both sides of the question, which give his books much of the eerie feeling of an Eisenhower press conference or a Nixon speech. But perhaps the narrow election of Kennedy and the fact that some of Golden's reviewers are becoming mildly irritated both point to the same surfeit of tranquilizers. As two of his readers have suggested, he should call his next book "Enough Already."

(1961)

Bernard Malamud:
The Old Life and the New

A few years ago Alfred Kazin wound up an essay in which he deplored the contactlessness of contemporary novelists, the tiresome diddling and doodling of the lonely ego, by pointing to the fiction of Bernard Malamud as a positive example of what still can be achieved by a writer who insists on imagining a world that men share and an ethics that joins them. Granting that there was plenty of cause for novelists, like most intelligent people in contemporary society, to feel disoriented and self-preoccupied, Kazin suggested that what sustained Malamud and made his fiction quick and resonant with feeling was a kind of "faith" in fiction itself. This enabled him to go his own way, creating a dim, half-legendary ghetto as an extreme case of the human condition, bringing characters into decisive relations with each other, asserting humane values clearly and firmly. As a result, Malamud has come to be a positive resource not only for younger writers but also for readers who still look for a renewed consciousness of moral experience from supposedly serious literature rather than for further dazzle, perverseness, and disgust.

Perhaps the most original feature of Malamud's previous work has been his tendency to place the contemporary search for the possibilities of personal connection and growth against a background of deprivation and despair that seems to be a composite of immigrant neighborhoods, the darker side of Russian fiction, and winter days in the 1930's. In his best-known stories in *The Magic Barrel* as well as in his second novel, *The Assistant*, he creates a kind of modern folk litera-ture by making a spectral version of New York body forth the ethos of poverty, irony, and salvation that the East Euro-pean Jews preserved in a virtually pure and congruous form. Along with providing for his needs as a fantasist, this timeless ghetto has also served his purposes as a moralist, for it en-ables him to cut through the fog of relativism, and to study men who have been stripped down to their irreducible inten-tions, conflicts, and mistakes.

The New York of Malamud's imagination is like a secular version of Purgatory. Morris Bober, the righteous grocer in *The Assistant*, goes to his death with the realization that "I gave my life away for nothing. It was the thunderous truth." In a story called "The Mourners," a landlord comes to evict a wretched old man and stays to join him in mourning, each grieving for his withered heart. In "The Magic Barrel," love finally comes to the careful Rabbi Finkel in the person of a whore. Malamud's figures have, or gain, an expert knowledge of suffering, whether in the flesh from poverty and illness, or in the mind from frustration and remorse. Their character is almost invariably formed by hunger, and they are connected to each other not by normal social ties but by a common fate of error and ill-luck and sorrow, of having lost much by their sins and gained little by their virtues. But their lives are suffused with an earnestness of feeling and are directed by an assurance of moral order which enables them to be cast whole and to restore the drama of conscience to fiction.

From where does this earnestness and assurance come? Most of the figures who embody them are unassimilated Jews, which is less to the point than might appear since Mala-mud's Jews are creatures of a particular moral vision that is as accessible to Christians as to Jews. To be sure, one can make (as Malamud himself sometimes explicitly does) a correla-tion between the nature of their lives and the norms of Jewish experience and values. Yet Jewishness is a source of Malamud's sensibility rather than the object: just as his characters are almost entirely detached from any real Jewish community—of the past as of the present—so are the causes and purposes of their conflicts. There are times when Malamud's feeling for the immigrant melancholy and ethos, and for its idiom and wit, produce a classic "Jewish" story such as "The Magic Barrel." But, in general, Malamud uses Jewishness as a type of metaphor for anyone's life—both for the third dimension of anyone's life, the one of the spirit, and for a code of personal morality and salvation that is more psychological than religious. To the extent that the Jew and his problems become a way of envisaging the human condition, he becomes more symbol than fact—that is, fashioned to the service of an abstraction. Hence, when, at the end of *The Assistant,* Frank Alpine gets circumcised and becomes a Jew, the whole point is not that he will now *daven* or move into a neighborhood that has a synagogue but that he has changed his inner posture and become an upright man. In effect, the Malamud Jew is partly Jew and partly construct—a way of viewing the relation of conscience to deprivation and devotion, of exploring the resources and process by which, as Ihab Hassan phrases it, "a man can become a *mensch.*"

Which is also to say that, for all the touches of folk art in his fiction, Malamud is nevertheless a contemporary American writer—detached, introspective, preoccupied with the problems of contactlessness and self-integration, for which each man's experience in his own gospel. "each in his prison/ Thinking of the key": the lines of Eliot suggest the burden of Malamud's vision, the consistency with which his chief figures are confronted less by the world than by themselves.

His first novel, *The Natural,* opens with this bit of description:

Roy Hobbs pawed at the glass before thinking to prick a match with his thumbnail and hold the spurting flame in his cupped palm close to the lower berth window, but

by then he had figured it was a tunnel they were passing
through and was no longer surprised at the bright sight
of himself holding a yellow light over his head, peering
back in.

The image is a kind of centering point of Malamud's
imagination of life. It foreshadows the fate of Roy Hobbs—
whose fabulous and brief baseball career is to be but another
stage in an endless train ride through his experience, marked
by obscure awakenings and illuminations which reveal only
himself. But more, this opening sentence indicates the main
locale of Malamud's vision. As in the romances of another
moralist, Nathaniel Hawthorne, there are a good many mirror and light images in Malamud's tales, and they signify
much the same preoccupation with those moments when the
distinction between the objective and the imaginary is suspended and the spirit sees either itself or, in Hawthorne's
term, its "emblems." Around this core of revelation the other
elements are placed, the action moving toward and away
from self-confrontation, the tone either controlled by or
within easy reach of the introspective and hallucinatory.
However, the psychology is in the service of a moral intention: the Malamud hero who sees himself sees his chief adversary, and what he learns from the experience determines his
life.

Spelled out in the terms of his most characteristic fiction,
this preoccupation creates the story of the loser who struggles to reclaim and redirect life against the powerful drag
of the old hungers and habitual errors. Thus Malamud's
fiction is often set in the crucial period when disabilities of
the past contend with fresh possibilities, the old defeats with
new aspirations. In *The Natural*—which is usually read as a
wacky mock-heroic satire on baseball but bears deep parallels with Malamud's other work—the heroine, Iris, tells
Hobbs, "We have two lives . . . the life we learn with and
the life we live with after that. Suffering is what brings us to

happiness. It teaches us to want the right things." Roy Hobbs suffers for fifteen years for one mistake before he gets his chance to play in the major leagues and become a great star. In *The Assistant*, Frank Alpine, an orphan and another drifter, has his chance to learn through his relations with Bober and his daughter, after he has robbed the upright, impoverished grocer and more or less raped Helen. Alpine and Hobbs are Malamud's loose men (usually Gentiles) who, lacking self-control, go on making the same mistakes. There are also the tight men (usually Jews) such as Rabbi Finkel and Fidelman (the art scholar in "The Last Mohican") whose lives are overly regulated and narrow, who are armored heavily against the dangers of desire. Each of these two is anxious to change his life—Finkel to marry, Fidelman to redeem his failures as a painter by producing a work on Giotto. They have "principles" but the wrong ones, and they are torn apart, no less than Alpine, by the fantastic figure who in each case enters to teach them about misery and passion. Alpine finds his own way to the pit: with the stricken Bober lying unconscious on the floor, the air filled with the wails and screams of his wife and daughter, the young Italian puts on the old grocer's apron: "I need the experience," he says.

Suffering can kill feeling, as with Hobbs, or educate it, as with Alpine, who emerges from his ordeal capable of relationships, of respecting the bonds of sympathy and trust. "Our life is hard enough," Alpine learns from Morris Bober and his situation. "Why should we hurt somebody else? . . . We ain't animals." With tenderness for others come Alpine's awareness and aspiration and, finally, his wisdom and self-control—the freedom to see and do the right thing. Without this freedom conferred by connection and self-integration, life dribbles away; the will struggles but remains attached to habits of lust or defensiveness and each man lives out his faults and despair. However, morality, in Malamud's view, is a slow and bloody business and has little noticeable effect on fortune. He is too intelligent a moralist to freeze his vision of failure into a formula and too saturnine to exaggerate the benefits of regeneration.

Roy Hobbs suffers, but doesn't learn; cut down in his youth by a sexy psychopath, he makes the same hungry mistake fifteen years later with the corrupt Memo and destroys himself by throwing the last game of the World Series for her sake. However, there is also the better Iris, who pays for her adolescent error with a stranger in the park, sacrifices her life to raising her daughter and hence to learning about the "right things," only to be left at the end almost exactly where she started—seduced by another stranger in the park, made pregnant, and probably abandoned. What makes Malamud so cogent in his treatment of these matters is the complication he can give to character, and to morality, by subtly bringing out the covert impulses which tie a man to his mistakes and frustrations and make his face stare back at him even as he awakens to new possibilities. He persuades us of the gravity of a single act of moral decision (or, as Alpine puts it, "how easy it was for a man to wreck his whole life in a single wrong act") by making us aware of the determinisms of guilt and self-deprecation, the ease with which circumstances overcome the weakened will, to lead a man away from his resolutions and back into his chains.

Further, the man, like Alpine, who does break out is left with little else besides his new wholeness and freedom. Along with Bober's humaneness, Alpine has received the grocer's way of life and the grocery store on a dead street, the Jew's justice and charity but accompanied by the rut of his days. The store is still a "fate." Such an outcome seems a little pat and in excess of the facts, a weighting of the scales of fortune that becomes a defect in Malamud's otherwise clear moral intelligence. But it is also the defect of Malamud's very particular virtue. The source of power in his fiction is, finally, in his struggle toward affirmation—his faith in the resources of the human spirit contending against his deep-seated sense of limitations, so that in the end liberation may only be measured in small degrees of change, shades of gray. Malamud's pessimism, in other words, tests and validates his main idea that a man is not necessarily defined by his limits.

Most modern thought, as exemplified by Marx and Freud, has conditioned us to accept the idea that a man's limitations are the main truth about him. The technique of modern fiction, stemming from Flaubert, is designed in good part to disclose the determinisms of history, society, and psychology. If *The Assistant* came as a revelation, the main reason was that it restored a sense of the mystery of character and of the older intention of fiction to show the ways men change. Despite its small compass and thinness of social reference, *The Assistant* thus took on some of the power and positiveness of the great Russian novels by its graphic depiction of Alpine's development from a bum to a man of principle.

That Malamud's fiction has been able to support its heavy moral interests is due to other resources as well. He has a particular gift for portraying the obsessive kinds of relationship that lead his characters into themselves or otherwise dramatize the ambiguities of their hearts. The resonance of such brief tales as "The Loan," "The Bill," and "Take Pity" result mainly from Malamud's uncanny sense of what people belong in the same story, of the subtle and unexpected ways in which relationships bind and influence. His sense of character, like his sense of episode and place, is abetted by a subtle grasp of the demonic—the kind of spiritual inventiveness and wit that creates a debauched Negro angel named Levine to test the faith of a Job-like little tailor. His imagination, in fact, seems most highly charged before the extremes of personal confrontation and crisis, which he presents as a mordant if not macabre comedy, the humor leavening the desperation and thereby enriching the tone and preserving it from the melodramatic and sentimental. Out of these situations come his semi-hallucinatory adversaries such as the *macher* in *The Assistant* or Susskind in "The Last Mohican" or Salzman in

"The Magic Barrel," who provide the electrifying element of Malamud's vision and enable the tale to reach into and dramatize the depths of the theme. Similarly, the moments to which one assents in *The Natural* are usually those in which Malamud gives up the horseplay about baseball and produces the tortured and truly wacky images of Hobbs's inner life.

In general, the special achievement of Malamud's technique has been the movement back and forth between the grimly plain and the fantastic, the joining of the natural to the supernatural, the endowing of his abstracted version of the commonplace with the entanglements of a dream. Similarly, his most characteristic style has been blunt New York speech, with a twist of Yiddishism so that it resonates, lit here and there by a sudden lyrical or bizarre image. The reality of his best work has come from the gray atmosphere in his vision which from moment to moment seems to take the place of the realist's eye for physical detail. The slow, grueling development of Frank Alpine unfolds against the mood of a vacuous Bronx neighborhood and of the mixed morale of bleakness and aspiration, discipline and defeat within the Bober household, where even the lovely and vital Helen "fights a sense of mourning to a practiced draw."

Similarly, in his religious stories Malamud manages—as much by abstraction as by detail—to create a vividly spiritualized reality. In a recent story, "Idiots First," for example, a dying man draws on "his cold embittered clothing" and goes off into the night to find $35 so that he can send his idiot son to a relative in California. As usual in Malamud's "New York," the city is deserted, the son is "hungrig," the pawnbroker and philanthropist are gross and hardhearted, the atmosphere is eerie with portents, one of which wears a beard and is named Ginzburg. At the gate to the train Ginzburg materializes as the gatekeeper and bars their way, for the dying Mendel is already past his time and Ginzburg is the Spirit of Death. Mendel begs for pity for his son, but gets nowhere:

"I got enough to worry about without worrying about somebody on one cylinder," says Ginzburg. "I ain't in the an-
thropomorphic business. . . . The law is the law." With a
sudden rush of hatred and in the name of "what it means
human," the dying man hurls himself at the mocking angel
and wrestles with him for the idiot's fate. The force of the
story comes from Malamud's uncanny ability to wind himself into this phantasmagoria of life at the very brink and,
through the sustained unity of the writing, to bring Mendel's
timeless struggle and the iron gates of Pennsylvania Station
within the same mixed realm of being.

Yet this story, however remarkable, leaves one with the feeling that Malamud can now write it with one hand tied behind his back. One of the difficulties he inevitably faces in
sticking to such material is that it comes to his mind with
events, emotion, and values all so intimately related that the
stories become variations of a common theme of striving and
suffering. Moreover, though Malamud's tales from this imaginary ghetto have brilliantly solved the problem of relating
his immigrant background to his development as a sophisticated modern artist, they leave him little ground on which to
carry the relationship between the man and the writer forward in time. Most of his mature years have been spent in entirely different circumstances of American life, and having
made his way, as it were, in this world, he can only choose to
write about it. It is precisely at this point that a number of
very gifted earlier Jewish writers, such as Henry Roth and
Daniel Fuchs, have foundered. Thus, when it was reported
that Malamud was writing a novel about a contemporary college teacher in the Northwest, where he himself had taught
for the past decade, there was a natural interest in what he
would make of this new subject.

As the title of the novel suggests, *A New Life* is again
mainly a study in the difficulties of undoing the hold of a
deprived and wasted past, of breaking "through the hardened
cement of self-frustration" to freedom and control. The hero

is S. Levin, an ex-drunkard and depressive from Malamud's New York, who has managed to pull himself out of the gutter by means of certain mystical revelations about life and an M.A. from New York University. Part Hobbs and Alpine in his melancholy impulsiveness and grossness of desire, part Finkel and Fidelman in being constantly on guard against his old habits, Levin has come to teach in the new world of Cascadia, whose mountains and forests and seasons are as stunning to him as its social and academic life is flat, frivolous, and intellectually inert. As a liberal and humanist as well as the Malamud *shlimazel* "who creates his own peril," Levin soon sees that he has more to worry about than the secret of his past. The time is 1950 and Levin's predecessor—another exotic from the "East"—has been fired for his radical views and for disturbing the peace of a school which is quite content —without any liberal-arts curriculum—to train engineering and forestry students and good football players. The leading question indicated in the early chapters is whether Levin will follow in the steps of the disgraced Leo Duffy. "I can't fail again," Levin grimly warns himself, but the question of what failure will and will not mean in Cascadia is portentous from the start.

However, the events that follow take a course not very different from Malamud's first two novels. There is the period of mixed achievements and satisfactions as the new possibilities of teaching, using his hands, taking hold in a fresh and promising environment fail to lay the old ghosts of dissatisfaction and guilt. "The past hides but is present," as Levin keeps finding out. "The new life hangs on an old soul." Behind the formidable beard he has grown and inside the diligent English-composition teacher lurks the mournful, clumsy clown, out of step with the opportunities but bursting with desire. After two near-misses, Levin finally comes to grief in much the same way that Hobbs and Alpine lunged past their resolutions in order to take an easy sexual advantage. After a weekend by the sea with a willing-enough coed,

Levin caves in, and in a scene strongly reminiscent of the self-confrontations in *The Natural* and *The Assistant*, S. Levin lies alone in his room and writhes:

> His escape to the West had thus far come to nothing, space corrupted by time, the past-contaminated self. Mold memories, bad habit, worse luck. He recalled in dirty detail each disgusting defeat from boyhood, his weaknesses, impoverishment, undiscipline—the limp self entangled in the fabric of a will-less life. A white-eyed hound bayed at him from the window—his classic fear, failure after grimy years to master himself. . . . More than once he experienced crawling self-hatred. It left him frightened because he thought he had outdistanced it by three thousand miles. . . .

As is also the case with several other Malamud heroes who pass through these crises, Levin's emotional life then begins to soften and run more clearly; charmed by the tender winter landscape and its connections to his own feelings, he gradually grows more in touch with himself. Still buttoned up in his raincoat but looking for a "triumph over nature," he is drawn into a love affair that begins in the woods with the wife of the man who hired him. A daughter of the modern American hinterlands—much as Memo embodies the neurotic and corrupting success offered by the baseball world of *The Natural* and Helen Bober the hungry but earnest world of *The Assistant*—Pauline Gilley is at first an "object of experience" for Levin, "not necessarily of commitment." But eventually love and its problems come to overwhelm Levin, and he goes through the Malamudian fire of passion and frustration, sacrifice and insight. In the end he emerges disciplined enough to choose the encumbrances of marriage to Pauline, abandoning his former illusion of liberation in return for the possibility of love—"the short freedom you had in the world, the little of life to be alive in." Unlike Hobbs, who spurns Iris, the honest woman, to chase after the flashy

Memo, Levin succeeds in saving himself through Pauline; but it is a success, like Alpine's, that is qualified to the bone. Just as we leave the newly circumcised grocer limping around in Bober's "tomb," so we last see Levin going down the highway with a pregnant woman he may have already fallen out of love with, and her two children, and burdened by the promise he has had to make to get them that he will never again teach in a college.

The point of this summary is that the dramatic and moral core of *A New Life* is less related to the specific social and ethical issues of teaching and living in Cascadia, America, than it is to the themes of Malamud's other work. To be sure, Levin comes a cropper in Cascadia because he not only takes Pauline away from her husband, the departmental whip, but also eventually takes a stand against the department's inane conservatism. However, the novel is only slightly more convincingly in touch with this subject by the end than *The Natural* was with major-league baseball. The book's failure to make good on its early promise of contemporary reality could be attributed to the possibility that Malamud is out of his proper element, as he was in major-league baseball in *The Natural*, where he used various literary and sub-literary sources (from Homer to *Dime Sports*) to do much of the work of detail and definition. However, the descriptions both of the Northwest and, up to a point, of the community are among the finest features of *A New Life*. Levin is perhaps most comic and moving, certainly most of a piece, in those passages that register his reactions to the huge, fertile beauty of the country and the modifications it produces on the spirit of a city man whose life had all but dwindled away in New York's parks and seasons. Similarly, the early scenes in which Levin is introduced to Cascadia College are very nearly perfect in their evocation of that special mixture of blandness, coziness, and pomposity common to third-rate colleges and of the eager-beaver compulsiveness of a highly organized English-composition program. Some of the narrative interludes are equally brilliant, such as Levin's frantic trip over the mountains to get to his coed. All of which is to say, though, that the writing is most solid when it is least concerned with the major problem that Malamud has set for himself—to transpose his themes and treatment of deprivation, suffering, and regeneration to the green and pleasant doldrums of Cascadia College.

Beneath the inventive but unsteady language of most of the book, one senses Malamud's struggle to bring the two elements together and at the same time preserve their given qualities. But the attempt to align Levin—the taciturn, desperate man who enters the novel—with Cascadia—dull, contented, moderately corrupt—soon creates another Levin and another Cascadia. The ex-drunk with a miserable past to overcome begins to fade into and out of another image—that of the academic innocent from N.Y.U. with stars in his eyes about the liberal arts and the humanistic tradition, eager to know the score, to get involved, to take a position. The college, on the other hand, begins to double as a chamber of intrigue and polite horrors in order to function in the unwieldy and elaborate plot and to provide scope for Malamud's moral interests as well as for his new social ones. In time, each new disclosure of English Department policies and politics becomes both another turn of the screw with which Levin is being tormented and tested and another betrayal of the goals of higher education. The passages of self-confrontation are always on tap and often are drawn not because anything very critical is happening but because S. Levin is constantly being confronted with the static question of whether he is "Sy"—the solemn faculty screwball and radical *naïf*—or "Sam"—the hard case with his "last chance," who emerges hamstrung but resolute at the end. Meanwhile, Malamud wrestles for an attitude and tone that will hold the two types in the same characterization, and finally relies mostly upon a type of literary clowning which doesn't fill the gap between satire and seriousness that the split in Levin opens in the novel—"the sorrows of Levin: his mouth thickened with thirst."

Without a steady, coherent grasp of Levin and Cascadia, reality and feeling keep running out almost as soon as they are re-created, and in the end Malamud can only again pile the burdens on his hero which he has implausibly arranged and send him on his way. In the process the powerful themes of *The Assistant* are reduced to a series of platitudes about the responsibilities of love and the holiness of life and the beauty of morality, along with some weighty pronouncements about liberalism and the humanities. And there is also a kind of underlying, nagging discontent with Levin as there is a more overt hostility toward almost everyone and everything else in Cascadia, except the landscape and a character who loves Sterne, that makes the novel finally seem designed less to explore the "new life" than to settle some grudges.

But in a number of ways, Malamud's novel also illustrates the perplexities of the novelist today that Philip Roth points to in his recent essay "Writing American Fiction." The question Roth poses is how is the writer to do justice to the spreading streak of absurdity in American life—how, indeed, is he even to compete with it? Clearly, in *A New Life* Malamud has had difficulty in presenting Cascadia College to stand from beginning to end as a contemporary institution rather than as a vague collection of academic types and stock grotesqueries. But, further, *A New Life* also suggests that to write about Cascadia today one must be prepared to receive its life directly rather than to try and plug it into another set of preoccupations and values. This last is what Malamud has done. "The past hides but is present"—in the end the statement defines Malamud's difficulties in writing of a new life more than it does Levin's rather arbitrary difficulties in trying to live one. Venturing into the strangeness of contemporary Cascadia, Malamud spends much of his novel unpacking and examining the luggage he has brought from his other world as well as using it to arrange and order the life issues. As a result, the book struggles from beginning to end to discover what it is really about and what its proper tone and treatment should be. Now strikingly comical and touching, now turgid and sanctimonious, now opening out resourcefully to grasp new areas of life, now withdrawing into pat attitudes and narrative habits, *A New Life* finally founders because Malamud is unable to give himself up to a much more indeterminate and ambiguous experience than he has dealt with before.

Which is only to say that Malamud is in the same quandary with the rest of us. The surfaces of life still look stable enough, but, underneath, massive and dizzying changes are obviously at work that undermine our bearings. What attitude to take, what orientation to adapt to? Between the cautious concern for the factuality of the contemporary world and the felt conviction of its special fluidity and speciousness, the sense of reality runs out and the mind struggling for purchase grasps at its own fixed ideas. Meanwhile the ties that hold a man to a place and confer a steadiness of purpose and perception—even in places like Cascadia—are lost in the telling. The sense of contactlessness makes us exaggerate.

In *A New Life* fixed ideas take over. I don't believe after the first chapter that S. Levin was once a drunk—not only because he doesn't behave like one but because he doesn't need to. His hunger and frustration are cogent enough simply in terms of the ambiguities of his making his way out of the ghetto by means of an education and then finding in the world only a mixed and possibly corrupting vocation as a teacher of English. The real interest of the novel—all but buried under the moral theme—is the encounter, not infrequent today, of the post-ghetto Jewish intellectual with the culture of the hinterlands. The word "Jew" is never mentioned in the novel, but Levin is the only Jewish name in the book and when his chairman tells him to go back to New York, he has something else in mind than its "stinking subways." Conceived more freely, *A New Life* might have cut more tellingly into the situation of S. Levin, whose problems of uprootedness and adaption have a primary and multiple significance today. Still, there is a good deal of opening up in the writing of *A New Life*, a risking of autonomy for the sake of flexibility, a brave and poignant effort by Malamud to update his imagination and bring it level with his experience. I imagine that, in true Malamudian fashion, the ordeal of writing it will prove to have given his art a new lease on life.

(1962, 1963)

Jewish Camp

A few years ago, I palled around with a group at the University of Chicago. Most of us were graduate students in English, either active or lapsed, and most of us were also Jewish. The latter tie was one that we seldom dwelt on as such, so engrossed were we in more immediate problems of identity, one of which was to confirm the belief that we were contemporary literary intellectuals, wholly at home in the society and its culture, as well as the legitimate heirs to at least one period of English or American literature. However, every so often we would let all that go, and at a party or some other boozy occasion, we would begin to turn each other on by telling Jewish jokes. Once the spirit of Jewish exotica descended upon us, we could go on for hours, taking even the chestnuts from adolescence and investing them with elaborate character portrayals, cunning nuances of accent and idiom, bizarre twists of the formerly simple plot line, and even an occasional stab at the more bitter implications of growing up Jewish. As a result, the punch line was often the weakest point in the joke, a small mouse of irony all but done in by the exaggerated labors to produce it. However, even when we were not all that amusing to each other we could count on the fascination of those in the room who were not Jewish and who seemed to regard their ability to get with the manias of life behind the candy store, or the hypocrisies in "Rabbi's

88

study," or the mutual bewilderment of Jews and Negroes, as a mark of their sophistication.

No doubt one of the reasons why we carried on in this way was that there was a particular satisfaction in the idea that being Jewish had suddenly become a very interesting thing to be in the eyes of our Gentile friends. This was the period when all of us were reading Bellow, Malamud, Singer, *et al.* with a great sense of discovery. No doubt, too, these protracted bouts of jokes and anecdotes also furnished some relief from the various kinds of protective camouflage we wore from class to class, and from the paper on George Herbert to the one on Henry James. And, further, these sessions provided a broad opportunity for expressing that admixture of affection and wryness, curiosity and knowingness, sentimentality and scurrility toward things Jewish that appears to be the final reflex of Jewish identity as it sinks beneath the sands of assimilation. However, since most of us comedians were writers in hiding, I think that the main incentive and satisfaction were that Jewish character and color and idiom served to spring our imagination: the gags and memories became a virtually free opportunity for mimicry and fantasy, one that played with a range of personal feelings without the pressure of social roles or the demands of serious representation. In short, what goes by the name just now of "camp."

These sessions of ours came back to mind as I was thinking about the vogue of contemporary American-Jewish fiction, and specifically of two recent examples of it—Jerome Charyn's *Once Upon a Droshky* and L. S. Simckes' *Seven Days of Mourning.* The jacket copy of each of these first novels emphasizes its close relation to the tradition of Jewish humor and art and also its exuberant inventiveness. The novels themselves are both set in the heartland of Jewishness —the Lower East Side—presented in its most indigenous and "wild" aspects, or at least what remains of them. Charyn's *Once Upon a Droshky* is a takeoff on a surviving remnant of the Second Avenue theater and cafeteria scene as it passes before the eyes and through the memory of an old madcap Yiddish actor. Simckes' *Seven Days of Mourning* is contained entirely within a Broome Street flat and provides a slice of Jewish family life so decayed and weird as to belong to both the ages and the present. In short, both novels look like the real thing—*Yiddishkeit* with a modern twist—at least to the foreign eye. I suspect that this is the main reason why they were published by Random House and McGraw-Hill respectively, and why both these houses, which pride themselves on their taste as well as enterprise in fiction, should have had high hopes for them. "Jewish" fiction is caviar for the happy few; it is also "seminal" in somewhat the same way that Southern fiction was said to be a decade ago. One imagines that the audience envisioned for these two novels is a mass version of those sharp young intellectual types who were so easily amused and moved by those performances of ours in Chicago.

Nor would Charyn or Simckes have been out of place among the performers. Charyn is a graduate student at Columbia; Simckes is at Harvard. Though Simckes is said to come "from a long line of rabbis," I doubt if he knows much more about Broome Street than I do or that Charyn knows about the recondite culture of the Café Royale and the plays of Jacob Gordin. Since both are obviously talented young writers, trained in literature, the only reasons I can adduce as to why each of them has chosen to launch his career with such thin, improvised versions of the immigrant folkways is that there is a literary premium on them today and that each in his own way has fallen under the facile spell of Jewish camp. Although *Seven Days of Mourning* drags some sort of momentous meaning in tow, while *Once Upon a Droshky* is burlesque occasionally cut with literary sentiment, the essential impulse of both novels is an impersonation act. Here is Charyn, crouched inside of Yankel Rabinowitz, relating the origin of the actor's fatal feud with Pincus, the critic:

I'm telling you the midget was insane. The biggest actresses fell in love with him, one after the other. Like flies! But he wanted only Shaindele! And when he wrote her messages, who do you think he picked out to deliver them? Me! And when I appeared at the dressing room with Pincus' messages, she chased out all the other chorus girls, closed the curtain and dragged me over to the couch. Why should I lie? You think I didn't enjoy myself! A John Alden I never was, and I'll never be! . . . The girl wore me out! What, at least at the *Silver Draidl* I had time to relax. . . .

And so forth. With his John Aldens and *Silver Draidls*, Charyn re-creates his "world" as a comedy routine that relies on frequent references to Tomashevsky, Ben-Ami, Joseph Buloff, the names of theaters, plays, and streets as well as to cockroaches, pushcarts, and borsht and boiled potatoes. After a promising start the characters fall into a series of flat exotic types—the gentled ex-mobster, the demented peddler, the avaricious landlord, the crooked lawyer, the slovenly cafeteria owner, the superannuated chippy, the rich but obese widow. There is a plot of sorts which keeps Yankel scurrying between the "Golden Age Center" in Washington Heights and Schimmel's Cafeteria somewhere around Second Avenue, where his old gang of Yiddish ne'er-do-wells has taken its last refuge against the forces of urban renewal and corruption. The thinness of Charyn's material inevitably drives him to increasingly crude and bizarre yocks to tart it up. The net result is a kind of animated cartoon of the fading Second Avenue scene that, unlike Grace Paley's "Goodby and Good Luck," reveals less of a sense of that life's natural and rich character than of the author's straining sense of humor.

Seven Days of Mourning, on the other hand, is mainly repulsive. Lacking Charyn's gift for mimicry, his intuitive, if trivializing, feeling for the flavor and accent of Yiddish-American culture, Simckes attempts to get along by rendering

Jewish marginality as disease and its religious traditions as a
psychiatric cure. No Zionist of the old school, railing against
the pathology of the ghetto, could begin to conceive of the
grotesque Shimanskys locked up together in their flat and
their dementia. In a race with nausea, I shall try to be quick.
For the conventional domineering mother and the ineffectual
father of the immigrant household, Simckes brings forward
an obese little monster of persecution and a skeleton in underwear who survives by weeping, shivering, and choking fits.
Along with the feeble-minded daughter who has been shut
away and killed herself and the narrator who is permanently
crippled, there is an older daughter who is a slightly more
winning version of her mother, her husband who suffers from
brain damage, and their hysterical child who also has reces-
sive testicles. To complete the picture there is a grandfather
who lives alone and spends his time draining his wens, and a
neighbor who likes to demonstrate the mysteries of life by
taking the Shimansky children into the bathroom with her.
In case anyone should miss what is known in creative-writing
courses as the "point of view," Simckes alludes at every early
opportunity to the animal-like nature of his characters, drawing his analogues mainly from the lower phyla—snails, liz-
ards, kitchen beetles, spiders, and so forth—and joins the
action to the theme by focusing upon the characters' marginally psychotic oral and anal fixations.

Into this Jewish menage—or, better, menagerie—is eventually introduced Vossen Gleich, a deformed quack who
brings with him rabbinical light and group therapy. Since
everyone has to be a psychic freak to stand on this sharply
tilted stage, Gleich is sane mainly by comparison and through
the requirements of the theme, which is that only by properly
mourning the death of the daughter and by having, as they
say, pity and love, and a bit of genital sex, will the family be
cured. (At the end Gleich is fixing up the narrator with a
humpbacked dwarf.) With the appearance of Gleich the
book suddenly swells with those hints of profundity that my

friends and I in Chicago liked to toss in every so often: "Life is a misfortune . . . ," says Gleich, "but we must make it sacred." Or: "I am Gleich . . . if I wound, I heal." Or: "Like your mother, you're bitter. And like your father, you don't want to change." The traditions of Judaism and psychoanalysis are whispering to us. But no earned possibility of change is reached: how could it be when not even Dorothy Day could help Simckes' Shimanskys? The whispers, along with a thought or two from Norman O. Brown, are merely part of the camp and make Simckes' venture into Jewish folk life intellectually as well as artistically vulgar.

Two blurbs are to be found on the back of *Seven Days of Mourning*. Bernard Malamud describes the book as "imperfect" but still "an original feat of the imagination. It cleanses and purifies through love for the human being." The other comment is by the critic Albert J. Guerard: "At his best [Simckes] challenges, for outrageous and ruthless invention, both Isaac Babel and Bernard Malamud. The novel is sad, funny, insufferably and excitingly human." Ordinarily, blurbs aren't meant to mean much and it's a cheap tactic to take an advantage of them, but these two happen to signify pretty well the terms of the appeal of American-Jewish fiction, which even a book such as Simckes' seems able to profit from.

This fiction, so its reputation goes, is full of "invention" (imagination, vitality, wildness, etc.) and it is "human" (compassionate, loving, radiant with insight, etc.). Since genuine vitality and humanity are in short supply these days in fiction, as everywhere else, one can understand why they should be so much appreciated and why pretensions to them should be so easily confused with the real thing. However, as conventions of a new genre of Jewish folk writing represented by these two novels as well as by, say, Norman Fruchter's *Coat Upon a Stick* or Edward Adler's *Notes from a Dark Street*, they derive from a patently tenuous and arbitrary, when not also narcissistic, relation to the folk material that provides their basis. The truth is that as one moves from Babel to Malamud to a writer like Simckes, the use of this material becomes increasingly exploitative ("outrageous, ruthless") in the separation of supposedly Jewish values and modes of behavior from the actual culture in which they were part of a coherent way of life and through which they gain their authority as aspects of human behavior and value as such.

"I was, with God's help, a poor man," says Sholem Aleichem's Tevye, with the complete aptness, the lack of literary distortion given to a folk artist who is in perfect touch with his world. But once the common folk life and the expressive purposes to which it is put become separated, either through the writer's intention or ignorance, he enters the realm of the inauthentic, which takes a great deal of art to redeem. For folk material has a way of taking its revenge upon the writer who is exploiting it. In the case of Adler and Fruchter it dries up and becomes abstract; in the case of Charyn it flickers intermittently and goes out; in the case of Simckes it quickly sickens, dies, and rots in his hands.

(1964)

Napoleon Street

Saul Bellow's *Herzog* is such a rich book, brimming with wit and thoughtfulness and feeling, that one can go on reading it over and over. So I have been doing, off and on, for the past three months. I am prepared to say that its interest is inexhaustible—one of the tests of literature. However, I also have to say that it is much easier and possibly more rewarding to re-read passages than to try to hold them together in your mind. Its principle of composition is that of overflow: Bellow's consciousness of life, much of it no doubt his life, caught at the flood, with the form of the novel kept wide open to receive it. There is an action that develops briefly in the middle, but its purpose is mainly to effect a transition in thought and feeling, and the meaning of the book remains embedded for the most part in Herzog's memories, reveries, and especially in his letters to the world which have only a fragmentary connection to one another. On the other hand, the writing is so clear, the sensibility of Herzog is so amazingly visible, the bearings of his situation are so graphically drawn, that one should be able to say something more interesting than "Go read it."

The trouble, of course, is Herzog himself. He is one of those European-type intellectuals who teach at the New School in New York or the Committee on Social Thought at Chicago (where Bellow is currently employed), whose minds are like the Mafia—interests everywhere. Then, too, he is a cuckold, and there is nothing like that to make a man think strange obsessive thoughts. But even so, what do Herzog's grievances have to do with "the plebeian stage of evolutionary self-awareness," or with "the fact that so much of 'value' has been absorbed by technology itself," or with "what Heidegger calls the second Fall of Man into the quotidian or ordinary"?

Well, to make a start, Herzog can be viewed as a high-class version of Bellow's other recent heroes: Tommy Wilhelm of *Seize the Day*, Eugene Henderson of *Henderson the Rain King*, and Philip Bummidge of the play *The Last Analysis*. They are all trying to recover from a crisis of middle age in which a man is overwhelmed by a happening that makes a mockery of his settled contrivances and assurances and that testifies once and for all to the previous mismanagement of his life. Wilhelm, a salesman, loses his job; Henderson, whose vocation has been to exercise his powerful vitality, is seized by the dread of his imminent death; Bummidge, the TV comic, can no longer stand his own jokes; Herzog, student of Romanticism and apostle of "heart," has been undone by his wife's love affair with his best friend. All four men are impulsive, self-dramatizing types who are impatient with their adversities. What King Dahfu says of Henderson is no less true of the others: "Everything about you . . . cries out 'Salvation, Salvation. What shall I do? What must I do? At once. What will become of me?'" Still, they *have* laid waste their powers and each is near the end of his emotional tether. The principal problem of Bellow's fiction, stated in *Dangling Man*, his first novel, as "How is a good man to live?" has thus come down to the more specific and desperate question stated in *The Last Analysis* as how is a middle-aged failure to be "reborn from an empty heart?"

Willy-nilly, then, all these later heroes of Bellow are gluttons for pain—for what hurts is still alive and still has the possibility of renewal. They are all also trying to reach the deeper sources of grief and impulse, to reconstitute the past in order to shed it, to clear away the cultural conditioning that has deflected them from a simple understanding of their desires. Herzog's case, however, is a much more complicated one. He has so many roles and self-images, is so divided among them, that simplicity is well-nigh impossible. A child of the immigrant Jewish ghetto, to which he remains so tied, he has written his first and only book on *Romanticism and Christianity*. A bookish, urban type, he has tried to turn himself into a New England country squire. A scholar, a footloose intellectual, a lover of fancy women, he is also a dutiful man around the house and a patient caretaker of his wife's neurosis. No wonder he has problems of identity. He is a Romantic who sets great store by "the heart"—a term that is constantly on his mind—but he is also a Rationalist who has more principles of ethics than Spinoza. His innocence is no less phenomenal than his sophistication. How can a man who is an expert student of his own character turn over his wife's diaphragm to his best friend? How can he then bring the friend with them to Chicago and find him a job, consult him about his wife's moods, finally be booted out and supplanted, and still not seriously suspect? No wonder Herzog wishes to give up "the crushing burden of self-development." No wonder the time for a serious reckoning has come.

The problem, though, is not only that Herzog has to come to terms with his high-minded and tender-hearted childishness. He also conceives himself to be a representative contemporary individual as well as a serious humanist whose breakdown has a general significance. For Gersbach and Madeleine are not alone in cheating and degrading him, of robbing him of his belief in "faithfulness, generosity, sacred quality." There are his lawyer and his analyst, both of whom exploited him in bad faith and in their respective and typically modern styles of contempt for human nature. There are also his more impersonal enemies such as the politicians and nuclear gamesmen who hold his life in their callous hands and increase his private citizen's feeling of impotency and rage by building missile sites on public beaches and making plans to blow up the polar ice caps with hydrogen bombs to get at their oil deposits. There is the huge, amorphous, unreal public life itself that dispenses freedom without content, culture without nourishment, the cynicism of Madison Avenue and the "potato love" of Eisenhower. Herzog's angry sense of grievance from his cuckoldry rises and spreads in all directions as he busily scribbles his dispatches of protest to a society and an age that has less and less room, use, and respect for the traditions of humane and personal being, for true individuals like Herzog.

Though Herzog realizes that many of his ideas about the heart and its prerogatives are as hapless and mistaken as his life has been, he wants to continue to believe in something better than the grimy pseudo-realism of the new "mass men"—people like his lawyer, Himmelstein, to whom all men are whores, all truth is facts, and all facts are dirty. Nor does he wish to fall back into the malarial pessimism of the Wasteland view, "the cheap mental stimulants of Alienation, the cant and rant of pipsqueaks about Inauthenticity and Forlornness," the "shivery games" people today play with themselves in advocating apocalyptic views, crisis ethics, the theology of dread. "I can't accept this foolish dreariness," writes Herzog to his friend Shapiro, who has apparently produced another fastidious treatise on the decline of the West, the nightmare of history, the death of God, the pathology of culture, etc. "We are talking about the whole life of mankind. The subject is too great, too deep for such weakness, cowardice."

However, the tone of Herzog's protest is unsteady; he lacks confidence. He recognizes that the facts of contemporary history and society are dead against the humanists. War and genocide have reduced the sacredness of the individual life, the significance of the civilizing virtues to a hideous mockery ("Limitless massacre!" Herzog reminds himself. "I never understood it, did I, because it was not compatible with my aims.") Then there is the other side of the coin: the revolutions of population growth and technology, the rapid transformations of culture and value that are necessary to help more people live a little better on this planet: "Would you deny them the right to exist? Would you ask them to labor and go hungry while you enjoyed delicious old-fashioned Values? You yourself are a child of this mass and a brother to all the rest. Or else an ingrate, dilettante, idiot." "A merely aesthetic critique of modern history?" he rages against Shapiro. "You are too intelligent for this. You inherited rich blood. Your father peddled apples."

However representative Herzog's crisis of belief may be, it takes on force only through being an expression of character and not merely a series of constructs to explain his failure as a man. Most of his ideas are too sketchy, in any event, to stand on their own. Herzog cannot write sustained discussions while he is supposed to be cracking up, though one wonders if Bellow himself doesn't want to have it both ways—to portray the "eager, grieving, fantastic, dangerous, crazed and to the point of death, 'comical' " Herzog, who will eventually be rushing around Chicago with murder in his eye and a gun wrapped in old rubles, and at the same time to provide an important if fragmentary set of notes toward the definition of post-modern culture. He is indulgent toward Herzog's habit of broad speculation as he is toward nothing else about him, and the novel tends to become cluttered with "brilliant" thoughts at the general expense of narrative power and clarity. Be that as it may, one of Herzog's ideas is that "Romanticism is the form taken by plebeian envy in modern Europe." I don't think that this was true generally, but it is true of Herzog. He comes directly from the one segment of the formerly repressed masses who immediately set about to possess the wealth, manners, and cultural heritage of the elite. Bred in Herzog's bones is the romanticism of the Jewish Emancipation: it connects the deluded "Graf Pototsky of the Berkshires," as he calls himself, to the somewhat presumptuous scholar trying to crack and revise Hegel's "Law of the Heart." The ground of his complexity, Herzog's Jewishness,

is also what finally connects the gifted analysand to the blind
husband, and the comic victim with his "immoderate, heart-
flooded way" to the gaunt and earnest seeker after Otherness.
It enters into his grandiose conceptions of himself and into
his stinging self-irony; it is the source of his moral sentimentality, on the one side, and of his vestiges of sternness with
himself, on the other.

Herzog's Jewishness is the one thing about him that goes
deeper than his ideas about his life and so is seldom discussed
as such. It emerges solidly, naturally, authentically, from the
family experiences that he remembers so vividly and that
function not as another construct but as the main province of
his temperament. Herzog's prototype is his improvident
father, the princely timid bootlegger, who rushed around
town calculating "percentages at high speeds," much as
Herzog rushes around in his "delirious" profession of intellectual history, making his quick, summary formulations and
judgments, usually to much the same profit that his father
earned. He is also the disciple of his tender, unworldly, and
not very honest mother. In Montreal, he grew up on Napoleon Street—a name that evokes not only one of the archetypal figures of Romantic individualism but also the Code
that enabled the Jews to leave their ghettoes and enter the
mainstream of Western culture and history on which Herzog
feels himself being swept along. The ambience of Herzog's
early life is beautifully encapsulated by the song the tragic
family boarder sang when he returned from his nightly
drunk, his wife and children having been swept away forever
in the Russian Revolution:

> *Al tastir ponecho mimeni*
> I'm broke without a penny.
> Do not hide Thy countenance from us
> Vich nobody can deny.

In the humor of Ravitch's song, there is something not a
little crazy, with its dizzying leap across the ages, the desperate irony of its transitions from the sacred to the profane, the

old world to the new, its feeling of cosmic loss and social estrangement which is both acknowledged and spoofed in the last line. Remembering Napoleon Street, "the bootlegger's boys reciting ancient prayers," Herzog thinks: "Here was a wider range of human feelings than he had ever again been able to find." And one is tempted to add, "Yes, and what gaps between them." Ravitch's profound division of consciousness bespeaks a culture in which all things are alienated from themselves and irony takes on the status of an ontological principle. This is the famous Jewish marginality that is currently being so much exploited and trivialized. However, it is the real thing in *Herzog* and he is its product.

The Herzogs have standards of "heart," and Moses has been one of those "young Jews brought up on moral principles as Victorian ladies were on pianoforte and needlepoint." All of which has helped him to know a great deal about life and to understand very little: the narcissism of his ambitiousness and the narcissism of his unworldliness are endlessly in conflict. Just as he is a natural for a profession in which "the main instrument is your opinion of yourself," so his inner life is regularly flooded by the self-enclosing emotional system of the ghetto, in which so much feeling circulates within the family, so little flows out to the bleak and hostile and corrupting world. Thus, though Herzog lives in the world, he has been able to spare himself real understanding of the vast range of human experience that exists outside his self-regarding categories. Similarly, his morality has remained one based on evasion and repression. It is only when he strays into a criminal courtroom and suddenly comes up against genuine sordidness and evil that he begins to realize how insulated he has been by his feelings, not only against the life of the drug addict or the child murderer that is revealed to him but also against his own balked desires that rise up in him as an evil taste in his mouth.

The jolt in the New York courtroom is followed by an automobile accident in Chicago in which Herzog almost kills himself and his little girl and is apprehended by the police for carrying his useless gun. These are the blows by which truth generally comes in Bellow's fiction. The first sharply teaches Herzog the limits and shallowness of his "essential human-ity" in the face of what is merely another routine day for a criminal judge. The second brings him back from his danger-ous preoccupations with his indignities, his rights, his need for justice. Returning to his abandoned country house and living amid the owls and butterflies and field mice, Herzog finally begins to move toward simplicity: a proper estimate of the interest of one small and ailing Self against the claims of all that there is in this world that is not Moses Elkanah Herzog; also a due respect for the mystery of experience that does not yield to explanations, much less to a "good five-cent synthesis." "Everything of intensest significance," he writes to God. "Especially if divested of me." Though Herzog ends the novel where he began it, flat on his back, he has come a distance in learning to keep still, to curb his vanity, and to let his heart fill of its own accord.

But the elegiac prose of the closing section is so gentle and moving that one tends to overlook the fact that it is quietly burying most of the issues that earlier had been raised in con-nection with Herzog's relations to society. At the end, he rests more firmly and spiritually in his passivity, but it is still passivity. He has taken Adlai Stevenson, among others, to task for being one of those "who think a good deal and effect nothing," but one wonders what Herzog is now able to effect besides another marriage to a woman lavish in all things, in-cluding advice on how he should live. True, he has begun to believe in the God of his friend Nachman and of his fathers, but isn't he merely availing himself of the solace of faith without committing himself to its substance? "I am pretty well satisfied to be, to be just as it is willed," says Herzog. One wonders what will happen when the trees of Ludeyville turn bare and Herzog's mind fills again with its dilemmas. God requires more desire than Herzog has to give; so far he hasn't abandoned the old Self but merely found a healing illusion of having done so.

I suspect that the same discursive looseness of structure that has allowed Bellow to indulge his flair for ideas has also ended by allowing him to indulge his flair for optimism. Like Herzog himself, the story of his recovery lacks the true opposition of Otherness, just as his protests remain too much the worldly discontents of an unworldly man. The finest thing about it is Bellow's incredible grasp of the individual intellectual plight—of the crisis of belief that lies beneath the complex surface of Herzog's behavior. As such, the novel is a great portrait of the contemporary humanist, Jewish-style, whose relations with the modern world are as increasingly hapless as Herzog demonstrates them to be. It's too bad that Bellow was driven to turn such a searching question of a book into a comfortable but evasive answer.

(1964)

Ship of Fools:
Anatomy of a Best-Seller

Whatever the problems were that kept Katherine Anne Porter's *Ship of Fools* from appearing during the past twenty years, it has been leading a charmed life ever since it was published late last March. In virtually a single voice, a little cracked and breathless with excitement, the reviewers announced that Miss Porter's long-awaited first novel was a "triumph," a "masterpiece," a "work of genius . . . a momentous work of fiction," "a phenomenal, rich, and delectable book," a "literary event of the highest magnitude." Whether it was Mark Schorer in the *New York Times Book Review* delivering a lecture, both learned and lyrical, on the source, sensibility, and stature of the novel ("Call it . . . the *Middlemarch* of a later day"), or a daily reviewer for the San Francisco *Call Bulletin* confessing that "not once [had he] started a review with so much admiration for its author, with such critical impotence"—in the end it came to the same sense of bedazzlement.

Propelled by this initial acclaim, *Ship of Fools* made its way to the top of the best-seller lists in record time and it is still there as I write in mid-September. During these four months it has encountered virtually as little opposition in taking its place among the classics of literature as it did in taking and holding its place on the best-seller lists. A few critics like Robert Drake in the *National Review*, Stanley Kauffmann in the *New Republic,* Granville Hicks in the *Saturday Review,* and Howard Moss in the *New Yorker* decided that *Ship of Fools* fell somewhat short of greatness, but only after taking the book's claim to greatness with respectful seriousness. A few of the solid citizens among the reviewers, like John K. Hutchens, found the novel to be dull and said so. Here and there, mainly in the hinterlands, a handful of skeptical spirits such as Mary Louise Aswell suspected that the book was a mammoth failure. But otherwise the applause went on and on.

Prominent among the circumstances which helped to make *Ship of Fools* a runaway best-seller and a *succès d'estime* was the aura of human interest that Miss Porter's long struggle to write it had produced. Most of the reviews began in the same way: a distinguished American short-story writer at the age of seventy-one has finally finished her first novel after twenty years of working on it. As this point was developed, it tended to establish the dominant tone of many reviews—that of elated witness to a unique personal triumph. The more so-phisticated critics approached the novel mainly in terms of the expectancy that Miss Porter's previous work had created. In Mark Schorer's words, *Ship of Fools* had been "eagerly awaited by an entire literary generation," which may over-state the matter but does point to the fact that over the years Miss Porter has become one of the surviving figures of the golden age of modern American letters—"the stylist of the 1920's to the last," to quote John Chamberlain's review. Her two splendid novellas "Pale Horse, Pale Rider" and "Noon Wine," along with her finely wrought stories such as "Flow-ering Judas" and "The Jilting of Grany Weatherall," con-tinue to be anthology pieces, part of everyone's education in literary craft and taste, as well as emblematic of an era when imaginative freedom and disciplined prose went hand in hand. In some ways Miss Porter has seemed like a very femi-nine counterpart of the early Hemingway, and her return after two decades of silence provided a rallying ground for old loyalties and affections. In reading the reviews, one had the feeling that almost everyone in the English departments and the New York literary circles was either awed by or pulling for her—particularly those "in the know" who were aware of the troubles that she had had in writing her novel.

If the first paragraph of the reviews was likely to dote in one way or another on Miss Porter, the second was likely to dote upon the universal dimensions of her new book. More often than not, this universality was demonstrated by quoting the Preface: particularly Miss Porter's statement that at the center of her design is nothing less than the "image of the ship of this world on its voyage to eternity." However large the claim might seem, the reviewers accepted it without question and lauded *Ship of Fools* as a novel whose theme "is the human race," as a "parable of a corrupt faithless world," as "a great moral allegory of man's fate," and so forth. That the only real sign of allegory in *Ship of Fools* is provided by the Preface (there are a few other details—the German ship's name is V*era,* etc.) and that the novel itself is a straightforward and grimly realistic account of a voyage from Veracruz to Bremerhaven in 1931, that the characters are drawn as literally as one could imagine, that the surface of the narrative is completely univalent, that the book is tied together by an attitude rather than by any conceptual scheme—none of this stopped any of the more enthusiastic reviewers from finding themselves in the presence of a great symbolic vision of human life and destiny. As Dayton Kohler, an English professor writing in the Richmond (Va.) *News Leader,* put it, "*Ship of Fools* is an attempt to confront the mystery of being. . . . Here in microcosm is the world man has made."

Another feeling repeatedly expressed by the reviews was that the return of Miss Porter had ended a long winter of discontent with recent fiction. Some viewed it as a welcome contrast to the genial popular novel that neatly solves the problems of its characters. But more often *Ship of Fools* was viewed as a kind of antidote to newfangled and noxious fiction by writers like Nabokov and Henry Miller. In their desire to behold again the "solid" novel that they had been deprived of by the idiosyncrasy and morbidity of contemporary fiction, such reviewers were inclined to see in *Ship of Fools* a somewhat different book from the one Miss Porter had actually written. If *Ship of Fools* does not have a "flimsy plot" (Winston-Salem *Journal and Sentinel*), this is only because it does not have much plot at all. If it has no "case histories" (Winston-Salem again), its cast of characters nevertheless includes a dipsomaniac (Herr Baumgartner), a nymphomaniac and drug addict (La Condessa), a religious maniac (Herr Graf), two paranoids (Herr Rieber and Herr Löwenthal), two child psychopaths (Ric and Rac), and—transfixed by their frustrations, compulsions, and illusions—a dozen or more feeble neurotics. Similarly, one needs to read only the first ten pages to see that Miss Porter re-creates "persons and events on their own terms" (Chicago *Sun-Times*) about as much as her title would indicate. For these reasons, among others, the novel has very little power, "rugged" (*Newsweek*) or otherwise, and its "myriad insights" (*Newsweek* again) all lie along the same rigid line of vision and impart much the same narrow judgment of experience.

Yet it is not hard to see what these reviewers had in mind. *Ship of Fools* suggests many of the qualities of the traditional "solid" novel that has virtually dropped out of sight in recent years. Like the nineteenth-century classics, it comes at life in a straightforward and comprehensive way. There are many characters and they all have the uncomplicated distinctiveness, bordering on caricature, that allows the reader to keep them straight and to know where he is with each of them. Miss Porter's steady, clear notation of the strongly marked and banal manners and attitudes of her German burghers, pedagogues, and naval men, of her American natives and expatriates, of her Hispanic priests and revolutionaries, aristocrats and peasants, thus provides the sort of large-scale social inventory that used to be one of the leading features of the major novel. Though she has dispensed with the old-fashioned elaborate plot, she does contrive an almost continual movement of the narrative among the characters which serves much the same purpose as complicated plotting once did: it brings different classes (in this case, nationalities) and types into relation and into the kind of revealing patterns of connection and conflict that can take on a large public significance. And tied as the novel is to crucial historical events such as the world-wide depression of the 1930's and the coming of fascism, the over-all effect is that of a novelist, as confident in her sense of moral order as Dickens or Balzac, creating the private history of an age.

Seen, then, from a respectful distance, *Ship of Fools* can easily look like the real thing come back again—a spacious, resonant, self-assured novel that the reader can settle down with instead of the highly mannered, oblique, claustral novel of recent years, confined to the academy or the suburb or a vaguely specified limbo, equivocal if not hostile toward the respectable values. At the same time, the unconventional anecdotal structure eliminates the Victorian furniture of an elaborate and artificial "story" and gives *Ship of Fools* a lean, functional, modern look. In other words, it is a book not only for the coffee table but for the room whose main point of taste is the well-upholstered Danish armchair and the print from Picasso's Blue Period.

All of which provides a few of the more obvious reasons why Miss Porter was able to win over about eighty percent of the reviewers and presumably the hundreds of thousands of readers whose currents of taste the reviewers both direct and mirror. The other reasons are more subtle. Virginia Pasley, book editor of *Newsday*, a Long Island daily, remarked that the novel's lack of an immediate story interest and its "incisive indictment of humanity" would put off many readers. "It was not written to please. It won't," she concluded. Yet Miss Pasley was completely wrong—for many of the reviewers chose to recommend *Ship of Fools* precisely for the two reasons that she had dismissed it as a possible best-seller. Indeed, the reception of the novel seemed a good deal less like another gathering of the philistines than a massive act of aspiration—even of conversion. It was seized upon as an opportunity both to move the level of popular literary appreciation up a full notch, and to declare, once and for all, that the human race has come to be as unsatisfactory and immoral as Miss Porter "objectively" pictures it to be.

The efforts at literary enlightenment turned mainly upon the discussions of the novel's action—the absence of a developing narrative, of any appreciable dividend of suspense, cumulative interest, or reversal of expectations that results from the highly episodic structure and the panoramic treatment of the characters. There was a good deal of talk about "the interplay of character" taking precedence over "the strategy of plotting," of "vibrant tension" rather than mere "suspense," of the writer's "vision of chaos" and use of "thematic structure." All of which indicated that a half-century after the innovations of Proust, Joyce, Kafka, Mann, et al., the idea that the happenings in a novel are far less significant or even moving than the underlying design, usually symbolic, to which they point appears to have filtered down into the popular literary mind. But the result of this theorizing was to shift the ground of discussion almost immediately from the novel's narrative qualities to its themes, which led most of the reviewers to overlook its crucial weaknesses as a novel.

The main such weakness is that no effective principle of change operates on the action or on the main characters or on the ideas, and hence the book has virtually no power to sustain, complicate, and intensify any real responsiveness to it. Several reviewers have compared *Ship of Fools* to Mann's *The Magic Mountain*, but the comparison immediately suggests the differences between a plot of ideas that changes with the development of the central figure and a collection of incidents that are strung along a few static themes. In *The Magic Mountain* there is an order of development whose nature is uncertain and problematic as the central figure, young

Hans Castorp, passes through a series of intellectual and spiritual influences that resume much of the cultural history of pre-World War I Europe. The slow, subtle transformation of Castorp's consciousness holds the various episodes together and also provides for a kind of intellectual suspense that reinforces the unfolding drama of his relationships with such powerful figures as Naphta, Settembrini, Peeperkorn, and Clavdia. In *Ship of Fools* there is little such drama or suspense, for no character or idea is kept open long enough to provide for them. As Mary Louise Aswell noted in the Phoenix *Gazette*, Miss Porter's narrative technique betrays at almost every point the hand of the unreconstructed short-story writer. Over and over again she isolates a single point of significance in an incident (people's failure to communicate, their self-deception, their emotional barrenness, moral bestiality, intellectual folly, etc.) and one or two salient traits in a character (Denny's bigotry and prurience, Mrs. Treadwell's boredom and indifference, Captain Thiele's childish authoritarianism, Fraulein Spöckenkieker's stridency, etc.). As a result, the personages on the ship soon become predictable, and when their behavior is not merely repetitious, it is usually abortive and inconsequential, leading to no significant alteration or complication and merely further illustrating one or another of the themes of human hunger, animality, or evil. The sense of sameness spreads like a yawn and, as one of the characters remarks herself, "this voyage . . . must undoubtedly be described as somewhat on the dull side."

But then *Ship of Fools* was mostly applauded for its gallery of great characterizations. In general, two claims were made in behalf of this extraordinary collection of boors, malcontents, and moral cripples who are mixed in with the grosser pathological cases. The first was that they were all superb creations ("any one or two of which," as Louise D. Rubin remarked, "would be the making of a lesser writer's reputation"); the second was that they are, individually and collectively, ourselves.

The favorite characters of the reviewers appeared to be La

Condessa and Dr. Schumann. The former, with her young men and her drugs and her wise heart, is actually little more than a stock theatrical voice crooning or shrieking in the wilderness inhabited by the fallen ladies of literature. Dr. Schumann—for all that he is supposed to be the main figure who experiences the truth of the substantial reality of evil by virtue of his sober, humane intelligence and his corrupting passion for La Condessa—is too enfeebled by a weak heart and a prudish malaise to have much force either as the victim or as the analyst of man's sinfulness. Also this good gray physician becomes not a little absurd during the course of the banal romance—a kind of higher literary soap opera—that he and La Condessa are given to act out:

> ". . . oh do you know what it is, coming so late, so strangely, no wonder I couldn't understand it. It is that innocent romantic love I should have had in my girlhood! . . . Well, here we are. Innocent love is the most painful kind of all, isn't it?"
>
> "I have not loved you innocently," said Dr. Schumann, "but guiltily and I have done you great wrong, and I have ruined my life. . . ."
>
> "My life was ruined so long ago I have forgotten what it was like before," said La Condessa. "So you are not to have me on your mind. . . . I shall find a way out of everything. And now, now my love, let's kiss again really this time in broad daylight and wish each other well, for it is time for us to say good-bye."
>
> "Death, death," said Dr. Schumann, as if to some presence standing to one side of them casting a long shadow. "Death," he said, and feared his heart would burst.

The other two characters often singled out for special praise by the reviewers were the two American women, Jenny Brown and Mrs. Treadwell. What the reviewers sensed, though tended to sentimentalize, is that both women possess

an intermittent autonomy, denied to the other characters, by
virtue of a special strength of feeling that Miss Porter has for
them. Jenny, an embittered and hollow version of the earlier
autobiographical heroine (Miranda in "Old Mortality" and
"Pale Horse, Pale Rider," Laura in "Flowering Judas"), is
shown in the grip of a personal despair whose force is sufficient to shake her alive from time to time, so that she becomes something more than the stereotype of the liberated
American and reveals something deeper and less predictable
than her foolishness. To a lesser extent, this is also true of
Mrs. Treadwell, an emotionally fragile divorcee with the rest
of her life to kill. Otherwise, the characters lead lives on the
ship that are tightly circumscribed by the baleful vision of
human folly in which they are suspended, by the particular
disfigurements, both personal and cultural, that they are fashioned to reveal. Unlike Dante's Brunetto Latino, or Chau-
cer's Pardoner, or Shakespeare's Angelo, or Stendahl's Sansfin
(Miss Porter was compared to these and other masters by the
reviewers in hailing her understanding of human nature), her
figures are cartoons of moral infirmity and as such have only
so much to reveal. After fifty pages they are predictable; after
a hundred they are less revealing of human nature than they
are of Miss Porter's remarkably shallow design and sensibility.

In fact, once the characters begin to be brought into relation or to have their innards exposed at all, the attentive
reader can smell the formaldehyde. Thus Frau Rittersdorf
comes aboard the *Vera*. Her first act is to take over the lower
berth, though she has been assigned an upper; her second act
is to place in vases "two enormous floral offerings she had
sent herself" with cards from two male admirers. After dressing and ogling herself, she opens her diary and writes:

So in a way, let me admit, this adventure—for is not all
life an adventure?—has not ended as I hoped, yet nothing is changed for indeed I may yet see the all-guiding
Will of my race in it. A German woman should not

marry into a dark race. . . . There are the fatal centuries in Spain when all too insidiously Jewish and Moorish blood must certainly have crept in—who knows what else? . . .

Elsewhere on the ship, Herr Rieber is already defending German honor and frolicking with the shrieking Lizzi Spöckenkieker ("How he admired and followed the tall thin girls with long scissor-legs like storks striding under their fluttering skirts, with long narrow feet on the ends of them"); William Denny is leering at two "Chili Queens"; and David Scott, Jenny's cold-hearted lover, is instancing his hatred of her and his horror of life ("There was no place, no place at all to go"). In one stateroom Frau Baumgartner is taking out her hostility to her husband (a helpless alcoholic and hypochondriac) on their sickly little boy, whom, despite the intense Mexican heat, she has kept dressed in a heavy leather cowboy costume. (" 'Mayn't I just take off my jacket?' he persisted hopelessly.") And nearby, the supernaturally pedantic Professor Hutten is lecturing to his wife about their bottle-fed bulldog Bébé ("We need not look for any radical change in his organic constitution"), while "in round maternal tones" she croons to the dog: "Don't think your little Vati and Mutti are deserting you, my precious one."

And so it goes for the next 460 pages, with only a few time-outs for an act of relative sanity, dignity, or even of complexity. All of which is supposed to constitute a true picture of human nature, and so it was generally taken to be.

This is the most remarkable feature of the reviews. One wonders which of these hapless or vicious grotesques Mark Schorer (who said that "It will be a reader myopic to the point of blindness who does not find his name on her passenger list") found to represent himself, or what qualities Louis Auchincloss ("how easy it would be for anyone to turn into even the most repellent of these incipient Nazis") would own up to that bring him so close to Herr Rieber with his clownish lust and serious wish to throw the steerage passengers into gas ovens. Moreover, one wonders why so many of the populars reviewers ("Katherine Anne Porter has seen all of us plain") took as gospel the most sour and petty indictment of humanity to appear in recent memory.

My hunch is that something more than reviewers' cant was involved here. The willingness of the reviewers to see themselves in Miss Porter's characters bears a remarkable resemblance to the reaction of the American press to the disclosures of the Eichmann trial last year. Bypassing the specific circumstances that had produced and empowered an Eichmann, most of the editorial writers hastened to phrases like "man's inhumanity to man," which collapsed all political and moral distinctions, not to say the purpose of the trial itself. And in the mood of moral malaise that the trial seems mainly to have inspired, it apparently became increasingly easy to assert that we are all Adolf Eichmann, which immediately transformed Eichmann from a very special kind of twentieth-century political figure into merely one more example of the imperfectibility of man.*

By and large, *Ship of Fools* was read as another brief in the same abstract trial of mankind, vaguely centering upon the Nazi treatment of Jews. "In 1931 the foulness [of the world] was the rise of pride-injured German nationalism . . ." (*Time*). "To the author, anti-Semitism of any description is only one form of humanity's general failure to perceive the commonness of all humanity" (*Newsweek*). In some cases the reviewers were proceeding on the basis of a statement Miss Porter made in 1940 that the stories collected in *Flowering Judas* were part of a "much larger plan" whose ultimate purpose was "to understand the logic of this majestic and terrible failure of the life of man in the Western world." But they were also reading the novel. That Miss Porter has

---

* I am indebted for this point to a study, prepared for the American Jewish Committee by Midge Decter, of the response of the American press to the Eichmann trial.

no use for her Germans is perfectly clear, and in almost every case they are seen to be well along the road to Nazism (the book is set in 1931). But since she has no more use for most of her Mexicans, Swiss, Americans, and Spaniards, the road to Nazism soon becomes part of a six-lane highway to hell that runs down the middle of her novel. The only power of active evil is given to the troupe of Spanish dancers; in the main, the Germans merely sit nervously at the Captain's table and speak their different varieties of Aryan cant while they bolt their food and look for chances to devour each other. There is no sense at all of the *force* of that monstrous romanticism, of the potential for *active* evil in the character of German nationalism, with its commitments not only to the purity of order but to the purity of chaos and self-immolation. In his recent novel, *The Fox in the Attic*, Richard Hughes understands these matters far more deeply than does Miss Porter. Hughes, too, sees the ludicrous pretensions of the early Hitler and his cohorts, but he also grasps the relentless energy of that "insane idealism" of hatred and love that created *Lebensraum* and death camps. It is the argument of *Ship of Fools*—indeed, the main theme of the book as Dr. Schumann states it—that most people's "collusion with evil is only negative, consent by default," and that it is the "mere mass and weight of negative evil [which] threatened to the rule of the world." This last may be merely Schumann's own proto-fascist proclivities, but it is difficult to distinguish his attitude from that of the writer who has been speaking through him. In any event, Miss Porter's theme of man's paltry sinfulness, once translated, say, into the figures of Captain Thiele and Herr Rieber, produces merely a bilious stuffed shirt whose fantasies of violence come from American gangster movies and an impotent buffoon who eventually cavorts around the ship in a baby bonnet. The threat of "the terrible failure of the life of man" that lurks at the Captain's table is far less that of genocide than of boredom and gastritis.

This insistence upon a "general failure" of humanity creates not only a feeble portent of Hitler's Germany but in time a brutally indiscriminate one. Among the Germans on board the Vera, there is none more wretched and repulsive than the Jew Julius Löwenthal, with his whining, puny hatred of the goyim; his lack of curiosity, much less passion, for anything in life save kosher cooking and the opportunities to make a killing off the Catholics; his tendency to spit disgustedly into the wind. A caricature of Jewish vulgarity, Löwenthal is otherwise coldly reduced to an abstract tribal paranoia. Thinking himself snubbed by Captain Thiele, he broods for hours:

> He wished for death, or thought he did. He retired into the dark and airless ghetto of his soul and lamented with all the grieving wailing company he found there; for he was never alone in that place. He . . . mourned in one voice with his fated people, wordlessly he bewailed their nameless eternal wrongs and sorrows; then feeling somewhat soothed, the inspired core of his being began to search for its ancient justification and its means of revenge. But it should be slow and secret.

In other words, this successful peddler to the Catholics is the stage Jew of the modern literary tradition whom other Christian writers of sensibility (among them T. S. Eliot) have dragged out of the ghetto to represent the vulgar and menacing dislocations of traditional order:

> *My house is a decayed house,*
> *And the jew squats on the window sill, the owner,*
> *Spawned in some estaminet of Antwerp,*
> *Blistered in Brussels, patched and peeled in London.*

Far from exerting any understanding of or sympathy for Löwenthal—which he might have claimed if only because of the far from "nameless wrongs and sorrows" that he and his people will soon have to face in Germany—Miss Porter uses him in a situation whose implications are both historically misleading and morally vicious. At the dramatic center of the novel—both in terms of placement and by being the only conflict in the book that affects any appreciable group of characters—is an incident in which Herr Freitag, Miss Porter's other well-intentioned but ineffectual German, is removed from the Captain's table because it has been discovered that his wife is Jewish. He is then seated with the isolated Löwenthal, who immediately begins to persecute him and his absent wife:

> She's the kind of Jewish girl that makes disgrace for all the rest of us. . . . I never laid a finger on a Gentile woman in my life, and the thought of touching one makes me sick; why can't you Goyim leave our girls alone, isn't your own kind good enough for you? . . . Be ashamed, Herr Freitag—when you wrong Jewish girls, you wrong the whole race. . . .

While Löwenthal baits him, Freitag thinks, "Here it comes again, from the other side. . . . I can't sit here either." And indeed the hostility toward him that he has also found in his wife's circle, along with the contempt he receives from his fellow Germans, has begun to make him repent of his marriage and renew his identification with the mentality and destiny of the Fatherland.

Thus, the historical significance that *Ship of Fools* is designed to possess—and all of its detail of national and cultural traits as well as its supposed symbolic resonance are nothing if not pretensions to such significance—becomes a matter of implying that the fate of Germany and its Jews reduces to the encounter of two particularly obnoxious breeds of inhumanity, with the decent but weak German liberals caught in the middle, where they become the victims of their own milder impulses toward evil. Such an implication (and there is little to complicate, much less correct it, in the course of the novel) bespeaks not simply a failure of historical understanding, but what is more inexcusable for a novelist, it indicates a failure of consciousness, a glib refusal to acknowledge any of the imponderables of Löwenthal's fate:

> All he wanted in the world was the right to be himself,
> to go where he pleased and do what he wanted without
> any interference from them [the goyim]. That no race
> or nation in the world, nor in all human history had en-
> joyed such rights made no difference to Herr Löwenthal:
> he should worry about things none of his business.

Such a passage is bad art and stupid history; it also expresses
the fretful and trifling caricature of Jews that is a hallmark of
genteel anti-Semitism. But the treatment of Löwenthal is
only one example of Miss Porter's compulsive tendency to
simplify and close her characters and issues, to look down
upon life from the perspective of a towering arrogance, contempt, and disgust.

It is just here that the reviewers went most astray in reading and puffing the novel. As some of the cleverer ones saw,
Ship of Fools is not a novel of action or character or ideas,
but one that is held together and given significance by its
point of view—that is to say, by the direct presence and pressure of Miss Porter's sensibility. However, the personal aura
of Miss Porter, that I began by noting, was particularly misleading in this respect, for it guarded her against direct criticism of the main weakness of the book—the bilious spirit in
which it was written. To judge this spirit was inevitably to
judge the "gracious . . . gentlewoman," "the distinguished
humanist" of acquaintance and reputation. The better critics
—such as Stanley Edgar Hyman and Stanley Kauffmann—
stopped just short of doing so. The others spoke of Miss
Porter's "compassion" and "concern," "candor" and "objectivity," "wit" and "humor." The critic who went to greatest
lengths to define and exult over Miss Porter's sensibility was
Mark Schorer:

> There is nothing (or almost nothing) harsh in her
> book. There is much that is comic, much even that is
> hilarious, and everything throughout is always flashing
> into brilliance through the illumination of this great
> ironic style. At the same time, almost everything that is

comic is simultaneously pathetic . . . moving to the point of pain, nearly of heartbreak. No, all that is conceivably harsh in this book is its magnificent lack of illusion about human nature and especially the human sexual relationship. Even that is not really harsh because all the sharp perception and unsparing wit is exercised by an imaginative sympathy that is not withheld from even the greatest fool, not even from the Texan oaf, Denny, whom the gracious Mrs. Treadwell, suddenly outraged beyond endurance, beats into insensibility with the sharp heel of her lovely golden slipper.

The remarkable thing about this passage, from what must have been the most influential review of the book, is that it does not contain a single point that is true. The humor in *Ship of Fools* is not hilarious but snickering, and its pathos is represented by the type of artful corn that was quoted some pages back in connection with La Condessa and Dr. Schumann's relationship. Seldom does anything "flash into brilliance," for the "great ironic style" of the author who wrote "Noon Wine" no longer belongs to Miss Porter. Under the cold, smooth plaster of her prose is not a "magnificent lack of illusion about human nature," but an alternately smug or exasperated or queasy hostility toward most of the behavior she is describing. The art of the book lies mostly in the covert little ways it has of showing up and putting down the characters, and almost any passage of description or dialogue brings out some of them. As I said earlier, Jenny Brown is one of the few characters that her author has any feeling for; yet not even she is allowed to escape from Miss Porter's subtle, habitual snideness:

She hesitated and then spoke the word "soul" very tentatively, for it was one of David's tabus, along with God, spirit, spiritual, virtue—especially that one!—and love. None of these words *flowered particularly* in Jenny's daily speech, though now and then in some *stray* warmth of feeling she *seemed* to need one or the other;

but David could not endure the sound of any of them.
. . . He could translate them into obscene terms and
pronounce them with a sexual fervor of enjoyment; and
Jenny, who blasphemed as *harmlessly as a well-taught
parrot,* was in turn offended by what she *prudishly* described as "David's dirty mind." . . .

My italics underscore the small jabs, the relentless cattiness of
Miss Porter's "sensibility." The most persistent and revealing
example of her "sharp perception and unsparing wit" is in
her comparisons of almost all her characters to a whole menagerie of animals and birds—the idea being that their behavior is at bottom no different from the chain of greedy,
malicious animosity that has been illustrated in the opening
pages by the relations between a cat, a monkey, a parrot, and
a dog. As for Miss Porter's "imaginative sympathy," one can
read the frigid description of the incident Schorer notes in
which the "gracious" Mrs. Treadwell, having alternately
teased and pushed away a young officer on the ship through a
whole evening, and having drunk herself into a stupor in her
stateroom, squats over the unconscious Denny. With "her
lips drawn back and her teeth set, she beat him with such
furious pleasure [that] a sharp pain started up in her right
wrist. . . . "

Mrs. Treadwell's violence is not directed at Denny so
much as at "the human sexual relationship" which she fears
and hates and which he, like most of the other characters,
embodies in a particularly hideous manner. Miss Porter's attitude in this respect is most apparent in the treatment of the
Spanish dancing troupe who are the evil characters in the
novel, the focus of most of the speculations about original
sin. From the moment they appear on the scene, the girls'
"sleazy black skirts too tight around their slender hips . . .
their eyes flashing and their hips waving in all directions," a
sense of fascinated revulsion settles into the tone of the narrative and continues throughout the novel as the dominant
strain of Miss Porter's outrage. In its most overt form, it

fixates upon the incestuous relations of the two six-year-old psychopaths, Ric and Rac; upon the malign sexual power and corruption of the adult dancers as they glide about the decks; upon the wildly lascivious Concha teasing one of the young passengers nearly to the point of murdering his grandfather in order to get some money to sleep with her; upon the sexual relations of the dancers themselves:

> Their supple dancers' legs writhed together for a moment like a nest of snakes. They sniffed, nibbled, bit, licked and sucked each other's flesh with small moans of pleasure. . . . She saved herself like a miser in the dull plungings and poundings of those men who were her business, and spent herself upon Pepe, who was tricky as a monkey and as coldly long-lasting as a frog.

However, this chilled, queasy attitude toward the sexuality of the dancers and the accompanying imagery of revulsion radiate outward from the dancers to condition each of the other sexual relationships. La Condessa croons seductively to Dr. Schumann and he has "a savage impulse to strike her from him, this diabolical possession, this incubus fastened upon him like a bat." Even when the incredibly stuffy Huttens make love, the reader finds himself back with Pepe and Amparo: the same stressed male violence, the same abased female satisfaction, the same description of their bodies "grappled together like frogs." Sex on Miss Porter's "ship of this world" is Denny's constant goatish leer; it is the chasing of the "pig-snout" Rieber after the "peahen" Spöckenkieker; it is the "monkey-faced" snickering of the Cuban students and the impassioned face of La Condessa, "her eyes . . . wild and inhuman as a monkey's"; sex is Jenny's gesture, "unself-conscious as a cat," of slapping her inner thigh; it is the Baumgartners' terrifying their child who lies awake in the next berth; in sum, it is David Scott's moment of introspection when "slowly there poured through all his veins again that deep qualm of loathing and intolerable sexual fury, a poisonous mingling of sickness and death-like pleasure."

This "deep qualm" is what Miss Porter's "magnificent lack of illusion" boils down to. It also plays a large part in deflecting her sensibility to its incessant quarrel with human nature and in leading it by inevitable stages to a vision of life that is less of vice and folly than of a hideously choking slow death. (In the words of E. E. Cummings, "Freud knows why/and so do I.") Miss Porter's versions of political action, artistic creation, religious belief, teaching, and so forth are no less skewed and embittered than her versions of copulation. Further, this clammy connection between sex and evil appears to rule out any feeling toward her characters that goes much beyond a nagging exasperated irony, and to remove the possibility of any struggle toward deeper insight. As a result, the consciousness that is operating in the book, for all its range of view, is standing, so to speak, on a dime, and has little contact with the sources of imaginative vitality and moral power—erotic at their core—that renew a long work of fiction.

One can begin to understand, then, why *Ship of Fools*— apart from problems of technique and theme—remains so stagnant and repetitive; why there is neither the humor nor the pathos that Schorer raves about; and why there is nothing either "majestic" or "terrible" about Miss Porter's image of human failure. Far from being a profound account of the "ship of this world on its voyage to eternity," *Ship of Fools* is simply what it is: an account of a tedious voyage to Europe three decades ago that has been labored over for twenty years by a writer who, late in life, is venturing, hence revealing, little more than bitchiness and clever technique. "*Ship of Fools* is a work of mechanical art," as Elizabeth N. Hoyt of the Cedar-Rapids *Gazette* put it—cutting through the sentimental and pretentious obfuscation which has surrounded the novel from the start—"but the soul of humanity is lacking."

(1962)

The Integration of Bigger Thomas

As I begin to write about *Native Son*, it is the first day of spring, 1964. My consciousness of the fact comes from a news broadcast in the next room: two brief reports announce the arrival of spring, in these times of ours, and foreshadow the days ahead, more surely than do warm winds or budding branches. In Birmingham, Alabama, two Negro ministers are making the first protest march of the year. In Jacksonville, Florida, Negro youths have been rioting in the streets through most of the night. And so, in the turning of the year, our society itself begins to turn again and to confront what Richard Wright referred to twenty years ago as "the shadow athwart our national life." Perhaps twenty years from now this shadow will have finally moved to the stern and Wright's *Native Son* will be simply another social-protest novel from a distant and benighted time. So it was generally taken to be during the past decade. But in March 1964 one inevitably tries to read it as a document that bears upon present realities, upon the feelings that rise like the sap of the trees in Birmingham and Jacksonville and all the other cities and towns, North and South, that will shortly again be in the news.

However, if *Native Son* bears upon our crisis, it clearly does so in a problematic way. Indeed, it is still all too easy to experience the book as a symptom of the social disorder it seeks to record and illuminate. Many readers will identify its shock and violence, its crudity and simplicity, with the period of its conception: the closing years of the Depression, when the conflict between the races existed in a more primitive and repressed form than it does today. The social mood of the novel is that of an American city just on the eve of the race riots of the early 1940's, which had no content other than the sudden explosion of hatred. The focus of its interest is almost entirely restricted to the characterization of Bigger Thomas: the Negro as an isolated and dehumanized being whose only mode of protest—indeed, of freedom—is crime, rape, murder. Through most of the novel Bigger is made to stand before us in all of his anger, hostility, and remorselessness, his deprivations so acute and complete as to constitute a type of depravity. Bigger is, of course, partly redeemed in the final section, but the dramatic power of the novel, the force that determines which of its themes will be driven home, is almost entirely in the service of emphasizing Bigger's savagery: his attack on his friend Gus, his conscienceless behavior after killing his employer Mary, his coercion, violation, and murder of his girl Bessie, along with the other details of moral affectlessness that bind his character to his crimes. In short, if Bigger is anything at all dramatistically, he is the creature of the "shadow" of racism, unrelieved by any hope save the vain one of working-class solidarity.

Little wonder, then, that the image of the novel that stayed with me for many years after I first read it as an adolescent was that of a baleful Negro crouched over the decapitated body of a white girl, like an animal over its prey. Most of the other characters reinforce the lurid racial melodrama, for they, too, are mainly cut from the same fabric of fantasy and myth that twenty years ago made up most of the consciousness of Negro-white relations in the North. If Bigger seems to answer to the most grotesque stereotype of a white racist, the whites correspond no less completely to the stereotypes of a Negro racist. With the exception of Max, a Communist humanitarian who probably elicited more assent in 1940 than he does today, the white race is represented by whited sepulchers or fools or devils: the do-gooding Daltons who are slumlords, from on high, the incredibly doltish and teasing Mary, the vicious Britten, the corrupt Buckley, the ghoulish reporters, the Chicago populace screaming for Bigger's blood. Over the very landscape of the novel broods much the same hallucinatory atmosphere; the hulking, abandoned tenements and the mournful, strangely deserted streets of the Black Belt, watched over by the huge picture of State's Attorney Buckley, his finger pointed in accusation of one and all.

No doubt the sensationalism of *Native Son* helped to shatter the indifference of its readers in 1940, but one can hardly justify the necessity for it today. On the contrary, the immediate effect of Wright's melodrama is to revitalize prejudices and projections on both sides and to contribute to the apocalyptic aura that inflames the imagination of our crisis but distracts from and weakens an understanding of it. Nor does it seem to me very useful or even accurate to celebrate *Native Son*, on literary as well as social grounds, for bringing to light the gruesome sexual content of our cultural nightmare, or for placing the plight of the Negro in its proper fantastic setting, or for hurling the violence that accumulates in the Negro spirit into the teeth of white apathy. All of this contributes to the power of the novel but, at the same time, is inseparable from the rage and hysteria that Wright was sometimes unable to control and that deflect his interest and ours from the social and psychological issues with which he was most concerned. In his essay "How Bigger was Born," Wright remarks that he kept a number of "improbable scenes" because they "revealed enough of what I felt . . . in spite of [their] unreality." The result is an unsteady combination of naturalism and crude expressionism in which the accumulations of realistic detail suddenly melt away and the Black Belt environment and the white world beyond seem to become mainly an extension of Bigger's fearful inner life and of Wright's outrage. Similarly, the character of Bigger is both that of "a [symbolic] monster created by the American republic," "a near-subhuman indictment of white oppression," to quote James Baldwin and Ralph Ellison respectively, and a convincing portrait of a trapped and hopeless Negro slum kid whose emotional life has been stunted and fragmented not by the angry hand of Richard Wright but by the probabilities of his existence.

In order to look beneath the sensational surface of *Native Son* and to confront its meaning, it is best to pay some heed to what Wright himself thought he was trying to say. In his essay on *Native Son*, he defended the actuality of Bigger by identifying five of his sources, all of them hard cases of twisted Negro pride, ranging from bullies who acted out their aggressions against Negroes to those who somehow managed to strike back against the taboos of the South. The one who most foreshadows Bigger was a boy "whose only law was death," an isolated and unstable rebel who was alternately "agitated and depressed" by his ruling idea that "white folks won't let us do anything," and who eventually went insane. There are also other evident sources for Bigger in Wright's autobiography, *Black Boy*, including the main one, as we shall see—Wright himself.

All of these prototypes Wright knew in the South. It was only in the black ghetto of Chicago that the "type" itself fully emerged. Wright observed that the new Negro of the bitter Northern slums was driven to the extreme by the tensions of his uprooted and frustrated way of life. Both Baldwin and Ellison have criticized Wright for isolating Bigger from his ordinary communal ties, for depriving him of the accumulated folkways of behavior and consciousness, of Negro comity and faith that have sustained the spirit of his people through its oppressions. Wright was perfectly conscious of doing so, however, for he believed that one of the two chief characteristics of the new Negro was his "estrangement from the religion and folk culture of his race." Wright particularly had in mind the great migrations North of the Negro share-croppers and field hands that began in the middle 1930's: "never in history," as he wrote elsewhere, "[was there] a more utterly unprepared folk." Bigger, then, was meant to embody the dislocation, loneliness, and anomie of the suddenly expanded Black Belt, the unremitting bleakness of its days. Molded by this bleakness, Bigger is constantly prodded to revolt against it by the second new aspect of his lot: the tantalizing lure of the dominant society that comes to him through the magazines and movies to which he has grown addicted and through "the mere imposing sight and sound of daily American life." In this respect Bigger is the victim of the American dream of possibilities; his desires are no longer forbidden outright, they are only impossible to achieve and so they constantly tease his mind as fantasies. "I always wanted to do something," Bigger says at the very end, summing up in his own way the justification of his deeds as an assault against the baffling aspirations and alienation of his blackness.

In "How Bigger was Born," explaining why this ignorant young Negro was attracted by the reports he heard of Nazi Germany, Wright identifies him as one of the modern *Lumpenproletariat* whose "wild and intense longing to belong, to feel they were alive as other people were, to be caught up forgetfully and exultingly in the swing of events" made them the prey of a mode of politics that allowed them, in Bigger's words, "to do something." Partly, of course, Wright was imposing upon Bigger's fate a standard insight of leftist sociology, but he was also approaching a more personal awareness of how violence can become the defining mode of being for the modern lost soul, white as well as black, who feels that he is being shut out by his society. In the novel itself, Bigger first rapes and then kills Bessie for no other reason, really, than to regain the feeling of weighted significant action that had followed the killing of Mary. These acts, as Wright understood them, were partly the product of Bigger's alienation: a hunger for a fullness of being that could only be satisfied "on the plane of animal sensations," an adjustment to the loss of personal security and faith that took the form of an intoxication with extreme feelings and sensations, of emotional highs and lows, that kept "him drowning daily in a perpetual nervous agitation."

If Wright was struggling to find a more general social meaning in Negro violence than its legacy of hate and fear, he was also attempting to explore the nature of human freedom within the context of Bigger's panic, flight, and fate. Both themes are not sufficiently thought through, much less dramatized, to run clearly in the novel, and they are easily lost amid the more overt strands of Negro protest, social determinism, and the conventions of naturalism that make Bigger into a monster and victim. However, readers in France such as Sartre were quick to detect the deeper implications of *Native Son*, and Bigger Thomas is still regarded there as one of the major heroes of existentialist literature. It is evident that Wright structured *Native Son* to provide for the examination of Bigger's movement toward individuality and freedom rather than to emphasize his entrapment and destruction by his environment. The murder of Mary comes early in the novel, and the social causes of its commission are far less evident than its consequences of discovery and growth. For all of the didactic deadwood that it drags in tow, the form of *Native Son* is that of tragedy: the movement of its parts follows the "tragic rhythm" that Francis Fergusson has described of "purpose, passion, and perception."

In order to explore Bigger's progress toward freedom and at the same time keep him sufficiently insensitive to remain within the social meaning, Wright perforce surrounded Bigger with his own consciousness. More than that, his depiction of Bigger—far from being merely that of the dehumanized "nigger" he is still usually taken to be—was adapted from the ruling issue of his own life: the freedom that he had won for himself.

Wright tells us next to nothing about Bigger's early life,

except that he grew up in Jackson, Mississippi—the town where Wright dwelled longest during the frequent moves and broken homes of his childhood. It is clear, however, that Bigger, like Wright, was unable to develop the "delicate, sensitive controlling mechanism" that enabled Southern black boys "to shut off their minds and emotions from all that the white race had said was taboo." Wright wrote of himself in *Black Boy* that by the time he reached adolescence

> my inability to adjust myself to the white world had already shattered a part of the structure of my personality
> . . . blocking the springs of thought and feeling, creating a sense of distance between me and the world. . . .
> Nothing challenged the totality of my personality so much as this pressure of hate and threat that stemmed from the invisible whites. . . . It was as though I was continuously reacting to the threat of some natural force whose hostile behavior could not be predicted.

Over and over again the same point is reiterated about Bigger, who "passed his days trying to defeat or gratify powerful impulses in a world he feared," whose character is such that "never in all his life . . . had thought and feeling, will and mind, aspiration and satisfaction been together," and whose sense of the white world is not of people but of "a great natural force."

As Wright goes on to tell us in *Black Boy*, his own fantasies of violent retaliation, however remote from reality they might be, constituted a necessary mode of resistance that prevented his fear from thoroughly violating his being. The more he came in touch with the white society through his various jobs, the more it loomed before him as a "huge, implacable, elemental design" toward which his hate was futile. Yet his desire to assault it persisted. The result was to keep his mind wound up with tension that could be sprung more completely by white kindness than by hate. Eventually he seizes upon an idea that will allow him to rebel against white authority and liberate himself from it: he will escape to the North and become a writer. To achieve his freedom, he resists the lures and snares of a career as a schoolteacher and a place in the comfortably enslaved black bourgeoisie of Jackson, just as he resists the conventional compensations of his working-class lot: religious resignation, on the one hand, and debauchery, on the other. He alienates himself from his own people and daily takes his life into his hands with whites, for to harbor his aspirations and allow them to shape his inner life was to experience a consciousness of being that "the state of Mississippi had spent millions of dollars to make sure that I would never feel," and that was punishable by terror, private when not public, once it became known that he had desires beyond the "darky's" lot in the South. To wish to reclaim his life by an act of liberation from its constraints was to assert his humanity, which in Jackson and Memphis was nothing less than to assert his equality. Wright becomes increasingly aware of the danger in which he lives; at the same time, to live with and work for these furtive aspirations, to contain and discipline the extreme stresses that they bred, to associate in his reading with writers like Mencken and Lewis and Dreiser, who put him in touch with the vague possibility of his own place and fulfillment among men, were themselves the beginning of his liberation from both the repressions of white society and from the shamed and unstable image of himself that they fostered. "In what other ways," Wright asks himself at the end of *Black Boy*, "had the South allowed me to be natural, to be real, to be myself, except in rejection, rebellion, and aggression?" But true self-knowledge is still beyond him; it awaits some meaningful intercourse with an actual freedom and community.

As Wright wound his way into the character of Bigger Thomas he used many of the same perceptions to explain the nature of Bigger's crimes, to fix in the cold, sullen depravity of what Bigger had done the tangled skein of a destructive effort to liberate himself from fear, to experience a full consciousness of being, to claim his humanity. Early in the novel, as he stands on a streetcorner with Gus and acts out his resentment at being a Negro and his hopeless fantasies of what it means to be white, he exhibits the "pensive, brooding amusement . . . of a man confronted and tantalized by a riddle" whose answer both escapes him and prods him to seek its solution. This is the inchoate inkling of self-awareness that will eventually expand and clarify itself through his crimes and the release they provide, and through his flight, incarceration, trial, and imminent death and the successive stages of consciousness they provide. Bigger does not have Wright's resources, only his needs. In *Black Boy*, Wright observes that the kindness of a white salesman to him merely exposed "the yawning shameful gap that loomed between us," that his solicitude was "more dangerous" than any abuse he could have handed him; and it is just such an experience—the heedless friendship of Jan and Mary—that gives Bigger the hideous consciousness of his true place in the world. As Wright noted at the outset, "the moment [Bigger] allowed what his life meant to enter fully into his consciousness, he would either kill himself or someone else."

In the throes of shame and fear, of hate and self-hate, whose intensity overwhelms him, Bigger trips the mechanism of violence that has been prepared in his small acts and large fantasies: he kills and "creates a new life for himself"—that is to say, he almost immediately begins to experience an entirely new range of relations with the white world and with himself. "The hidden meaning of his life" has been sprung open by the act that has released him from his bondage to fear and shame, that has made his *being* count in the world and hence enabled him to begin to see himself as the agent of his own destiny. It pays not to sentimentalize here. Bigger may now begin to feel human, insofar as his life is now directed by his own consciousness and will—but he is not human in his sensibilities. His guilt is almost totally subconscious—lurid images of the murder: consciously, he feels no remorse. Experi-

encing the confidence, fullness, and freedom that his crime
has conferred, he imagines killing others, such as his brother
Buddy, and eventually kills Bessie, less out of any necessity
than to rekindle his sense of power and to blot out the "stillness, isolation, meaninglessness" of another Negro life.

Meanwhile his own panic is still always on tap. He has begun to learn how to exploit his blackness in forestalling suspicion of him, but he is still in its grip. The gap between
thought and feeling has only temporarily been bridged and
the connection is swept away again in the anguish of his
flight. Early on the morning that he has killed Bessie, Bigger
looks out upon the freezing, snowbound world of the South
Side, a model of the white world that he realizes has denied
him real consciousness and wholeness by shutting him out:

> He did not want to sit on a bench and sing, or lie in a
> corner and sleep. It was when he read the newspapers or
> magazines, went to the movies, or walked along the
> streets with crowds, that he felt what he wanted: to
> merge himself with others and be a part of this world, to
> lose himself in it so he could find himself, to be allowed
> a chance to live like others, even though he was black.

Much of the final section, apart from the trial, traces the
growth of Bigger's "wayward yearning" and "obscure need"
to be at home with people in order to validate his feelings
and understand their relation to the life he has led. The
hunger for full consciousness of himself and full connection
begins to be satisfied in his relations with Max. Firm in his
rejections, he pushes aside the consolation of religion: he is
looking for a place in the human community where he can
lodge his emotions so that he can die with the awareness of
having, however briefly, lived in it. The "Popular Front"
homilies in which Bigger's final liberation is expressed should
not distract us from the profound insight behind them.

What Wright saw in the fate of Bigger, as in his own
struggle for freedom, was that only in the acknowledgment of

his humanity by other men could he expect to join the
scarred and fragmented elements of his emotional life, to reconstitute what society, through its prejudice against him,
had shattered. It is to the credit of Wright's honesty that he
grants to Bigger only enough consciousness to acknowledge
and integrate the feelings that he has had nurtured in this
world, not those which he has not. "What I killed for, I *am!*"
This is as much freedom as Bigger has been given to achieve.

Two decades later we come again to our own yearly confrontation with the algebra of hatred and guilt, alienation
and violence, freedom and self-integration; and in the
struggle for what is called today "civil rights" the meaning
of Bigger Thomas and of Richard Wright continues to reveal itself.

(1964)

Irving Howe and the Socialist Imagination

Over the past decade or so there have seemed to be two Irving Howes. One is the literary scholar and journalist: the author of the fine critical biography of Sherwood Anderson, the intricate interpretation of Faulkner, the erudite and mostly disinterested book on *Politics and the Novel*. This is the Howe who appears in journals as diverse as the *New Republic* and *Hudson Review*: his crisp, meticulous prose, his skill at literary description, his grasp of the relevant issue quite equal to any serious book or audience. He is almost always telling you something sound and worthwhile and he is almost always as clear as glass: he is the only critic I can think of who is not somehow defeated in writing for the *New York Times Book Review*. The other Irving Howe is, of course, the radical thinker and publicist: the co-author of books on American Communism and the U.A.W., and more prominently, the embroiled editor and chief house writer of *Dissent*. This is the polemical Howe, the irascible idealist of the Thirties joined to the rueful realist of the Fifties—the enemy still in view but strengthened and camouflaged by affluence, his own position in need of reorientation and restatement, most of his best colleagues from the 1930's either demoralized or on long leaves of absence or succumbed to the blandishments of conformity. Amid his small band of hard-core socialists, disaffected social scientists, and surly graduate students, the political Howe is more natural but less masterly, more spirited but less intact, than the literary one. His *Dissent* prose typically comes on with its collar open, its sleeves rolled high, even a bit of shirt-tail hanging out—the hasty, edgy style of a militant radical eager to be back on the barricades and wide open to provocation.

Now and then the two Howes have seemed to inhabit the same essay. His famous pioneering attack on the conformity of the intellectuals begins in systematic cultural analysis and winds up in that special tone of lead-pipe sarcasm that helps one to live with his regrets at having missed all the "fun" of the Thirties. Howe's recent essay on Richard Wright, James Baldwin, and Ralph Ellison is a more subtle but even more damaging combination of literary judgment and activist polemic. However, in reading through the rest of the essays in *A World More Attractive*, which brings together for the first time his literary and political writing, I was struck much less by divergences of purpose and discrepancies in tone between these two sides of Howe's work than by the strength of their relation, the complicated but intimate terms on which they relate to and support each other. Like certain good marriages that don't quite make sense until you observe the couple living together, Howe's purposes as a man of letters and a socialist make up a close communion and, at their deeper levels of effort and perception and bias, a moving one.

On the most immediate level of subject matter and approach, one sees that his view of the modern element in literature proceeds from and returns to the general perspective of his Marxist-Trotskyist background. For Howe, the dominant "style" of modern writing, like that of the age itself, is one of "extreme situations and radical solutions," and its content is most typically the strange and bitter fruit of an "unprecedented" crisis of experience and perception, conduct and belief. We all like to say, particularly when we sink back into the swamps of the soul, that we are living in an age of crisis, but few are able to sustain the conviction and fewer are able

to discriminate its proper terms and to develop them meaningfully. Thus, most "crisis writing" merely reveals the dark-
ling plain of the modern literary mind where clouds of vague-
ness clash with mists of banality. Howe, on the other hand, is
a true scholar of the twentieth-century imagination of "experiment and disaster, apocalypse and skepticism . . . rebellion,
disenchantment, and nothingness." His main advantage is
that he is rooted in the intellectual tradition which has been
best able to grasp the inexorably turning revolution of modern consciousness:

> Constant revolutionizing of production, uninterrupted
> disturbance of all social conditions, everlasting uncer-
> tainty and agitation distinguish . . . [this] epoch from
> all earlier ones. All fixed, fast frozen relations, with their
> train of ancient and venerable prejudices and opinions,
> are swept away, all new-formed ones become antiquated
> before they can ossify. All that is solid melts into air, all
> that is holy is profaned, and man is at last compelled to
> face with sober senses his real conditions of life and his
> relations with his kind. . . .

Nothing very "antiquated" about this statement, though it
was made of the "bourgeois" epoch of 125 years ago by the
two fathers of the socialist perspective. In the later writings
of Marx and Engels, as well as of their followers and critics,
the disintegration of custom and tradition and the manifold
conditions of alienation were often used for crude polemical ends, but the *problem* of bourgeois culture as it affected
ideas and behavior continued to provide one of the deeper
currents of Marxist thought. Howe's attempt to forge a coherent perspective from the complicated relations between
the literature and the politics of modern culture, and to explore its major poetry and fiction as testaments of the personal experience of severe public disorder, grows out of and
extends this major contribution of the radical tradition. No
doubt someone better versed than I am in its literature could

see more of Howe's indebtedness than what he has chosen to make explicit in using, say, Mannheim's concept of "functional rationalism" to explore the recoil from utopianism in Orwell, Huxley, and Zamiatin; or Simmel's concept of the hero to focus the specific character and general significance of T. E. Lawrence's career; or insights from Marx, Durkheim, and C. Wright Mills to develop descriptions of the postwar mass society as it questions the socialist vision or attracts and stymies our novelists. However, one need not be a specialist to spot intellectual authority and to admire the pertinence, precision, and scope of Howe's investigation of the evidence and implications of the "uninterrupted disturbance of all social conditions."

As a literary critic, Howe is not a "Marxist" in the standard sense: he is much too concerned usually—though not always —with the individuality of a writer, and with the complexities that necessarily involves, to insist upon the class relations of a Céline or Hemingway, a Frost or Wallace Stevens as the principal source of his attitude toward experience. Still, the focus of his criticism of these writers is basically a more subtle and searching version of the view that Trotsky develops—and vulgarizes—in *Literature and Revolution*: in Trotsky's words, that "the rearrangement of classes shakes up individuality," that "Nature, love, or friendship" are closely connected with "the social spirit of an epoch," that "a profound break in history" both decimates and renews the arts by establishing their fundamental problems from a new angle. Howe has read, and no doubt lived, with this view for so long now that it functions as an *intuition*—in the sense that Croce used the term to designate the source of true literary perception—of the specific effect on a writer of the loss of "ancient and venerable prejudices and opinions" and the impermanence of "new-formed ones." This intuition makes him a penetrating interpreter of Wallace Stevens and Frost, as well as of the more obvious cases of Fitzgerald, Hemingway, and Faulkner, in their common struggle to capture some tentative basis for existence, or, in Frost's phrase, "some momentary stay against confusion."

It is also evident that Howe's European socialist orientation has provided him not only with many of his general ideas but also with his method of reasoning with them. His skill at dialectical thinking is mainly responsible for the clarity and flexibility with which he deals with the literature of crisis. It allows him to control abstract and essentially fluid ideas within a tight logical framework and, at the same time, to give them sufficient play to capture the distinctions and nuances that make for accuracy and depth of characterization. His essay on Céline, for example, is a stunning example of dialectical steadiness and agility. He begins by sorting out the principal contradictions that make up the temperament of the classical underground man and measures his general import in signifying "the end of the belief that the human being can be understood . . . as a unique ensemble of traits [rather than] as a history of experiences that are often impenetrable and gratuitous." Noting the progressive deterioration of the type from Dostoevski's "whole man"—analyzing as well as suffering the burdens of consciousness—to the legion of modern nauseasts, Howe takes Céline as the most complete example of revulsion from the world and the self. He then reasons his way to the core of Céline's major work by shuttling between the opposing elements that produce its distinctive character of "exuberant disgust," while relating them to themes and style. Eventually Howe arrives at the central insight that it is Céline's compulsive but powerful preoccupation with his own "biological ignominy" that both provides the energy of his disgust and sharply limits its satirical range: "the nausea that makes him recoil from experience is linked to the comedy that makes him relish the experience of recoil—beyond that he cannot go." Having reached both the source and the limits of Céline's savage burlesque, Howe then sets up the final link of the chain. Trotsky had suggested that the resolution of Céline's impasse would lie in his choice between "an aversion to the lie" and "a disbelief in the truth." Much less tendentious about "the truth" than Trotsky was, Howe restates the prediction in terms of the decisive inferiority of Céline's intellect to his imagination which inevitably led to an attrition of his powers and to the eventual transaction between his nihilism and fascism. "Unable to transcend the foulness which was his authentic and entirely legitimate subject, he made 'his peace with the darkness.' And not he alone."

I have paused over this one essay not only because it points up Howe's ability to zero in on a subject with an orderliness and precision of thought that is by no means usual in literary criticism, but also because it serves as a partial paradigm of the political-ethical bias that underlies and charges his method. For the imagination of "extreme situations and radical solutions" is, to some extent, the source as well as the object of his thought. In his short essay on Norman Mailer, Howe speaks of the bland, insulated circumstances in which most cultivated Americans increasingly live, with a "minimum of courage or failure, test or transcendence," and, in an unusual personal aside, he testifies to the disorientation and dismay of "those of us raised, or ruined, by the ethic of striving, dissatisfaction, and renewal." The formulation suggests the emotional core of Howe's perspective: the dialectic both of immigrant Jewish aspiration in which he grew up and of the Trotskyist ethos in which he came of age. Similarly, he characterizes the climate of contemporary socialism as one of "crisis, doubt, and reconsideration." Conditioned by these climates, he writes as a man who has become habituated to the uneven conflict of one's best hopes with the recalcitrance and betrayal of the world. In almost every one of the essays in A World More Attractive, the underlying focus of description and judgment is fixed upon the drama of the individual writer struggling to wrest from the disorder of the times and the disarray of his own convictions some brave principle of transcendence or, failing that, of moral realism, in which to lodge the freedom of his spirit. In two of his most recent essays, those on T. E. Lawrence and Edith Wharton, the pressure of Howe's own stake in this ethic seems to break through the usual restraints of his rationalism and provides a new feeling of personal attachment to it. This is Howe at his very best, a literary socialist stirred to eloquence by the spectacle of another "writer struggling with a vision he can neither realize nor abandon." Sometimes in his other essays he tends to take the theme of crisis for granted, so habituated has he become to it, and writes too patly and imperturbably about what were, after all, matters of spiritual life and death to his subjects.

This, then, is one side of the relation between Howe's literary and political purposes. The other side is his effort to bring imagination and complexity to socialist doctrine. For example, his essay, with Lewis A. Coser, on "Images of Socialism" makes use of his grasp of the truth and forae found in oppositions to provide a more dynamic and visionary concept of socialist ends than that of the highly centralized and spiritless pig-heaven which is already in the process of being realized by the post-capitalist mass society. To provide motive for the doctrine, Howe and Coser attempt to re-argue the relevance of socialism in terms of providing opportunities for social striving, tension, and productive conflict. Along with Richard Crossman, they affirm that the aim of socialism is "not the pursuit of happiness but the enlargement of freedom."

Thus, the theme of effortful aspiration and conflict in Howe's literary approach joins to his faith in a hard-headed utopianism of liberating social struggle. In the main he has been attempting to introduce something of the literary imagination of the modern world into socialism in order to rescue it from the "functional rationalism" of its dream of collective security, which, whatever its sources of human misery and hopelessness in the nineteenth century, grows more and more dispiriting, it not ominous, in the shadow of twentieth-century technology and bureaucracy.

To my mind, the body of Howe's work collected here

would have been better titled "The Socialist Imagination." The phrase, of course, ties in with a famous collection of essays from the last decade on literature and society. A comparison between Irving Howe and Lionel Trilling is not likely to endear one to either party. However, one can say that both men have been involved in the similar enterprise of being teachers of their tribes of liberals and socialists respectively and that each of them has tried to re-state the nature of his political tradition by emphasizing its original impulse to human liberty and recalling it, in Trilling's phrase, from "the impulse to organization." Thus their common emphasis falls, to quote Trilling again, upon "variousness and possibility, complexity and difficulty." The last term, perhaps, is one about which contemporary socialists need no further education. In essence, though, Howe's new "image" of socialism is as committed to the possibilities and burdens of freedom as is Trilling's critique of American liberalism, and it is dependent in much the same way on literature as "the human activity that takes the fullest and most precise account of variousness, possibility, complexity, and difficulty."

But if the main motive in Howe's work is to enlarge and quicken the socialist imagination along these lines, then his recent discussion of Baldwin and Ellison is particularly misbegotten. Speaking at the time—and, I suspect, under the spell—of the first unmistakable evidence of a civil-rights revolution, Howe accuses the early Baldwin and Ellison of having written from the meliorist ideology of the Fifties rather than from their experience of "plight and protest" as Negroes. The operative term for the essay itself is "protest." The "jug," as Ellison subsequently put it, into which Howe was trying to force him was not so much his Negro identity as such as it was the imperative of "extreme situations and radical solutions"—that is to say, of militancy. Certain serious weaknesses of vision immediately follow wherever Howe's radicalism ceases to be critical. On the literary level, for example, he mistakes the tacit but powerful protest at the end of *Invisible Man* for one of the run-of-the-mill affirmations of the past decade. And on the political level, he battens upon the weaknesses in Baldwin's earlier writing in order to get in another blow at the ideology of conformity, but fails to bear down at all upon the much more relevant and disturbing incoherencies in the ideas of *The Fire Next Time*. Finally, he subverts his own philosophical basis for socialism—and, presumably, for Negro freedom—by prescribing, in effect, the limits of a Negro writer's freedom of consciousness. "What, then, was the experience of a man with a black skin, what *could* it be in this country . . . ? The 'sociology' of his existence formed a constant pressure on his literary work . . . with a pain and ferocity that nothing could remove." But what, then, was the experience of the Yiddish ghetto writers, one wonders, except usually that of poverty and fear and oppression, of quelled pain and outrage and of the saving dignity of silence and irony? In his essay on Sholem Aleichem, Howe is a long way from suggesting that this great, impassive Yiddish writer was less than fully in touch with his experience.

Howe asserts at another point of attack on Ellison: "As if one could *decide* one's deepest and most authentic response to society!" But such a decision is precisely the one that he himself has made and kept to for so many years now in having to regard socialism, in his words, mainly as "a commitment to a value and a problem," and his own efforts as a struggle to "will" its image. Indeed, as I have tried to show, Howe's own value as a literary man as well as a radical derives in good part from his keeping independent faith—through a period of affluence and conformity—with his own "deepest and most authentic response to society."

(1964)

Wrestling with Trotsky

When Trotsky died I was eleven years old, and since there were no Trotskyites in my petit-bourgeois world, his death, like his life, completely passed me by. Thus I am among the readers for whom Irving Howe has edited this collection of Trotsky's "basic writings"—one of the generation "who did not live through the experiences" of his career. In choosing to write "lived through," Mr. Howe is referring to something more, and to some extent other, than merely chronology. Since Mr. Howe must have been only nineteen or so at the time of Trotsky's death, he himself could not have lived through the train of events that forms the background of Trotsky's basic writings: the October Revolution or the defense of Petrograd, the emergence of Stalin and the shattering of the left Opposition, the NEP and the First Five Year Plan, the abortive revolutions in Germany and China or the struggle for power between the Left and the Right in the Europe of the early Thirties.

Yet Mr. Howe could not write about Trotsky as he does without having "lived through"—however retroactively and vicariously—the fateful politics in which Trotsky was involved and the awesome peripeties and discoveries of his career; he may very well have done so more intensely than if he had been twenty years older and a citizen of the USSR. A few years ago Lionel Abel wrote about the Thirties in New York as the period when the city packed up and went off to Russia. And if Union Square could become Red Square, so could Trotsky's relations with Zinoviev hum with immediate relevance ten years after the fact.

Indeed, it was Trotsky, more than any other figure, who made the Russian Revolution and its aftermath an experience that adolescents in the Bronx "lived through," since he was both its star and its consciousness—the walking image of radical thought and action and of their power and peril. In the pages of his "History" the Marxist dialectic becomes flesh and blood, an actual and inevitable proletarian revolution, and the Leninist dream of a potent and righteous alliance between peasant and worker becomes cogent and eloquent. In "My Life" the development of the "young eagle" Trotsky as theoretician and agitator, polemicist and orator, the mover of men and the shaker of history provides a haunting example of the possibilities open to outsiders in a society who dedicate their talents to a "great idea."

But even more than his writings, Trotsky's life came to personify the great, tearing forces that the Revolution had unleashed and the bitter struggle to make its original intention prevail. For the objective theory of the "permanent revolution," he provided the subjective component of the permanent revolutionist: the man of destiny, however lonely and beleaguered, armed only with a pen, a voice, and a doctrine. Moreover, just as Trotsky tried to tie the fate of the Revolution to the proletarian struggle, so did he embody, particularly in the Thirties, the beguiling dream of an international movement, and at the very least an international radical consciousness, as relevant to modern literature as to bourgeois politics. Finally, and perhaps most importantly, there was the Trotsky who preserved the Marxist vision against the Stalinist corruption and made it possible to remain a Communist without forfeiting one's intelligence or probity. All of this, and more, is implied in the feeling of having "lived through" the history with which Trotsky was associated. Someone like

Mr. Howe was probably among the last to be able to do so, for by the end of World War II, Trotskyism, for personal as well as political purposes, had vanished like Villon's snows, and with it much of Trotsky's relevance and apparent stature.

What, then, is it like to read him today, to come upon him cold, as it were? Well, one does not read him casually: one confronts him, and it is a slow and bruising business. Mr. Howe tells us that he has deliberately avoided Trotsky's more recondite and polemical writings; he has generally made his selections from those documents that Trotsky struck off during the various crises that formed his career and has clearly tried to emphasize the Trotsky who of all his roles was most at home, according to Mr. Howe, in that of "the independent political analyst, historian, and literary man." Nonetheless, a reader like myself is likely to find that Trotsky is a good deal more abstract and a good deal less winning than he might have expected. Partly this effect may be the work of his translators, most of whom seem indifferent, to put it mildly, to Trotsky's reputation as a gifted stylist. Still, Trotsky's mode and tone of discourse are quite foreign to what one expects from an "independent" intellectual. Once past the sections from "My Life" and the "History," one begins to grasp the fact that through the main part of his writings Trotsky was "most at home" as the apostle of "Marxist science" and as the apologist of Bolshevism.

Thus: "The strength of the compulsion exercised by the masses in a workers' state is directly proportional to the strength of the exploitive tendencies, or the danger of a restoration of capitalism, and inversely proportional to the strength of social solidarity and the general loyalty to the new regime." As Marxist doctrine this is unexceptionable: one of the standard formulations for the "withering away of the state." Trotsky, however, is advancing it in 1937, after twenty years in which the difference between "the masses in a workers' state" and "the new regime" was not one of terminology but of systematic deception, coercion, and terror.

Trotsky immediately continues: "Thus the bureaucracy . . . —that is, the 'privileged officials and commanders of a standing army'—represents a special kind of compulsion which the masses cannot or do not wish to exercise, and which, one way or another, is directed against the masses themselves." And so one wrestles with Trotsky: what is the force of that "Thus"; where does that "bureaucracy" come from if not from the "new regime"? In point of fact, rather than of dialectic, hadn't an enormous "degree of compulsion" been exercised against the masses from 1917 forward by the "proletarian vanguard" who were also the "privileged officials and commanders of a standing army"? Yet the point of the essay itself is that "the bureaucracy" developed as the necessary "bourgeois organ of the workers' state."

Similarly Trotsky's much-acclaimed discussion of pre-Nazi Germany is almost completely devoid of any specific sense of the nation itself: only the names of the different parties and positions glow with any immediacy. This may be why Trotsky could write that the fascism of Hitler had "for its basic and only task the razing to their foundation of all institutions of proletarian democracy." Certainly, by 1932 it was clear that the motive forces of Nazism were not those of the class struggle but rather those of a rabid nationalism. True, Trotsky was a foreigner in Germany, but he was also a Russian and a Jew, and both experiences should have provided him with clues that Germany presented different sources of political power from those dreamt of in his philosophy.

But this was not the way Trotsky thought; nor was he disposed to notice, much less raise, issues that lay outside the realm of the class struggle. Beside Marx, in this respect, he was rigid and provincial and dry in spirit. If Marx regarded religion as "the opiate of the people," he was also capable of moving on to the awareness that it was also "the heart of a heartless world." Trotsky, for all his imagination, seems incapable of granting such a point, perhaps even of grasping it. Certainly he is blind to it in his essay on Gogol.

The main truth that comes home to one in reading Trotsky is that he was, after all is said and done, a Communist: an intellectual whose consciousness and conscience became almost totally identified with the seizure and rationalization of social control. "To a revolutionary Marxist," he writes toward the end of his career, "there can be no contradiction between personal morality and the interests of the party, since the party embodies in his consciousness the very highest tasks and aims of mankind." Such a statement is not merely a commitment to the Bolshevik mentality; in the case of Trotsky it represents what came to be his defense against self-awareness and its impingement upon his authoritarianism: or, as he puts it in one of the few inward statements in this book, "the dark night of the circumscribed I." Once he cast his lot with the Bolsheviks in 1917, his mind must have needed every bit of abstractness it could acquire.

In praising Trotsky as an intellectual, Mr. Howe tells us that he "believed in the power and purity of the word." Power, yes, but not purity. The other side of Trotsky's abstractness is a vehemence that is usually quite equal to the Communist notion of public debate, which is not to dispute with the opposition so much as to ridicule, vilify, and neutralize it. Under the justification of "our merciless fight against liberalism for influence over the masses," Trotsky indulges in the most flagrant kinds of intellectual demagoguery. Mr. Howe comes closer to the truth when he writes that "the common distinction between word and deed Trotsky scorned as a sign of philistinism, worthy—he might have added—of liberal professors and literary dilettantes."

If one reads Trotsky today, it is mainly to learn from his example of living by his ideas, of indomitably joining thought to action. When he writes, "Life is not an easy matter. . . . You cannot live through it without falling into prostration and cynicism unless you have before you a great idea which raises you above personal misery, above weakness, above all kinds of perfidy and baseness," one is very tempted to say, particularly at this point in time, Yea, verily. In recent years many intellectuals have begun to distrust, if not regret, their complacent retreat from any "great idea," for without it their skepticism has grown sterile and bitter, and their role in society has become similar in some ways to that of the chorus in a Greek tragedy, whose part is to discuss the actors, appreciate their predicaments, shudder at their mistakes, ponder the problem of reality, and eventually reassert the wisdom of the tribe. With the cues to meaningful action being provided these days by the civil-rights struggle and the renewed consciousness of the poverty that coexists with affluence in America, one becomes attracted by, at least, the strength of commitment that Trotsky represents. Reading him, however, gives one pause, for one becomes aware, finally, that the relation of thought to action is ultimately the relation of truth to power, and in the hard, cruel, authoritarian meshes of Trotsky's mind the former is remorselessly subservient to the latter. One need not be a "liberal professor" or a "literary dilettante" to take Trotsky's writings as a problem rather than as an inspiration.

(1964)

The Red Hot Vacuum

This past July a big, bright, and relatively notorious spread on "The American Literary Scene" appeared in *Esquire*. The magazine's view of this scene began on the cover, which featured one of those little cornsilk blondes who read for Alfred A. Doubleday and live for the Panna Grady parties: her cigarette holder poised jauntily, her eyes swooning with sophistication, her mouth avidly open, she gazes up into the hairy unbuttoned shirt of Allen Ginsberg and adds his name to those of the other members of the pantheon (Mailer, Albee, Styron, Jones, Nabokov) already in attendance. As it turned out, *Esquire*'s cover girl was an apt image of the Muse that inspired this issue, just as the idea of having it come on as a party provided a reverberating point of introduction to the literary scene itself.

"WRITERS! HOW CAN THEY LIVE LIKE THAT AND WORK TOO? THIS ISSUE TELLS ALL." The coverage began with two picture stories of writers—East Village and Hollywood, respectively —their pads, their haunts, their girls. Despite certain obvious differences at these extremes of the literary life, both John Filler and George Axelrod clearly had their respective worlds by the tail. "None of these photographs has much basis in reality. My reality is loneliness, poverty and anguish," beatnik John Filler blurted out as the fellows from *Esquire* closed in with the klieg lights and the models. But the editors were too hot for glamour, titillation, and savvy to be much concerned with that kind of "reality," and the party bubbled along at the level, and with the concerns, of conversation that literary parties have. Terry Southern gossiped about Mickey Spillane playing Mike Hammer, Robert Linscott gossiped about the real Faulkner, Eleanor Perenyi told her Edmund Wilson stories, Gay Talese went on at length about the *Paris Review* jet set in the half-reverent, half-arch tone that characterized the *Esquire* treatment. James Jones and William Styron were even overheard talking to each other about writing, and there was a peek at what Cheever, Albee, and Nabokov were writing at the moment. There was also Norman Mailer's latest appraisal of the competition—a piece which was so perceptive and meant, so intransigently in character, that it gave the lie to most of the proceedings, like a speech by SNCC leader Bob Moses to a convention of the Urban League.

In the midst of the *Esquire* coverage was an article and chart by its fiction editor, Rust Hills, which provided the lowdown on the "literary power structure." As Hills made explicit, he was talking about a *literary* establishment, the significant reputations, "literature with a capital L." But what one got was mainly a great many names dropping like snow—the names of the agents, the editors, the hipsters, as well as of the writers and critics—and, like a snowstorm, burying former distinctions of terrain into amorphous mounds and drifts. Community within this "structure" was represented by the magazines or creative-writing centers with which authors were vaguely or temporarily associated and by the stables of the publishers and agents. Authority, or power, was seen to be mainly a matter of informal arrangements between a book editor, an agent, a handful of willing blurb writers, most of whom inhabit "the red hot center" of the establishment and who are easily mobilized to introduce or sustain a reputation. Not that the difference between Grace Metalious and Grace Paley is simply a matter of which people get together for lunch to promote them; there are also "values" which filter down from the academic critics and theorists, and through the literary journalists and such "red hot" journals as *Partisan Review* and *Paris Review*, so that the reputations are eventually shaken out and changes occur.

Though Hills made no attempt to formulate what these values were, it was clear that his own were derived from a firm regard for the relations between sales, publicity, and new wrinkles of taste that make a writer or tendency "chic." Thus: "the Cool World (Grove-Evergreen, etc.) has less commercial access now that Kerouac and Ginsberg have left off visiting Madison Avenue offices." And as in dinner jackets or sports cars, there are the right short-story anthologies and poetry awards, and at the very core of "the red hot center" of "literature with a capital L" are the agents that matter and the Writers Who Get in Columns.

And yet . . . and yet. One can fault this chart on matters of detail, one can be repelled by its superficial knowingness as one can by the trivial and promiscuous image of the literary situation that emerges from the rest of the issue, but in the end he will also have to admit that the dominant conditions and tone of this situation today are not very different from what *Esquire* exhibits them to be. One can argue that no "literary establishment" exists in America, that what Hills is talking about is a new and very fluid marketplace whose entrepreneurs are too busy trying to keep both ears to the ground to see very clearly or act very effectively; but he will be hard put to specify any genuinely significant center of literary associations and values that *Esquire* has slighted or whose influence is obscured by its view of things. Such centers existed not too long ago, but they have since fallen prey to the malaise that afflicts the old avant-garde and the random chills and fevers that afflict the new. Their decline and displacement by the entrepreneurs who have set up shop where Madison Avenue runs into Greenwich Village is what makes the idea of Hills's "establishment" plausible: the increase in the vacuity and confusion of literary opinion, the loss of serious community and authority, the merely reactive tendencies of the "cultural explosion," and the concomitant preoccupations with the issue or style of the moment, as well as with sales and reviews and writers who get in columns. *Esquire's* coverage represents accurately enough the shrinkage of extremes between the serious and the trivial, between hard thought and easy attitudinizing, between originality and novelty, relevance and chic, distinction and celebrity. With all due respect to the modesty of its editors, *Esquire* is itself "the red hot center" of our literary vacuum.

Since this vacuum has been growing for some years now, it is time we began to reckon with its presence, or, more meaningfully, with the absence it betokens of genuine community and authority. By a literary community I don't mean, of course, a group living in a particular locality, but rather a community of intentions, ideas, and standards that imparts purpose, energy, and perspective to the efforts of individual writers and to the literary culture at large. At the same time, there are usually affinities of temperament and background that confer some degree of personal connection and direction. Two such centers of community were to be found not too many years ago in the pages of *Partisan Review* and *Kenyon Review*, along with a few ancillary journals that supported their tendencies and spread their influence.

Briefly and broadly speaking, *Partisan* can be said to have represented the radical spirit and *Kenyon* the conservative one in modern literature. This difference was not only a matter of opposed political dispositions, though it was partly that, but also of different orientations to the intellectual and literary problems of the modern age. Up until the early 1950's the perspective of *Partisan* was principally the European Marxist and later post-Marxist one—that is to say, a perspective that took for granted the separation of the artists and intellectuals from the middle class at an advanced stage of the bourgeois epoch. In brief, this stage was marked by an ongoing social crisis in which the attack upon bourgeois institutions extended to the traditional beliefs and attitudes that supported them and from which a new consciousness of man's real conditions of life would emerge. The bearers of this consciousness—the advanced thinkers, writers, organizers —were unable to fulfill their historic destiny of identifying with and leading the proletarian revolution, but when this prospect was swept off the board, they found themselves even more alienated than before, more subject to the climate, in the words of Marx and Engels, of "everlasting uncertainty and agitation." Thus, a journal such as *Partisan* became particularly responsive to other revolutionary explanations of man's real conditions of life such as those found in Nietzsche, Freud, Mannheim, Reich, Sartre, and others, as well as to the great portraits of these conditions to be found in Kafka, Mann, Malraux, Lawrence, and others. The result of this development was an intellectually sturdy and imaginatively rich perspective that joined the radical element in modern thought to the experimental element in modern literature and art. In its more personal bearings *Partisan* reflected the spirit of the lonely urban intellectual, usually of recent immigrant stock, whose intellectual homeland was still European. As such, *Partisan Review* provided backing and orientation to many young writers who were attracted to the new, the provisional, the uprooted sense of existence that followed the upheavals of the 1930's and the cataclysm of World War II.

Kenyon, on the other hand, grew out of the social and literary relations that were advanced during the 1930's by the group of Southern writers known as "The Fugitives." Believing that a higher culture required a stable class society, they tended to formulate the cultural problem of the time as that of the widening separation of thinkers and writers from the concrete habits, customs, and manners of a traditional and parochial way of life such as that of the agrarian South. The political and social philosophy of this group was unable to develop much force of its own, but it did provide ballast to the literary perspective they developed, known as "The New

Criticism," whose approach to literature as self-contained structures was grounded in assumptions of the continuity and permanence of significant human behavior and values. As this approach developed in the pages of *Kenyon* and was joined to the later phase of American Humanism, it played an important role in demonstrating the spiritual authority of literature, in renewing the dominant traditions, particularly in poetry, and in enriching the conservative orientation with the perspectives of myth, religious belief, and aesthetics. In its personal bearings *Kenyon* tended to remain pastoral rather than urban, traditional rather than contemporary, Anglo-Saxon rather than European, rooted rather than alienated.

At the same time, there was considerable overlapping between these two communities, so that the writers identified with one published occasionally in the magazines of the other. However, the oppositions were genuine and were repeatedly engaged: throughout most of the 1940's and 1950's one can observe in the pages of both magazines a determined, if often implicit, debate with the other's assumptions. Together, they provided a kind of continuing dialectic which had an incalculable effect in strengthening literary thought in America and, to some extent, artistic performance. At the very least, they provided restatements of the cultural traditions that were relevant to the creative situation of the time, offered nurture to young writers, who generally start out in America ten years behind their counterparts in Europe, and imparted a vital tone of seriousness to the literary vocation itself.

All of which is much changed now. *Kenyon* and *Partisan* continue to be published, but neither provides anything like the community I have been sketching. The former ideas and values linger on as vague dispositions, without the energy or clarity they once had. It is not only that these journals have declined in quality; there is also a visible loss of independent purpose and vision through which they have come to resemble the literary culture at large. *Partisan* seems to be becoming mainly a journal of book reviews, *Kenyon* a random anthology of the brighter criticism being written by the younger members of the academy. That is to say, both are typical in their ways of the reactive and *ad hoc* character of the literary situation, its obsessive concern with the texts of the moment, its lack of direction, its impoverishment of ideas, whether critical or creative, its widening separation from its own traditions, including now the tradition of the modern itself.

To point to this decline of literary community and authority is not to say that the remedies are at hand if only we would have the seriousness to grasp them and the will to make them prevail. The qualities found in *Partisan* and *Kenyon* came into being through a slow accretion of cultural circumstances that allowed each of these centers to flourish in virtual independence of the mass society and to preserve, by its different lights, the integrity of art and intellect. Such independence is not likely to be given again, at least in an affluent mass society. Moreover, they had in their immediate background one of the major revolutions in thought and sensibility that has occurred in the West, and, as has been repeatedly pointed out, we are now perhaps only beginning to emerge from the long backwash of its impact. Perhaps the best that can be asked is that we become aware of the vacuity of the literary culture, that we cease trying so hard to jump with the *Zeitgeist* or to beat it at its own fragmenting and frantic game and begin again to restate the cultural tradition from the perspective of the present.

Such an enterprise, at the very least, would help to free us from the trap of the merely topical and chic revolt, with its tendency to bury genuine elements of dissent and experiment like quicksand, and from the trap of academicism, with its undue reverence for the settled judgments of the last generation. An effort in this direction has begun to be made in England, where a number of younger writers—Richard Hoggart, Raymond Williams, and others—have been attempting to move forward from the impasse that pitted Bloomsbury against the *Scrutiny* group by reintroducing the broader and more dynamic social vision of nineteenth-century radicalism and by bringing the body of new and counter ideas it thus obtains to bear upon the present changes in English culture. Whether such a body of ideas will produce creative initiatives in literature remains to be seen, as does the possibility of a comparable undertaking in America. But it has already begun to provide that "quickening and sustaining atmosphere" of fresh thought which, as Matthew Arnold saw, is "the true basis for the creative power's exercise." For it is around such restatements of a cultural tradition that new viewpoints spring to life, true centers of literary community and authority begin to form, and works like *The Waste Land* and *Ulysses* and *The Magic Mountain* begin to be imaginable again.

(1964)

The Deadly James Purdy

Make it new," advised Ezra Pound. Many try, few succeed. One who has, in a quiet but unmistakable way, is James Purdy. Purdy is a naturalist of unusual subtlety and a fantasist of unusual clarity. These two strains cross repeatedly in his fiction, for his subject is most often the enigmatic borderland between innocence and depravity, and his characters are generally people who are cut off from the more or less normal life of humanity—orphans, invalids, Negroes, spinsters, homosexuals, failed artists, and other lost souls who have retreated into the weird logic of their illusions and privations, their pain and cruelty. Sometimes this logic is handled with great wit and charm, as in Purdy's iridescent novel *Malcolm*, a sort of high-camp version of adolescent initiation, more often with chilling objectivity as in his laconic tales of dead marriages and emotionally starved children, or in his small masterpiece of underclass sadism and effete corruption—"63: Dream Palace."

Like a number of his gifted contemporaries, Purdy has worked up his material less from a social subject as such than from his own intensely private way of looking at things. Eudora Welty, Flannery O'Connor, Bernard Malamud, John Hawkes, John Barth, Carson McCullers, William Gaddis are, like Purdy, characteristic of a development in recent fiction that seems to grow directly out of the increasingly divided

aspect of modern existence: the lonely, bizarre distance that
stretches between the past and the present, between the individual and society, between the natural and the actual.
Transmuting regional or ethnic or religious or sexual identifi-
cations, as the case may be, into personal styles of vision, such
writers seem to emerge suddenly from the interior of American consciousness with stories of a strange and violent misery
in this land. Confronted by the progressive unreality of our
mass society, novelists move farther and farther back into
their sensibility to get their bearings; it is almost as though
experience with any relevant human content to it cannot be
seen clearly through the eyes any more but only rendered in
dark synopsis by the imagination.

Until now James Purdy's America, whether located in the
sumptuous drawing room of Gerard Gerard, in the black and
ghostly streets of the Chicago slums, or in the prosaic vacuousness of Rainbow Center, Ohio, has been mainly the background of his vision of individual loneliness and of "the immense dreariness of things." His most powerful characters are
isolates who have suffered or are suffering the loss of an essential emotional tie and are thereby rendered vulnerable to the
depredations of others and to the ravages of their own sorrow
and rage. Dread, anxiety, perversion, grotesqueness, obscenity
—the characteristic motifs of modern writing—enter Purdy's
stories as naturally as they do nightmares, without any particular reference to contemporary society. The deliberateness
and detachment that have been the main features of his style
and the source of his emotional strength are partly due to the
firm distance he has kept from the local and topical. In the
story "Eventide," for example, a Negro woman mourns the
loss of her son who has disappeared for good into the white
part of the city. In the course of the story, as the flat that
Mahala shares with her sister Plumy fills with the darkness of
evening, Plumy suddenly sees before her the dead son that
she buried seventeen years ago. Envying Plumy her hallucination, Mahala thinks "how nice it would be if Teeboy could

also be perfect in death, so that he could belong to her in the same perfect way as George Watson belonged to Plumy." There is no trace of a social moral to the story; its intention is to explore the perverse recesses of grief, and the two Negro widows belong less to their race than to Purdy's desolate family of man: each of whom bears passive witness to "the something awful and permanent that comes to everybody."

In his new novel, however, Purdy has suddenly turned away from these private and timeless preoccupations. *Cabot Wright Begins* strikes out at the contemporary world with a vengeance, almost as though all of Purdy's hatred of it, which he had been suppressing for the sake of his art, had suddenly boiled up and spilled over. The novel begins as a brilliantly controlled spoof on American sexuality and book publishing, but ends as a wild, flailing, and finally hysterical attack on everything that bugs him, from the *New Yorker* to Miss Subways to Orville Prescott.

A used-car salesman from Chicago, Bernie Gladhart, is persuaded by his wife, who has begun to feel tied down by her fourth marriage, that he is the man to write a fictionalized biography of Cabot Wright, the Ivy League sex maniac, who has recently been released from jail and is now living in seclusion somewhere in Brooklyn. With a mixture of regret and relief at leaving the warm, smothering affections of his middle-aged wife, Bernie dutifully comes to New York and hacks away at his novel from old newspaper accounts of Wright's career, while waiting for his hero to turn up. Through the assistance of Mrs. Curt Bickle, a friend from Chicago, Bernie is "discovered" by the celebrated book editor Princeton Keith, who promptly takes the manuscript away from Bernie and offers Mrs. Bickle, who has her own failed writer to support, a fabulous sum of money to rewrite and complete the novel.

From Bernie's manuscript and then from Cabot Wright himself, Mrs. Bickle assembles the story of this contemporary American folk hero who, in the course of his short career, had raped "easily and well" some three hundred women, usually to their edification and often to their emotional profit. Graceful and well-scrubbed, looking as if he had just stepped out of a Coca-Cola ad, Cabot is an older brother of Purdy's Malcolm—another child of "suppositious" parentage who has been brought up by a prominent family. Before he took to the streets, Cabot was married to a brittle, high-stepping New York clotheshorse and worked in a brokerage house where he was directly under the thumb of a Wall Street magnate, Mr. Warburton, who concentrated in his frozen presence all of the tediousness of the WASP establishment. Gradually Cabot was possessed by a great weariness.

In time he placed himself in the hands of Dr. Bigelow-Martin, a specialist in treating "the tired feeling." Though the therapy consisted mainly of hanging Cabot on a huge hook, the results were as spectacular as Wilhelm Reich could have wished. Sweating furiously in public places and emitting a "sweetish rich animal-vegetable odor" much like that of tropical natives "before they were spoiled by missionaries, constricted clothes, [and] bottled drinks," Cabot embarked on his adventures in sexual hypnosis and gratification. "Get deadly," he muttered into the ears of his victims, ranging from teen-age visitors to the city all the way up to the lonely matron Gilda Warburton. A tremulous panic came over the streets of New York. "Women who thought of screaming did not. Those who began to run stopped short in their tracks. There was never any evidence of struggle after he had left. Many called the police, but more to share their experience than to register a complaint." Why did he rape? "Boredom," said Cabot on his way to jail, as well as from being fed up with the teasing, tittering pseudo-sexuality of the popular and literary culture.

All of this is very finely done. The first two thirds or so of *Cabot Wright Begins* is a cool, mordant, and deadly accurate satire on American values, as good as anything we have had since the work of Nathanael West. The deliberateness and subtlety of Purdy's stories have gone into creating a gallery of characters—the Gladharts, Princeton Keith, the Warburtons, Cabot and his wife, a predatory adolescent model, a lapsing Liberal minister—all of whom function as credible and telling caricatures of the blithering grotesqueness of our moral vices and sexual follies. Through a marvelously flexible, yet clearly drawn plot line, moreover, Purdy keeps the narrative steadily on the track of its subject. But having sprung his indignation, Purdy eventually allows it to get out of hand. Losing the objectivity of his art, he continues to pour it on and pour it on: characters and situations become inflated and pointless with exaggerations, and the comic themes give way to a cackling and obscene rhetoric. In the end, Cabot Wright regains his potency and saves his sanity by rolling on the ground with laughter at the spectacle of the hidebound and horny republic that has so violently turned him on and then cut him down. It is a fine moment in contemporary writing as well as healing counsel to one's beleaguered consciousness. More's the pity that it didn't come directly out of the life portrayed in the novel rather than as an extension of the author's horse laugh that has been dinning in our ears.

Which is not to deny that a writer who takes on our culture today is hard put to maintain his wits amid the witlessness of his subject. But much of *Cabot Wright Begins* is evidence that it can be done, that the detachment and deliberateness of Purdy's art are as indispensable in exploring the awfulness of our mores as they have been to him in touching the "something awful" in each man's life.

(1964)

Alfred Chester: Daring and Doing

I am a ne'er-do-well, I suppose, a cynic, an immoralist, and therefore very contemporary. In a pinch, I would give up everything, because I value nothing, except my skin. . . . It feels so good, especially in the sun or in the woods or in the sea or against another. Philosophy, politics, furniture, books, paintings, human relationships, the whole of Western civilization—none of it feels so good, none of it is me."

Very plain and straightforward, that. It is also very contemporary in its tendency, though few writers as intelligent as Alfred Chester are as yet willing to dare themselves into quite such a corner. On the other hand, unlike most intelligent writers today, Chester knows where he stands, and without any beating around the bush he lets you know it, too.

In the last year or two he has made something of a reputation for himself as a sort of *enfant terrible* of the book-review columns, the man who described Rechy's *City of Night* as a "blow-by-blow account" or a trip across America. In the monthly column he contributes to *Book Week*, Chester reports on his loves and griefs and exacerbations in Tangier with much the same display of uninhibited style, and he has now brought out a collection of stories, *Behold Goliath*, most of which involve the efforts of a lonely but true-blue sensualist to hold body and spirit together by living his life as Nature, for all apparent purposes, intended him to, and by keeping your world and mine at its bloody distance.

In short, *Behold Goliath* is mainly about the skin and about those out-of-the-way and not very sanitary places and lives where the kingdom of its desires still reigns. "Cradle Song" tells of a girl who is so smitten by the skin of her lover that she murders their newborn infant in order not to lose it. "As I Was Going Up the Stairs" is a fantasy of a boy's struggle with social authority and repression to avoid being turned into another sensible middle-class ghost, and of the illumination he receives from a pregnant gypsy, a demented angel of the carnal underworld. The title story presents a series of vignettes on the alienations and resources of a female impersonator, while "From the Phoenix to the Unnamable, Impossibly Beautiful Wild Bird," "In Praise of Vespasian," and "Ismael" are studies in the *Realpolitik* of sexual relationships and, in the latter two cases, fairly explicit accounts of the adventures of the skin that lurk in the doorways along Greenwich Avenue or in the *pissotières* of Paris.

What makes Chester an interesting writer in these matters is that he often has the radical honesty that both children and deviant adults may possess. He is himself a very curious combination of innocence and depravity—a sort of cross between the Baron de Charlus and Huckleberry Finn, however odd that may seem. Thus he is able to write about perversion from a fresh and complicated perspective that gives all proper and enthusiastic due to the joys of the instinctual life, however a man chooses and needs to experience it, while at the same time remaining very precisely aware of the twists and turns and torments of its fantasies:

> . . . it isn't like the first time. We have lost our innocence, our anonymities. We (I) seek to please. Not only does my body want his, but my heart wants his, and his wants Frankie's, and Frankie's wants—whose? How many men are here with us in bed, flailing and laboring

with us, locked with us not only in the body's terrific
heat but in the heart's terrible romance? . . . [After-
ward] Am overwhelmed with gratitude, despise myself
for it.

Yet Chester's stories, on the whole, are less daring than
their subject matter and his attitude toward it would promise.
His celebration of his own forms of ecstasy as well as his snide
dismissal of the huffing and puffing routines of the straight
world will seem grossly offensive to the mass of readers who
have still moved up to only Grace Metalious. His more sophisticated readers, however, are likely to find that alongside
of, say, Céline and Genet, Chester himself seems tame and
rather vague and rhetorical in his imagination of deviancy
and in his revulsion from the ghostly squares. Indeed, in several of the other stories—of a dying girl who comes alive
through sex, of a loveless marriage that has reached its moment of truth, of a fantastic but lovable Polish piano teacher
—Chester seems to be writing with his coat and tie on, as if
to show that he, too, can produce a presentable story.

The main problem of the other stories, I suspect, is that
Chester has still not entirely liberated his perspective from
the defensiveness that he feels in making use of it. The free
flow of his sensibility circles around a certain inhibition of
aim and requires a forcing of attitude to move it along. Thus,
he tends to be a spokesman—indeed, at times an apologist—
for the sexual underground he inhabits, so that there is an
undue amount of explaining and arguing and position-taking,
and too little inventing and representing. And though the
world he describes and the levels of consciousness and tone at
which he approaches it are richly imaginative, the point to
which the reader is finally brought is usually the same. One
feels that he is being told the same thing over and over again:
that feeling—whatever pain and selfishness and perverseness
it breeds—is all that matters in life, that conventional society
—and its psychic surrogate, reason—deaden it and thereby

turn us into phantoms.

I admire the courage of Chester's efforts to naturalize homosexuality, to give it its legitimate place in the sum of human nature's possibilities for joy and tenderness as well as morbidity and cruelty, particularly so after reading a book like *City of Night*, which is undermined by its author's hypocrisy about the nature of his feelings. Still, when Chester comes to write, say, of one of his "Unknown Soldiers" of love, so much of it is covered over with literary decorations and editorializing that one wishes he would be daring enough to do what he is always telling the world to do: let his characters be.

In "From the Phoenix" one does begin to see the possibilities of Chester's fiction when he liberates himself from his defensiveness and allows experience and imagination to make his point. The story involves a triangle, the apex of which is a young Greenwich Village roustabout and poet whose wife has just left him and who turns to his former lover for consolation. In the course of re-enacting both relationships—mainly through the dialogue of the two men—Chester takes entirely for granted their equally normal-abnormal character and discloses their common basis in the illusions of vanity and dependency. Male to his wife and female to his lover, Mario takes on genuine and moving significance as a walking, lusting, suffering example of sexual ambivalence.

All of this Chester understands very well: particularly the inexorable logic by which the passions are subverted by the fantasies they breed. Homosexual passion is, no doubt, the genuinely tragic ground of this logic, since it is apparently so unmitigated by the other sources of human connection. However, in order to explore this theme, Chester will have to be really audacious: he will have to give up the easy out of rebuking our problems of feeling and begin to accept and dramatize his own.

(1964)

Hubert Selby's Kicks

It was only a few years ago that *Lady Chatterley's Lover* unexpurgated and *Tropic of Cancer* were the bold and shocking books. I can't imagine that either work would cause much of a stir today. Alongside the revelations of Genet, Durrell, Burroughs, Chester, Albee, Rechy, and now Hubert Selby, Jr., the intimacies of Lady Chatterley and Mellors seem almost idyllic, and Henry Miller's experiences and reveries in the cheap hotels and alleys of Paris have a kind of healthy eighteenth-century coarseness.

Indeed, any kind of writing that describes straight sexuality with a feeling of pleasurable excitement has begun to seem outdated and rear-guard. The new tack that the sexual revolution has taken, at least in literature, or that so-called experimental writing has taken with regard to sex, is in the direction of perversion, particularly homosexuality, whether in subject matter or in vision. Rather than banning *Fanny Hill*, the authorities should consider subsidizing it as a contribution to the maintenance of normal animal nature in difficult times.

In a recent essay in *Partisan Review*, Susan Sontag suggests that two minority groups are making the only significant contributions to contemporary culture: the Jews, who impart moral seriousness, and the homosexuals, who impart aesthetic style and playfulness. But it seems to me the homosexual imagination is having a more decisive effect in defining the moral as well as the aesthetic character of the age since its view of human nature seems much more arresting and convincing to our sensation-seeking, anxious, and cynical eyes than does the old-fashioned earnest humanism of Saul Bellow or Bernard Malamud. The darkest (deepest) truths about drug addiction come from William Burroughs, about Negro-white relations from Genet and Baldwin, about modern marriage from Albee and Tennessee Williams, about the disaffected young from Allen Ginsberg.

The latest extension of this perspective is provided by Hubert Selby, Jr., who carries it into the violent slums around the Brooklyn waterfront, where he casts a particularly lurid light upon juvenile delinquency, the homosexuality of everyday life, the degeneration of the family in public housing projects, the corruption of the unions, and, in general, upon the vicious, obscene, and cold-hearted propensities of modern man, not to mention modern woman.

Only two of the six stories in *Last Exit to Brooklyn* deal with inversion as such. "The Queen Is Dead" features an uncensored drug-booze-and-sex orgy between a circle of homosexuals and the local gang of teen-age hoodlums as seen mainly through the stoned eyes and told in the tremulous language of "Georgette," a young addict who wears a G-string but whose soul is with Edgar Allan Poe. "Her" passion is for Vinnie, a member of the Gang, who had knifed her in the leg a few days before in a typical bit of streetcorner horseplay; eventually Georgette has him, though in a particularly odious way that casts her farther out upon the thorns of life. Vinnie and the boys also figure in the other story in this vein, which chronicles the passage into homosexuality of one Harry Black, a ponderously stupid and officious shop steward in a union run by labor racketeers; Harry's good times come to an end with the settlement of a strike on which he has been fattening himself, and with his molesting of a young boy, for which he is beaten and maimed by the Gang.

Selby's other vignettes of the waterfront slums, however, are no less informed by the same loving and loathing fascination with "rough trade," or by other variants of sado-masochistic fantasy. "Another Day, Another Dollar" describes a typical night in the life of the Gang, highlighted by one of their encounters with some soldiers from the nearby base. Having cornered one of them and tried to run him over with the car, the boys form a circle over the prostrate man and they, like Selby's prose, warm to the occasion:

> Ya . . . cottonpickin punk, and a hard kick in the ribs turned him slightly and he tried to raise himself on one knee and someone took a short step forward and kicked him in the solarplexus and he fell on his side, his knees up, arms folded across his abdomen, gasping for air and the blood in his mouth gurgled as he tried to scream, rolled down his chin and spumed forth as he vomited violently and someone stomped his face into the pool of vomit . . . and their shoes thudded into the . . . bastards kidneys and ribs and he gasped as a kick broke his nose . . . and Freddy kicked him in the temple and the yellowbastards eyes rolled back and his head lolled for a moment and he passed out . . .

And so on.

As part of the publicity for *Last Exit to Brooklyn* there is a statement by Miss Sontag that Selby, like Antonin Artaud (the ex-maniac who conceived "the theater of cruelty"), "has discovered in cruelty . . . that which is absolutely necessary." I can't imagine that Selby's idea of its necessity is all that impersonal and philosophical. It takes a genuine compulsion to write the above passage, to yield up one's imagination so completely to the images and sensations of sadism, to identify so thoroughly by one's language with the mentality of the action. Whatever revulsion the passage is meant to convey is quickly absorbed by a cool excitement: it is, unmistakably, the prose of a man whom violence turns on.

Selby's best single piece of writing is the story of Tralala, a teen-age psychopath whose dumb and constant rage sweeps her from one gutter to another, from delinquency to prostitution and eventually into dereliction and destruction. As with his young hoodlums and queens, Selby creates Tralala from the inside out, so that the language of the narrative and of her own interior monologue merge in one long rush of flat, baleful expression:

> A couple of sailors asked her if she wanted a drink and she said what the fuck and left with them. They roamed around for hours drinking and then she went to a room with two of them and they gave her a few bucks in the morning so she stayed with them for a few days, 2 or 3, staying drunk most of the time and going back to the room now and then with them and their friends. And then they left or went somewhere and she went back to the bar to look for another one or a whole damn ship. What's the difference.

There is no femininity in Tralala, not a trace of tenderness and only a minimum of passion. In Selby's hands she takes on a repulsive but magnetic thereness by virtue of his being utterly faithful to the brutality of her nature and to the strong attraction that her nihilism exerts upon his imagination. As a result, he strikes a current of feeling and fantasy that carries him far beyond the point where another writer's imagination would be repelled and would cut out: the final scene in which Tralala finds her "whole damn ship" and is turned into a piece of mutilated human junk is hideous and yet emotionally valid.

Tralala is Selby's ideal character. She has none of the normal emotions that would offer opposition, contradiction, even ambiguity to the simple, destructive point he wants to make with her. Otherwise, Selby's characters soon begin to reveal less of their lives than of the narrow, habitual grooves in which their author's sensibility runs, just as the line of action almost invariably moves toward still another explosion of violence. The only feeling of human connection and sentiment wells up when Harry Black finally spends a night with a man or—improbably enough—when Georgette recites "The Raven" and briefly turns the orgy into a hushed poetry reading. The sentimentality of these passages is, of course, merely the reverse of the crude, tough tone that surrounds them and reinforces the awareness of how little range there is of thought and art in these stories, of how dependent Selby is upon the intense slant and twist of his emotions for his perspective.

The same is true of his ability to create. The world that exists apart from his own obsessions is conceived by a callow, banal, pointless loathing. "Lands End" tells of a neighborhood housing project that is inhabited by a gallery of stereotypes: a Negro stud who neglects his family and lives for his Cadillac and the next available wench; an Italian couple locked in a continual, screaming warfare (Georgette's dashing Vinnie fifteen years later?); a loafer who sends his wife out to work and spends his time swilling beer and peering hopefully into the windows across the way; a Negro woman who is hung up on respectability—she is, of course, frigid; and so on. There is also a kind of chorus of slatternly, evil-mouthed housewives who turn away in disappointment when a baby is rescued from falling off a window ledge. So much for married life. Turds in the elevators, babies in the incinerators, children tearing each other apart on the playgrounds: so much for social welfare and progress. Boredom and cruelty; neglect and bestiality, forever and ever, world without end.

Selby apparently sees some profound religious truth in all of this, for he prefaces each of the stories with a quotation from the Old Testament. None of them is apt: the one for "Tralala" comes from the "Song of Songs," of all things. I imagine that Selby wishes us to believe that he is describing a modern-day Sodom or Gomorrah, which of course he is, though from the point of view of a Sodomite. Like William

Burroughs dedicating his macabre and lubricious fantasies to the fight against drug addiction, Selby or perhaps his editor may merely be anticipating his day in court. But still it's a very false note. Nihilism is Selby's single true love, and one of the Grove Press crowd—Seymour Krim, LeRoi Jones, Terry Southern, John Rechy, etc.—who tell us how beautiful and true Selby is should tell him that if you're going to be like a nihilist, you can't work the religious shuck as well.

(1964)

The Development of Flannery O'Connor

I never met Flannery O'Connor, but from the memoirs published after her death last year at thirty-nine and from her friend Robert Fitzgerald's sensitive introduction to this collection of her final stories, I imagine her to have been from that breed of Southern girls whom I met in Ann Arbor or Chicago ten or fifteen years ago—the ones who looked as if they had stepped not out of a Salem cigarette ad but rather out of a continuation of *The Heart Is a Lonely Hunter*. Rather plain, buttoned-up girls, they usually sat by themselves in the back of the creative-writing classes and the graduate English courses, smoked a great deal and approved of very little, but every so often one of them turned up with a wickedly alive and deadpanned and original story or essay that made the rest of us green with envy. It occurred to me at the time, and still does, that all that emphasis on old-style femininity in the South which produced the typical "belles" had also produced an even more highly developed version of the "misfits."

At that time it was also a particularly good thing to be a Southern misfit, just as today it is helpful to be a Jewish one. There were Faulkner and Eudora Welty and Miss McCullers and Robert Penn Warren; there were *Kenyon Review* and *Sewanee Review* and Mr. Ransom and Mr. Tate; there was a sense of cultural authority and also a feeling that those who had grown up in Memphis or Highpoint or Tuscaloosa were genuinely in touch with the secret life of the American psyche, just as the Midwestern writers had been in the 1920's. So those "shy, glum" girls, as Robert Fitzgerald describes Flannery O'Connor at this period, seemed to have a great advantage, and I waited for them, and their male counterparts, to emerge into prominence and join the rest of the "Southern Renaissance."

Well, they didn't, and the one or two I've kept track of are writing advertising copy in New York or raising children in New Haven. This, too, in a way turned out to be the fate of the Southern Renaissance, which has ended up pretty much in the North, where it is spread with increasing thinness from Broadway to Berkeley. Meanwhile, the important individual careers lapsed or deteriorated or ended, and the Southern culture became a place to visit imaginatively rather than to live in, and then, in more recent years, not even that.

There is an essay by Isaac Rosenfeld, written as early as 1946, in which he points out the degree of withdrawal from the circumstances of Southern society which had already occurred in the fiction of Carson McCullers and Eudora Welty—"an unavowed double standard which divides the [folk] material used from the personal uses to which the author puts it." Rosenfeld went on to argue that such a split was inevitable because "the social contradictions of the South are . . . such that the whole society may be called the antithesis of art." A decade later when Southern politics began to visibly belie the metaphors of its literary men, when Faulkner's "cursed land" was shown to be not tragic but simply and pragmatically evil, when Willy Stark had faded into Ross Barnett and the formerly much-discussed civility and spirituality of the Southern tradition had passed into the keeping of Martin Luther King, it seemed that Rosenfeld had been unquestionably right in concluding, "I don't see how a serious Southern artist can really and truly feel at home in his home."

The one important writer, though, who stayed home, who evaded and then wrestled with and eventually triumphed over these "contradictions," was Flannery O'Connor. She, too, had gone north in the late Forties, but she returned a few years later, after being stricken with a rheumatic disease, and lived the last thirteen years with her widowed mother on a farm outside of Milledgeville, Georgia. Thus her residence was not a choice but a fate, and judging from the number of well-educated and bitter spinsters and bachelors in her later stories, who for physical and/or psychological reasons live cooped up with their mothers, it was not a fate that she accepted easily.

For a time, however, it probably made little difference where she lived. She was not writing about Milledgeville or from the genteel, Catholic perspective of her own background and circumstances. Since she had such a quick, deft, animating touch that brought her characters and milieu to life by means of a few details and the flick of a metaphor, it is easy to forget that she was not portraying Southern life so much as her own lurid sensations of religious life. Even in the rural South, where she sets her two novels and early stories, most people belong to something—to a community, a church, a family, a settled way of life—but her people are so solitary or isolated, their degree of alienation is so extreme, that they seem to know no one else except the other characters they meet in the tale. Divested of all social ties and acquiring none, they are the creatures of a vision, and though their speech, manners, and dress bespeak the Bible Belt, their real existence is meant to lie in the eternal mysteries of sin and redemption, which they grotesquely and usually blindly enact.

This weird procession of teen-age prophets, backwoods nihilists, and demented acolytes, as well as orphans and widows, frauds and psychotics, is intended to create a world that was as close as possible to pristine Christianity. *The Violent Bear It Away*, for example, depicts the transmission of a prophetic vocation from a crazed old bootlegger to his fourteen-year-old grandson whom he had kidnaped, baptized, and raised in the wilderness and who, though aided by the Devil himself, is eventually unable to resist the fate of baptizing his idiot half-brother by drowning him and trudging on "in the bleeding, stinking, mad shadow of Christ." Besides allowing Flannery O'Connor to let rip her talent for the vulgar and violent, her latter-day counterparts of Galilee and Nineveh enabled her to start at rock bottom, as it were, and put her much more rational Catholic beliefs through the fire of a barbarous and frequently perverse faith. It also kept her in a highly subjective, almost solipsistic relation to the South and made her seem like the country preacher she describes near the beginning of *Wise Blood:* "a waspish old man who had ridden over three counties with Jesus hidden in his head like a stinger."

Embodied in such defective human clay, moreover, the religious moral was often consumed in the fire of her grotesque melodramas. In *Wise Blood* a young backwoods ascetic is released from the Army, buys a glaring blue suit and a ministerial hat, travels to a city, where he immediately visits a prostitute and then sets forth in a broken-down jalopy to found "The Church Without Christ." The first thirty or forty pages are brilliantly unexpected, but the comedy soon breaks down into a macabre phantasmagoria of a sort of Baptist sideshow in which both faith and its perversions seem equally deranged. Though *The Violent Bear It Away* is a much more convincing and powerful book, it, too, suffers from being so claustral and freakish, as though, like beggars' children, her characters must first be lamed before they can function. Over the longer stretch of her novels, though neither is very long, Flannery O'Connor seems also to lose much of the sly casualness and wit that is the leaven of her vision of sin and the agents of timing and contrast in those two marvelous early stories "A Good Man Is Hard to Find" and "Good Country People," and instead fills in by piling up one lurid effect upon the other.

In most of the stories collected in *A Good Man Is Hard to Find* her consciousness begins to open out to full range and to contend with the actual disjunctions and disparities between modern Southern culture and "the Catholic sacramental view of life" that she regarded as her ruling perspective. I am thinking particularly of such stories as "A Temple of the Holy Ghost," "The Artificial Nigger," and particularly of "The Displaced Person," which seems to me to mark the turning point in Flannery O'Connor's career—the first full merging of natural and religious experience as well as a subtle assimilation of social meanings to anagogical ones. Paraphrasing "The Displaced Person" is like whistling a Bach cantata, but it is mainly a manifold study in uprootedness that connects the concentration-camp inmates of Europe to the itinerant farm laborers of the South and associates a Polish refugee, who puts a rundown farm in order and tries to marry his relative to a Negro farmhand, with Christ. "He's extra and has upset the balance around here," complains Mrs. McIntyre, the owner of the farm, to the old priest who has brought Guizac to her. Unable to bring herself to make the efficient refugee leave, she stands dumbly by while the native white farmhand, whom Guizac has displaced, runs him over with a tractor. In the aftermath, the Negro, the farmhand, Guizac's family, and eventually Mrs. McIntyre herself abandon the farm, leaving it to the Judge, her dead husband, who lies "grinning" under his desecrated tombstone, from which another farmhand had stolen an angel on his way through.

The complex funding of this narrative of modern uprootedness and human transience with Christological overtones so that the spiritual meaning is mysteriously embedded in the specific is carried out again and again in the final stories that have been collected in *Everything That Rises Must Converge*. This is a book by a major writer who in the last years of her painful and foreshortened life achieved a mastery of form and a strength of vision that enabled her to create tales such as "Parker's Back" and "Revelation" that raise a truck driver's tattoo and a housewife's sense of insult to the level of spiritual illumination. It is as though in the struggle against her illness she had come to find enough grotesqueness and grace in the common life of men and that she had no more time or talent to waste on merely being sardonic and bizarre.

Not that Flannary O'Connor became a balanced, serene writer. Of the nine stories in *Everything That Rises*, five end in a violent death. She did not lose her sense of melodrama; she severely disciplined it to weight the consequences of perverse wills and crooked passions. In the title story there is a fateful encounter between a Negro woman and another of Miss O'Connor's foolish but well-intentioned elderly daughters of the Old South. The bus they are riding on is integrated, and they discover to their mutual disgust that they are wearing the same hat. Both women are also visibly living through their sons—a little Negro boy, fancifully dressed, and a bitter young man, Julian, who despises his mother's fallen heritage as much as he secretly yearns to repossess it. Devious and sadistic, he torments her by scraping acquaintance with the Negro passengers and dreams of giving her a stroke by marrying a Negro girl. The stroke, however, comes when they all get off at the same stop and Julian's mother tries to give the child a penny. Furious, the Negro mother lashes out and knocks her down. Julian, in turn, vindictively bullies her until suddenly he realizes she is dying there in the street. He experiences a rush of love, but his mother is beyond that: "[Her eye] remained fixed on him, raked his face again, found nothing and closed," and he is left alone, "postponing from moment to moment his entry into the world of guilt and sorrow."

The story is so resonant with irony, so dense in social and moral implications, that it undermines complacency and cant on all sides of the racial question. All three people are right and wrong, but Julian is most wrong because his motives are corrupt. The story turns a stock political answer into a religious question.

But I do not wish to gloss these stories. They each exist on

their own complex terms and within their own profound
sense of the mystery of sin and grace. They steadily confront
the contradictions Rosenfeld spoke of, and then, as often as
not, by a visionary power transcend them. As such most of
these late stories conserve the integrity of the individual
fallen life even as they passionately reveal the divine order
that is immanent in its desires and fortune. They also demonstrate that not even the contradictions of the South are anti-
thetical to a major writer's sense of her task. Major writers
inevitably take major risks. Which is something one of those
"shy" girls could have told you all along.

(1965)

Witnesses of the Holocaust:
1. Anna Langfus and Piotr Rawicz

Piotr Rawicz's *Blood from the Sky* and Anna Langfus' *The Lost Shore* are both award-winning French novels by East European Jews who managed to survive the Nazi holocaust and whose vision and vocation as writers have been marked for life by the nightmare through which they passed. Rawicz's book is an original and highly symbolic account of the destruction of the Jewish community in a Ukrainian town and of the odyssey of one of its survivors in his dazed and tormenting efforts to remain alive in the charnelhouse of Central Europe despite a complete revulsion toward life. *The Lost Shore* is set in France immediately following the liberation. Having described in her first novel, *The Whole Land Brimstone*, a young Polish Jew's flight from and capture by the Nazis, Mrs. Langfus now portrays the more subtle, and in some ways more painful, horror of her heroine's return to the indifferent—and hence unreal—world of the living.

Though Rawicz and Mrs. Langfus are as different from each other as, say, Baudelaire is from George Sand, their respective books are joined at the middle by their common apprehension of the shadow regions of human extremity and by their common role as witness to the unassimilable—and hence easily repressed—history which they and their dead were forced to endure.

This vocation of Jewish witness, which in the case of a deeply sensitive writer like Rawicz or Schwarz-Bart or Elie Wiesel or Sydor Rey seems to be an irrevocable fate, is not simply a matter of writing directly about the holocaust itself, of telling what they remember and filling in a bit more of the record. Indeed, the imperatives of this vocation have least to do, perhaps, with the factual side of the history. By now there has been a glut of books and articles, reminiscences and diaries, documentary histories and objective analyses that tell us everything we need to know about life in the ghettoes and prisons and death camps; no survivor need feel compelled to assume the burdens of testimony to the degradation, torture, and murder that reiterate endlessly through these accounts and that finally dull and deaden consciousness of their import.

Were a knowledge of the facts enough to limn the nightmare and to approach its meaning, the world could long ago have closed this chapter on its depravity, and writers such as those I've mentioned would perhaps be freed to turn to themes other than the meaning of Jewish victimization and survival. What keeps this chapter open (as in the recent wave of interest around the Eichmann trial, followed by that around Hannah Arendt's account of it), and what compels some of its survivors to devote to it not merely their books but their innermost being, is that beyond the facts and our keen awareness of them yawns the mystery of genocide and our numb, if vaguely troubled, awareness of it: in short, our inability to *understand* rather than merely *know* what happened to the Jews of modern Europe.

What keeps our awareness numb is not only a psychological diffidence but also philosophical habit. To understand what happened to the Jews, to really heed the screams of the victims as they come down to us in the records and in the novels would of necessity shatter our pragmatic assurance that whatever happens in this world is explicable, that men, governments, and history are rational, that such episodes as the Nazi period are aberrations that prove the rule of Western humanism, whether in psychology, politics, or morality. Against this assurance, existentialist philosophy—not to mention its data such as the plight of the Jews or of the twenty-five million others who were killed within a period of five years—has scarcely made a dent. Perhaps in this modern world of ours only a Buddhist monk can *understand* what happened at Dachau or in the Ukraine. In the meantime such writers as Piotr Rawicz and Anna Langfus struggle as best they can to bear witness to those screams of ontological horror, whether those uttered by the women and children at the open graves or those continuing to reverberate in the memories of the survivors.

One might even say that the value of the witness is directly related to the force with which it disturbs the normal, rational ontology of the daily life. Again, this has less to do with subject matter—whether the writer chooses, let us say, to dwell upon the enormities of the death camp or the ambiguous inner life of one of the survivors in Paris—than with matters of attitude and tone and the techniques and talents he employs to express them. The mark of the true witness is that he is without reassurance: he is too aware of the dissolution of the conventional categories of being—"reality" and "illusion," "past" and "present," "good" and "evil," "life" and "death."

Like the dreamer of a nightmare, the witness has at best only a provisional and tormented relationship with the world of fact, which at any moment threatens to turn into the utterly strange and terrible, just as he has only a provisional and tormenting hold upon his own ego, which, as in the nightmare, is stripped of its defenses and senses the threat of its dissolution. The truth toward which the witness approaches is that of madness, that of the fundamental disorientation of being which Conrad speaks of as "the heart of darkness," or Bettelheim as "the extreme situation," or David Rousset in *Les Jours de notre mort* as the feeling that Buchenwald was ruled over by Ubu Roy, the surrealist maniac, or Rawicz's apprehension, amid the slaughter of twenty children, that "God is mad, stark raving mad. . . . The Belly of the Universe, the belly of Existence was gaping open."

In Mrs. Langfus' *The Lost Shore,* ostensibly the story of a doomed love affair between a young survivor and a gentle but obtuse middle-aged Frenchman, the burden of the meaning is carried by Maria's abiding sense of disorientation toward the things of this life, whether love affairs or careers, houses or subways. Early in the novel she begins one of her typical days drifting about Paris in search of a new stranger to follow: "I went down the steps leading to that subterranean kingdom which the living have filched from the dead and which they clutter with their impatient stridings and jostlings and raised voices, these last torn to shreds by the roar of trains eager to proceed on their way to nowhere—all in the very place where one would expect to find the silence and peacefulness of those who have finally arrived." In the case of Rawicz this disorientation is even more thoroughgoing: he thinks of his book as a "composition on decomposition," and tells us that "ambiguity—strained and creaking ambiguity—is the one remaining bridge which occasionally allows me to steal, in the evenings, into the encampment of the human."

It is one thing to live in the valley of the shadow of death, however, and another to make the reader experience it as such. The trouble with *The Lost Shore,* as with its predecessor, *The Whole Land Brimstone,* is that Mrs. Langfus' imagination is far too limited and literal to create much of a sense of the unique crisis of being that makes up her subject. She practices a more or less conventional realism inadequate to to those larger reaches of her material since it reduces the problems of terror and madness to the commonsensical and straightforward probabilities of motive and act, conditioning and response, that this method engenders. As a result, her two novels are halted far short of the illimitable and flatter our knowingness while impoverishing our understanding.

The Whole Land Brimstone has its intensities, but they are conferred more by the experiences common to the literature of the six million than by the author's particular vision. *The Lost Shore* is even more fatally harmed by literalness since it reduces Maria's plight to standard neurotic symptoms—remoteness, self-destructiveness, sexual queasiness, passive hate, vacuity—propped up by a conventional mingling of fact and fantasy, being and nothingness, along with the other routine categories of disorientation. In the end, Maria seems less like the witness to the nightmare of her people than another victim of the deadness that currently afflicts young women in French novels and movies. And it is no surprise that the suicide of an emotionally deprived young girl who has become her friend should be identified eventually with her own experiences under the Nazis. What is moving and true is the relation between Mrs. Langfus' two books: the horrors of her experiences as a fugitive and prisoner twenty years ago are related with a fullness and intensity of recollection that one feels from reading the thin, shadowy depictions in *The Lost Shore* will never be available to her in describing the life that has come after.

Blood from the Sky is something else entirely: the most freely created and sheerly brilliant treatment of the ontological issues that I know of in this literature. It seems less like a novel than a testament that has been written under a spell—so esoteric and multiple and yet so coherent is Rawicz's imagination of the Jewish terror and the world's disaster. It is a book to ponder at length, and I can do no more here than sketch some of its salient features.

The framework of this testament is provided by the author's commentary; he is one of a community of refugees and assorted derelicts who live in the Montparnasse cafés and nurse their exhaustion. ("Then there is the fellow with the beard who is jealous of Soutine. He should have been Soutine, but not be dead.") Into this atmosphere of pallid, macabre life and dead time, in which the only unquestionably real item in view to the author is a piece of red meat covered with black flies in a butcher's window, there comes another spectral but upright figure who makes for the author "like a magnetic mine for a ship." And so begins Boris' "tale of the tool," which the author will piece together from his friend's account as well as from scraps of meditation and poetry that are taken from his journal.

The two modes of narration are joined by the fact that Boris is blood brother to the author in his cool cynicism and disgust, in his passion for ultimate meaning, and in his capacity for "the art of comparison"—by which he uses the catastrophe of his community in the Ukraine as a kind of revolving prism that refracts the impalpable rays of cosmic horror into the dark and bloody colors of Jewish experience.

Both Rawicz and Boris are symbolist poets, and what unfolds in these pages is a sumptuous and scarifying tapestry of the last desperate days of the community dissolving into eternity. Boris belongs to a wealthy and highly cultivated milieu which furnishes the members of the council who preside, whether tenderly or brutally, over the community's destruction. Boris himself is both tender and brutal—an assimilated Jewish version of Baudelaire's dandy who observes the coming holocaust with a detached and ironic eye, a connoisseur of the carnality and spirituality that have been set aflame among the Jews and within himself. He learns from an astrologer that he will survive not through his blondness and impeccable German but through the fact that he is too detached from his people to deserve to die with them, that his fate will be to experience "the one true emptiness." He is then given a vision of the town, which he will bear with him as one of its survivors and witnesses, in which the bestiality and purity of its suffering life will have merged into the oneness of time. "Abraham, Isaac, and Jacob are here in this room," the astrologer tells him. "And so is the bleating of their sheep. What is the use of trying to fight it?"

The destruction of the community is viewed within these

two contending attitudes of cynicism and mysticism that together provide an extraordinarily vivid account of individual
behavior, on the realistic level, and of its universal import, on
the transcendent level. Among the portraits of the innocent
are those of the scoundrels and sadists; among the faces of
the dazed and ignorant victims is a gallery of lawyers, scholars, poets, and rabbis to whom the final pogrom is more an
illumination than a curse. As "Leo L."—the most articulate
member of the community and its leader—puts it, "human
beings have no worse enemy than the state of Being"—a
truth borne out from page to anguished page. At the same
time, the immediate and palpable specter of persecution and
death frames and focuses the question of Being, and amid a
riot of sensual and spiritual paradoxes Rawicz-Boris finally
raises the massacre of the Jews to that of genuine ontological
significance.

Thus, the first section closes with a particularly hideous
mass murder of children, to which Boris returns a few hours
later.

> Several mutilated children were still suffering. The nurse
> went around distributing death, like portions of ginger-
> bread stuffed with darkness. . . . [Boris] also compares
> the nurse to the gardener who fulfills the destiny of the
> flowers and the sunshine by picking them.

The second half of the novel recounts Boris' migration
with his mistress through Central Europe and his eventual
capture. The earlier themes are recapitulated and developed
further through "the tale of the tool." The "tool" is Boris'
genital, the vehicle and talisman of his fate. Upon it has been
inscribed "the sign of the Covenant"—the circumcision that
binds him to his community and that also finally betrays him
to the Nazis. At the same time, his genital is the one last
thing that attaches him to life and to any further desire to
penetrate its mysteries. And eventually it is his sexuality that
preserves his spark of life through the unspeakable tortures of

his months in prison and that restores him to the little joy he is still capable of and to the vocation that is his destiny to endure.

The erotic element, though, is more than the matrix of Boris' life force. It is also the matrix of Rawicz's imagination, the Ariadne's thread that guides him through the labyrinth of the world's derangement. To view the holocaust under the aspect of the erotic is not a perverse dandyism but rather a profound recognition that on the farthest edge of being the erotic impulse still throbs away and as such expresses the conditions of dementia and lucidity, depravity and transcendence with which it becomes compounded. *Blood from the Sky* is not another chronicle of Jewish suffering but rather a brilliant depiction of the paradoxes of desire at the brink of extinction. Yet it is the more scarifying for that. The gifted, haunted Boris stays in the mind long after his story is told, the adversary of our numbness.

(1964)

Witnesses of the Holocaust:
11. *Chaim A. Kaplan*

Scroll of Agony is the diary of an elderly Hebrew school principal—dry, bookish, but inspired—who lived in Warsaw during the Nazi occupation and died shortly after the mass deportations in the summer and early fall of 1942. There is an old photograph of Chaim A. Kaplan on the dust jacket; taken when he was perhaps in his thirties, it shows a very proper, studious Jewish professional wearing a pince-nez and a tufted beard—all in all, a model of the "refinement" that was once much cultivated by the emancipated class of East European Jews. Less obvious is a certain mournfulness around the eyes and, more distinctly, in the set of the lips that suddenly recalls an old-fashioned Talmudist. Somewhat shadowy and grainy, as though the photograph itself were an emblem of the now vanished world of Chaim A. Kaplan, his face holds one's attention: turned this way, it is "modern," that way, it is ancient; gazed at steadily, it becomes the face of an enigmatic culture.

Isaac Bashevis Singer, who lived in Kaplan's home as a young man, remembers him as a typical Hebraist of the period: prim, domestic, zealous, unworldly. Indeed, Kaplan's disposition was so gentle and imperturbable, his life so unexceptional, that when Singer learned that his landlord kept a journal, he wondered what Kaplan could possibly have to say in it.

Whatever Kaplan's earlier diaries may have been like, the ones he kept during the Nazi occupation are not the reflections of a spiritually timid man. Nor is he a particularly calm one. Though aging, diabetic, living in wretched circumstances, harrowed each day by "the Dantean scenes" in the Jewish quarter, he must have possessed great reservoirs of moral stamina simply to continue writing. He is by turns stuffy, cranky, lachrymose, grandiloquent, as well as wry, passionate, hard-headed, and eloquent. He tells us very little about himself, seldom mentions his wife and never his two children who were safe in Israel. But, being a man to whom an event and his reaction to it were virtually inseparable, he pours himself out into every sentence he writes. At one point, just after the Germans have condemned all the Jews of Warsaw from twelve to sixty to forced labor and almost certain death in the work camps, Kaplan sits in his unheated room in sub-zero weather and writes in his beautiful Hebrew script, which he never erases, as though he were inscribing a sacred text:

> The whole nation is sinking in a sea of horror and cruelty. . . . I sense within me the magnitude of this hour and my responsibility to it. I have an inner awareness that I am fulfilling a national obligation, a historic obligation that I am not free to relinquish. My words are not rewritten; momentary reflexes shape them. . . . My record will serve as source material for the future historian.

Kaplan's "scroll of agony"—the term is his own—is "source material" of a particularly valuable kind. There is not a great deal of factual material about the Jewish holocaust—indeed, Immanuel Ringelblum's diaries, which appeared in English as *Notes from the Warsaw Ghetto*, provide a more comprehensive and detailed account than we get from Kaplan's book, partly because Kaplan's journals from April 1941 to May 1942 have not been recovered, partly because

Ringelblum, a social historian and community leader, was privy to much more information than the secluded Kaplan received. The value of Kaplan's record stems from the continuity of those "momentary reflexes" of intensely personal reflection and expression that provide an authentic emotional and cultural context of meaning for the facts of the holocaust. The facts do not speak for themselves—not even ultimate ones—and without such a context, the tragedy of "the six million" dwindles to an abstraction—100,000 killed here, 800,000 there—and becomes the more susceptible to facile psychological or sociological explanation. *Scroll of Agony* restores the sense of the individual Jewish victim without which we cannot feel the meaning of the holocaust, and of the agonizing paradoxes of Jewish religious and communal traditions without which we cannot understand it.

There is not a false note in Kaplan's diary, not a response that does not immediately seem true to the man. Determined to perform his mission without "exaggeration or distortion," he responds to each of his facts and impressions with unaffected candor. When the German army enters Warsaw, he registers his awe at their "healthy appearance and marvelous uniforms. . . . You almost begin to believe they are fit to rule the world through power and strength." When the Jews are ordered to wear the Star of David, he is pleased and even proud that the Warsaw badge is blue and white, the Jewish national colors, rather than the yellow one of medieval times that must be worn by the Jews of Lodz. He is amused by the optimism and ignorance of the rumors that continually circulate in the ghetto as it waits deliverance from afar ("Rommel's hand, too, has withered. . . . The members of the ghetto have already encircled him, attacked him, and left him an eternal ruin"). He is contemptuous of the *Judenrat*—"strangers in our midst . . . sons of Ham who trample upon our heads . . . musclemen . . . nincompoops"—appalled by the Jewish police, who "exist on the same moral plane" as the Nazis. Increasingly shaken by the privations and havoc of the ghetto, Kaplan writes with a growing range and sensitivity of response to the small as well as to the huge aspects of his fate, and with greater justice to everything he feels, from tenderness to irony to outrage to horror.

Perhaps the most remarkable thing about this journal is that its author through three years of living in hell not only retained his capacity for self-expression but strengthened it; the somewhat strident lamentations of the first year give way to a more grave and measured voice, and the Kaplan of the final sixty pages who describes the terror and havoc of the nightly murders and the deportations speaks with the voice of the Prophets. But whether shrill or austere, mournful or sardonic, it is always the distinct voice of Chaim A. Kaplan, and any abstract notion one may have about the "six million" does not survive for very long. Kaplan's constant struggle to understand the catastrophe in which he has been caught up and to guide his own behavior almost invariably carries him back to the traditions of Jewish history, philosophy, and faith. The very Hebrew he uses enfolds the daily phenomena of persecution within the fabric of traditional consciousness. Thus he writes of the Polish cooperation with the Nazis: "Midian and Moab have joined forces to oppress Israel." Or again, though Kaplan has a sophisticated Zionist's knowledge of modern European politics, he relies finally upon a statement such as "because you drowned others, they drown you" —taken from the *Ethics of the Fathers*—to explain the dismemberment of Poland by Germany and Russia. More crucially, he repeatedly demonstrates that the organization and maintenance of life in the ghetto follow the timeless Jewish patterns of response to adversity: an outward compliance accompanied by an inner resistance. Kaplan often compares the Jews of Warsaw to the *marranos*—the Spanish Jews who accepted apostasy but many of whom continued to practice Judaism in secret; in Warsaw the Jews engaged in an enormous web of illegal activities ranging from smuggling to religious services: "everything is forbidden us, and yet we do everything." And, as he immediately notes: "This is the strength of eternal Judaism, that it continues to spin the fiber of our lives even in hiding." This tradition of conspiracy, Kaplan believed, was the manifestation of "our eternal tradition which commands us to live"—and he celebrates at many points the tenacity of the Jewish will to survive, no matter what the odds, as an expression of Judaism itself, of "the People of Hope."

Yet there was a terrible irony inherent in this behavior that Kaplan himself came to realize. In the early months of 1942 the "extermination squads" arrived in the ghetto, the deportations from the provincial towns had turned into mass murders, and the death camps had begun to operate. The hope of the Warsaw Jews that had kept the community functioning, had organized schools, had created an enormous relief effort to feed and house refugees, now became worthless, worse than no hope at all, for it placed the victims that much more securely in the hands of the killers. When the deportations from Warsaw began, Jews hurried to obtain permits to work in the war factories which would exempt them, though, as Kaplan lamented, "this is a tragedy as deep as the abyss—to help your enemy with your own hands, to save him from his misfortune so that he may turn around and kill you."

Kaplan not only perceived these paradoxes; he embodied them. The final weeks of his diary register the tragic experience of a man who has reached the outer limits of his character in trying to cope with his fate. His pride of identity lay in his being a Jew—in being guided by the moral ideals and communal wisdom that had preserved Judaism in the Diaspora. Thus he was able to maintain himself and his journal as a "holy" emblem of Jewish survival. At the same time, he remained true to his intelligence, refusing the false consolation bred by the rumors and fantasies that up to the end swept through the ghetto ("every ray of light . . . from afar unsettles our souls. . . . We have already been rescued from real freedom. A crumb of freedom is sufficient to make us

happy"). Driven to the extreme of conflict, he invents a
friend, an imaginary seer named Hirsch, who speaks the
naked, ultimate truth. "Like a mourner among bridegrooms,"
Hirsch gives the lie to the merchants holding on to their capital, the intellectuals busily buying up cheap rare books. As
the "political experts" study the Reuters broadcasts and
predict the fall of Hitler like so many cabalists predicting the
arrival of the Messiah, Hirsch tells them that it is Polish
Jewry whose days are numbered. And as the news filters in
(17,000 missing in Cracow, 40,000 in Lublin), Hirsch ex-
claims: "Cowards! A whole community of millions of people
stands on the brink of destruction and you keep silent. Protest! Alarm the world! . . . Is there any meaning to your
deaths?" But though Kaplan-Hirsch can come this far, he is
at the end of his forces. The terror of the ghetto—"suspended over nothingness"—engulfs him, and as he waits for
the Nazis and the Jewish police to come to his building, he
dreams of simply walking to the deportation center and turning himself in; but then thinks, "If my life ends—what will
become of my diary?"

These are the last words of this tragic book. One of the
things that tragic writing teaches us is to suspend judgment
in the presence of truths that are deeper than our experience.
For this reason alone, I hope that *Scroll of Agony* finds a
wide audience.

(1963)

Sartre: The View from the Void

Two collections of Sartre's writing, *Situations* and *The Philosophy of Jean-Paul Sartre*, have recently appeared. Read in conjunction, they provide a good introduction to his thought and temperament, particularly for the reader, like myself, who knows Sartre mainly through his fiction and plays. *Situations* is a collection of literary and political essays, written initially as prefaces to books Sartre admired or as contributions to his magazine, *Les Temps Modernes*. Along with his famous reply to Camus, there are lengthy studies of two other close friends and erstwhile partisans, Paul Nizan and Merleau-Ponty, through which Sartre develops his own views on and relations with the French Left of the past three decades. *The Philosophy of Jean-Paul Sartre* is mostly an anthology of passages from his technical writings, from the early studies in phenomenology to his recent massive critique of Marxism. Thanks to the coherent scheme of presentation worked out by the editor, Robert Cumming, and to his extremely lucid introduction, one can follow the main lines of Sartre's evolving system and begin to grasp the focus, range, and continuity of his view of the human condition. Mr. Cumming also includes some selections from Sartre's novels and plays which enable the reader to recognize the imaginative uses to which Sartre has put his abstract and often abstruse speculations. Further, a number of Sartre's own essays in *Situations* offer examples of the existentialist perspective in action as it isolates the issues of a man's life or attempts to elucidate, say, the fiction of Nathalie Sarraute or the art of Giacometti.

The two books also suggest why Sartre has become the leading intellectual figure of our time. One reason is that his work presents in a virtually total way the two crises that have haunted intellectuals in the twentieth century and converted their search for significant thought and action into traumas of uncertainty. On the one hand is Sartre's confrontation with the dizzying vortex of self-consciousness to which the contemporary mind has been led by the progressive emphasis on the inner life of the individual and, accordingly, on the accidents and peculiarities and distortions of his nature. Though we are still convinced that our endless preoccupations with the purely personal slant of our perceptions and feelings yield the only significant truths about existence, these truths typically bear a burden of hysteria or malaise, of what earlier writers took for granted as the fretfulness of the soul and went on from there. Sartre's own fiction, particularly *Nausea* and *The Age of Reason*, can be viewed as a brilliant systematic transformation of a neurosis into the condition of man and the state of nature.

On the other hand, Sartre's writings reflect, in only a somewhat less extreme way, the effort of the intellectuals to put an end to their alienation, undo their last ties to the hateful bourgeoisie, and immerse themselves in radical politics—that is to say, in the affairs of the proletariat, in the abstract, and, often enough, in those of the Soviet Union, in the concrete. Sartre himself came relatively late to this abyss. As he tells us in his essay on Merleau-Ponty, it was only in the early 1950's that he realized "I was a victim of and an accomplice in the class struggle. A victim because I was hated by an entire class. An accomplice because I felt both responsible and powerless. I discovered the class struggle in that slow dismemberment that tore us away from them [the work-

ers] more and more each day." This conflict, according to a
private note provided by Simone de Beauvoir in her latest
volume of memoirs, could not be resolved "without transcending his situation." Accordingly, in Sartre's words, and
in the parlance of his philosophy, which makes the statement
all the more poignant or, if you like, absurd: "I had to take
some step that would make me 'other.' I had to accept the
point of view of the U.S.S.R. in its totality and count on myself to maintain my own."

Yet what makes Sartre so interesting, as well as so representative, is just this profoundly divided character of his
thought: the unremitting effort, as he says elsewhere, to
think against himself; to transcend himself; to cast the amorphousness of the total "freedom" he posits into the iron mold
of a "situation"; finally to maintain general ideas while remaining convinced of the dizzying sweep of relativity, of
what Hegel called "the negativity of all singleness and all
difference."

At the center of his philosophy is an extreme subjectivism:
he tells us that the only thing we can be sure of is our individual existence, which is merely a ceaseless flux of consciousness. According to Professor Cumming, much of Sartre's subsequent philosophy can be traced back to his early
epistemology, where he tries to demonstrate that the mind
cannot be conscious of itself and consequently does not transcend its experience. From this he argues that there is, in
fact, no predetermined ego or self; there is only conscious
existence which is directed by its own intentionality—he
speaks of it as "a sheer activity transcending toward objects,"
otherwise "a great emptiness, a wind blowing toward objects." From this typically vehement *prise de position* (Sartre
does not take positions as much as seize them) the young
philosopher works his way back to a world of things, which
the howling void of consciousness requires to exist, and develops a complex dialectic of perpetual conflict between intentional subjects and objects—the "*pour soi*" and the "*en
soi*"—each man being a subject only by virtue of being an

object to other men. Thus, around the rim of this nothingness a self comes into being, though it remains a sort of
doughnut, constantly crumbling into its own void through
the permanent revolution that is consciousness and the
struggle with otherness that is existence.

Much of Sartre's mature philosophy, from *Being and
Nothingness* forward, can be viewed as an attempt to make
his way back along the edge of this void of philosophical nihilism, with its nauseated sense of the endless pullulation
and decay of material being, its lucid but arbitrary vision of
the disorder, contingency, uncertainty, emptiness, exploi-
tiveness, and despair of consciousness as the context of
human experience. As he remarks at the end of *The Words*,
his early effort to explore "the bitter unjustified existence of
my fellow-men" was a way of letting himself off the hook,
while the experience of the Occupation was to make him
aware that the situation of men in this world was a more determined and fateful one than he had dreamt of in his philosophy. There are, of course, various logical connections in
Sartre's thought between the "pernicious existentialism" of
his negative phase and the increasingly concrete and committed exploration of human freedom in the writings after the
war, but their main force seems less a matter of the extension of a system than of the exigencies of Sartre's discovery
that the hopeless division between himself and the world had
political causes and solutions.

Not that Sartre's politics emerge as all that concrete in *Situations*. The only specific issue he deals with is the Korean
War, which he attributes to MacArthur, Rhee, and the China
lobby. Disconcerted at the time by the fact that it was the
North Koreans who invaded, Sartre established "the truth"
that the "American troops in conjunction with the feudal
warriors of Seoul, set a trap for the Communists which the
latter fell into." The question of the Soviet labor camps
which Sartre himself initially protested against—is raised
twice: in his controversy with Camus, Sartre still finds them
"inadmissible," but no more so than is the use that has been

made of them to attack the Left. In a later essay he speaks of his erstwhile concern with the camps as a possible indication that the Soviet economy required them as well as the forced recruitment and exploitation of millions of workers every year—an accusation which he was subsequently able to disprove from his study of Russian production quotas. In short, the familiar dreary cant of fellow-traveling which is mimicked, sometimes almost word for word, by Simone de Beauvoir in *The Force of Circumstances*. Sartre was later to break his spell of remaining "as close as possible to the Communist party" during the suppression of the Hungarian revolt, and in his essays on Nizan and Merleau-Ponty he makes one aware of the desperate ambiguities of radical politics. Still, his later political thinking is disappointingly vague and overdetermined, and his method of defending himself against Camus is downright repellent.

The impression one gets of the committed Sartre from *Situations* is otherwise much more various and appealing. Whatever else there is to be said about his identification with the class struggle, it appears to have provided him with an enormously stimulating "situation." Like the image of consciousness in the early writings, the writer of these essays is constantly on the go, hurrying from point to point, subject to subject; fiercely intentional, his thought occupies, fills, and distends its material as he endeavors to lose and find himself in his encounters with other lives, disciplines, books, situations.

His long piece on Tintoretto is a case in point. In much the same way that he identifies with the alienations and self-alienations of Baudelaire and Genet, Sartre finds in the "lacerated heart" of this Venetian painter, formed by the culture of a great city which both employed and despised him, a partial reflection of his own character and fortune. Proceeding from a few facts and dates, but mostly from the evidence that Jacopo Robusti, the man known to us as Tintoretto, was eventually defeated by hate, Sartre builds up a portrait of an outrageous conniver and an indefatigable, fluent worker, a

cynical plagiarist and an original genius, an ostensible conformist and a determined revolutionary. Sartre's description
of Robusti proceeds partly along Marxist lines, taking the
painter as a son of the respectable working class who was
fighting to claw his way to bourgeois security and respectability and was therefore forced to subvert the exploitive relations between the painters' guild and the aristocracy. Most
of the coloring of this portrait, though, is done in the lurid
and sweeping style of existentialism to emphasize the decisive
event of rejection through which Robusti chose himself to be
the "frantic, hounded outlaw," the "opportunist gnawed by
fear." As the essay moves along, Sartre adds other characteristic features of his vision of the human condition: plagued
by the erosion of religious belief, by the introduction of new
categories of being—"distance, exile, alienation"—and by the
"bad faith" that resulted from these unassimilated changes,
Tintoretto's painting was "seized with dread." Sartre concludes:

> Nimble opportunism, resourcefulness, alacrity, talent
> —nothing was missing, but everything was corroded by
> an overwhelming void, by Art without God. This Art was
> ugly, wicked, nocturnal, the imbecilic passion of the part
> for the whole, an icy darkening wind, hissing through
> lacerated hearts. Inflated by emptiness, Jacopo was swept
> along on a motionless journey from which there was no
> return.

All of which seems to be more discernible in the literature
of Sartre (see, for example, the closing pages of *The Words*)
than in the painting of Tintoretto. But no matter. If he im-
poses himself on everything he touches, it is usually to our
advantage. Putting forward the image of his consciousness,
he provides us with ours: this little bourgeois revolutionary
with a hole in his center whose thought has whirled outward
to embrace and define his age.

(1965)

The Laughing German

As a people, the Germans have not been known for their self-irony, but during the past three decades or so they have grown exceptionally solemn. Throughout the Hitler years there was plenty of material but little opportunity for satire. With only a twist here and there, Chaplin in *The Great Dictator* was able to reveal the inanity that lay just beneath the surface of the Nazi mystique: all that was needed was to allow that goose-stepping and heel-clicking and jumpy saluting, those grandiose slogans and perfervid speeches to parody themselves as the antics and gibberish of nationalism run amok. But this was also the reason why social satire in Germany was one of the first of the democratic virtues to be driven underground, for—like all cases of megalomania, whether individual or mass—the hypnotic power of the Nazi will, much less its illusion of sanity, could be maintained only as long as nobody was encouraged to laugh. A similar phenomenon, though on a much more limited scale, occurred here during the McCarthy episode: it was only after the inadvertent comedy team of Cohn and Schine had demonstrated the silly pouting and preening that lurked behind the scenes of the Senator's crusade to save America that the spell of its passionate intensity was broken and McCarthyism came to be viewed in its proper dim light.

While McCarthy was eventually reduced to a comic villain

and hustled off the stage of history, Hitler was not. The manias of the Third Reich that were revealed in the period immediately after its demise were well beyond the ken of comedy or tragedy alike, and its case was properly turned over to criminal judges and political pathologists. One might have imagined, though, that the disorder and cynicism of the late Forties in Germany would have given rise to a mood of satire similar to that which swept over its artists and writers during the 1920's. But this was not in the cards. Thanks to the cold war, West Germany suddenly became the economic and political frontier in the struggle against Communism, and, with only a few snickers here and there, its people found themselves encouraged to resume a just estimate of their prudence, enterprise, and love of freedom. Thus, what was repressed by fear or zeal during the Hitler years came to be further buried by the earnestness and complacency of the "miracle" of reconstruction and recovery. Every so often a reminder of the recent past would rise to public consciousness as still another grocer or policeman was discovered to have assisted in the murder of another 20 or 2,000 or 200,000 Jews, or a government official such as Franz Joseph Straus regrettably tried to move against his critics with the former severity; but such stirrings merely made the cheese of obliviousness more binding. To be sure, there was a generation of younger writers who were struggling to remember and to remind, but their statements were usually too oblique and abstract, their evocation of the past too thinned out by symbolist techniques, to appreciably disturb the prevailing amnesia.

Finally, though, the lid was partly blown off a few years ago by *The Tin Drum*, the first novel of a flamboyant, raucous, and violent young satirist. Günter Grass had grown up in a Polish-German milieu in Danzig, had been thrown into the war and the Nazi cause in its last desperate years, and had knocked about in West Germany as a laborer and sculptor, his sense of outrage and betrayal remaining on tap. *The*

Tin Drum is the scarifying memoir of a midget drummer, writing from a mental hospital, who has a power of recall of the past thirty years of the Central European bourgeoisie that is equaled only by his voluble and sardonic contempt for them. In his mockery of the bakers and boy-scout leaders who had become Nazis, there emerges, as it were, some of the buried laughter and horror of the German consciousness itself. Tender and violent, spiritual and obscene, sportive and gruesome, Oskar's laughter covers virtually the whole range of human expression, but its two poles are cynicism and terror, the respective feelings with which his memoir begins and ends and to which his awareness of the meaning of his life constantly reverts.

For all of the intensity of Oskar's responses, Grass had the wit to come at the subject of the Nazi experience in Danzig and its aftermath in Düsseldorf from the side, as it were, rather than trying to confront it head-on. The first two thirds of the book, in particular, are packed with the domestic details of Oskar's family and neighbors in which he is far more absorbed than he is in the Nazi presence itself. The advantage of this method is that it enables Grass to present the appeal of fascism as a matter of course, another aspect of the hopelessly childish vanity, docility, and gullibility of the Danzig petit-bourgeoisie. Indeed, Grass's main insight in *The Tin Drum* is of the infantalism of German culture, in particular, and of the human animal, in general. The only character who doesn't appear as a case of thwarted development is Oskar himself, who has deliberately remained a midget to protect himself from becoming emotionally stunted by a "normal" family life and business career and also by virtue of his belief that the best place for a man, particularly in a mad age, is hidden under the skirts of a woman, a condition which his size is designed to facilitate. The purpose of his writing this memoir and of drumming up the past is, as he says, "to get back to the umbilical cord," and through his account of thirty years spent amid the storm and wreckage of recent history he is only at peace when he has found another warm, dark, sheltering place inside a woman's skirt, closet, cupboard, or bed.

Oskar's infantilism is not a conceit of the author, but the real thing: a powerful current of libidinal energy and purpose that drives him to turn his mother's lover over to the Germans and his presumptive father over to the Russians and to stab at the pregnant belly of the maid who is carrying either his brother or his son. Perverse, brutal, fetishistic, and macabre, he provides a perfect sounding-board for the history that unfolds around him, he being the reality of its unreality. Caught up in the society of Danzig, he would have been a ruthless Nazi; but since he contracted out at the age of three and remained a midget, his destructiveness becomes a sheer anarchism with a sentimental streak of Polish patriotism and Catholic mysticism. In later life he has a great success as a concert performer who hypnotically drums elderly audiences back to their infancy. Meanwhile the bad memories of his own actions and those of his age begin to pursue him and the various talismans of his libidinal career end by terrifying him. But from first to last Oskar is the various and irreducible image of the human animal—"childlike, curious, complex, and immoral." At the same time, he is intensely German— a grotesque, modern-day Goethe, crossed with Rasputin, as he himself reminds the reader—and he forms a scarifying mirror image of the "barbaric, mystical, and bored" culture that he satirizes.

Following *The Tin Drum*, Grass published a short novel set again in Danzig during the war years but written in an entirely different vein of feeling. *Cat and Mouse* is a tender, almost elegiac tale of one of the Danzig schoolboys whom the war draws out of the shelter of his decency; it exploits his masculine idealism and sends him off to the Eastern front. He fights bravely, wins the medal he has always coveted, but when he returns home on leave, he decides he has seen enough, and deserts, only to drown when he tries to return to his private sanctuary inside a half-sunken ship. Though Grass is seldom more than a paragraph away from his contempt for the Nazi mystique, the bitter laughter of *Cat and Mouse* becomes an aspect of his grief for his generation, so snared and so decimated.

The entrapment of Joachim Mahlke in the Nazi cause and his struggle to free himself anticipate the situation of Walter Matern, one of the two major figures in Grass's new novel. *Dog Years* is his most ambitious assault to date on the memory and conscience of contemporary Germany, as well as still another return to the Danzig of his own youth under the Nazis—a subject he seems bent on working and reworking until he has reached bottom.

Yet I wonder if he hasn't already done so, at least as far as his present lights go. For all of its epic dimensions, *Dog Years* is a thinner book than *The Tin Drum*, one that keeps piling up material around its periphery because it lacks the fully felt and developed center of each of the earlier novels. The book opens with an evocation of the Vistula River as a stream of legends and memories, bearing in its flood waters not only the debris of the present but also the mysteries of change and continuity. Thus, the narrator of this first of three sections, a mine owner named Brauxel, connects the river gods of Polish mythology, the different bands of famous knights that crossed the Vistula, and Napoleon himself to two boys who are playing around a dike. They, too, have already become part of the timelessness of his consciousness as well as of historical time, for the one boy, Amsel, is from an obscure family, possibly Jewish, and the other, Matern, comes from a proud line of Polish-Catholic bandits and anarchists. Matern then casually throws a penknife into the river, the knife with which a year ago the two boys had drawn each other's blood and sworn themselves to brotherhood. It is only 1926, but as Matern casually throws away Amsel's present to him for lack of a stone to throw, it is as though one of the more treacherous currents of European history has picked them up and separated them.

Yet there is something of a false magnitude in this open-ing, though it is very beautiful, just as there is a great deal of subsequent collapsing of time distinctions throughout the book to open up a historical perspective that remains narrow and repetitive. The first section is mainly an account of the developing ambivalent relationship between Amsel and Ma-tern and of Amsel's early career as a constructor of elaborate scarecrows. The second section, told by Harry Liebenau, a junior member of the Matern-Amsel generation, brings the story up through the war years, but readers of Grass's first two novels will feel that they have been through much of this before. The main difference is Grass's increasing penchant for portentous allegory, literary parody, and mixed prose styles *à la* Joyce. Matern has drifted into the Nazi Party, though he continues to befriend Amsel and even gives him old SA uniforms, with which he constructs mechanical storm troopers. Then, one snowy night, Matern leads a group of his cronies to Amsel's house, where they knock out all of his teeth and roll him in the snow. Meanwhile Tulla Pokriefke, whose father is a Nazi, is doing the same thing to Jenny Brunies, a girl whom a liberal schoolteacher has adopted.

Very well: Amsel is half Jewish and Jenny is the daughter of a gypsy. The historical anticipation is sound, if somewhat obvious. But why should both Amsel and Jenny undergo a transformation that renders them both slender and graceful, so that Amsel will go on to become a ballet master, among other things, and Jenny a leading dancer? Jenny's first success as a ballerina will come in a performance of *The Snow Queen* and she will later spend an entire night in an icehouse with-out feeling any discomfort. One traces out these different al-legories, but they usually confuse or distract from rather than clarify the main issues of the book. Similarly, the two central symbols—a line of three dogs and the mechanical scarecrows —which are intended to represent the bestial and automaton-like aspects of Nazism, respectively, throw little light on the actual characters in the novel and, consequently, become merely part of the elaborate rhetoric with which Grass keeps trying to fill out his vision. More's the pity since his powers of immediate observation are such that he can place a gang of storm troopers in a bar and in two pages of watching them get drunk and start a brawl, he can tell us more about the emotional basis of fascism than he can in all of his lucubrations about Harras and Prinz, the Führer's dog.

What saves *Dog Years* is the figure of Walter Matern. Once Amsel leaves the narrative about one third of the way through to become a mysterious presence on its periphery until he reappears near the very end as Brauxel, the manufacturer of humanized scarecrows, it is Matern who carries most of the interest. He is a fascinating study of the vestigial anti-Semite, of the internal émigré under fascism, and later of the militant anti-fascist who is attempting to scourge himself and his former comrades for their past crimes. From the moment in which he knocks out Amsel's teeth, his figure alters and he is, by turns, a purposeful and a hapless figure who is never able to extricate himself from his double image as persecutor and avenger. After the war he travels back and forth through West Germany seeking out his former comrades and superiors in the SA, taking his revenge usually by seducing their wives or daughters and, for a period of several months, passing on to them his venereal disease. For all of his determination, however, Matern is eventually worn down by the sheer shamelessness and complacency that reign wherever he goes.

Otherwise, though, *Dog Years* often seems more an exercise in writing than a vision of an era. It is strange that such a powerful and original satirist of German character should produce such a determinedly literary piece of work. Not that *Dog Years* isn't eminently worth reading; it's just that after reading *The Tin Drum* one feels let down by an all-too-German archness where one has come to expect the wit of a deeper terror and rage.

(1965)

A Kind of Survivor

If you are interested in contemporary intellectual life and are looking for intelligent direction, then *Language and Silence*, a collection of George Steiner's essays and reviews, is the book for you. Steiner has been mostly known for his two dazzlingly precocious works of scholarship, *Tolstoy or Dostoevsky* and *The Death of Tragedy*, but he now emerges as a cultural journalist who is as pertinent as he is erudite, a kind of latter-day Arthur Koestler. *Language and Silence* casts a bright and searching light into the murky disarray of current letters and literacy: it looks back to the period of darkness and disruption of Western culture two decades ago that continues to plague and challenge the moral purpose of literature, among other fields, and it looks forward to possibilities of art and thought that may carry us beyond our broken heritage. It provides an articulate and comprehensive discussion of the impact of science and mass communications on the ability of language to describe the realities of the earth and the world. It takes up such matters as the wages of pornography, both for letters and for the private life of feeling; the sociological as well as artistic conditions responsible for the crisis of the novel; the efforts of scholars and translators to come to grips with such classics as Homer, the Bible, Shakespeare, and Racine; and the complacent assumptions of literary study that threaten to make it as relevant to modern experience as is coin-collecting or alchemy. There is a sound introduction to those two obscure figures of our cultural future, Marshall McLuhan and Claude Lévi-Strauss, and a series of pieces on the relations between Marxism and literature that is free of the usual cant that one finds in most English and American journals. Steiner also manages to say something fresh about Thomas Mann and Kafka and something just about F. R. Leavis, and he firmly characterizes uncharted figures as Lawrence Durrell, Sylvia Plath, and Günter Grass. All in all, a remarkable coverage of topics and issues: the index of *Language and Silence* runs to thirty-one pages, from the mathematician Niels Henrik Abel to the novelist Stefan Zweig, and, though padded by unnecessary and repetitious items, still gives you an idea of the library of references this young writer carries in his head.

But what carries the reader through *Language and Silence* and makes it cohere is something more than critical intelligence, range, and pertinence. Many of the pieces are written with the cutting edge of feeling suggested by the subtitle, "Essays on Language, Literature, and the Inhuman," and the book as a whole is permeated with the sense of Steiner's effort—impressive, moving, and irritating—to carry on a cultural tradition that mostly went up in smoke twenty-five years ago at those terminals of European culture known as Auschwitz and Dachau.

In an essay titled "A Kind of Survivor," the emotional and in some ways intellectual center of the book, Steiner tells us that his parents left Vienna in 1924, five years before he was born, and Paris in 1940: "So I happened not to be there when the names were called out." But though he has spent most of his life in America and in England, where he teaches at present, Steiner regards his way of being in the world, like his way of being a Jew, as indissolubly tied to "the black mystery of what happened in Europe," just as he derives his sense of vocation from the mighty line of acculturated Jewish intellectuals of Central Europe and from their common practice of what he calls "radical humanism."

Some of the general strengths and defects of *Language and*

Silence can be traced to this identification, which is all the more potent for being as much a repeated act of Steiner's imagination and will as it is a natural carrying forward of a family background. To regard oneself as the heir of that extraordinary group of artists, scholars, and scientists means to take upon oneself an audacious, backbreaking, and momentous task. It means to place oneself in a line that includes Marx, Freud, and Einstein: Schoenberg, Kafka, and Wittgenstein; Heine, Hofmannsthal, Hermann Broch, and Walter Benjamin; Bergson, Proust, and Lévi-Strauss; Karl Kraus, Ernst Bloch, T. W. Adorno, Hannah Arendt . . . the list goes on and on, a veritable pantheon of modern genius. It means to master the languages and literatures that extend from Budapest to Paris, to grasp the range of intellectual achievements that runs from Cantor's mathematics to Lukács' Marxism. It also means to take upon oneself the restatement and reliving of "an inheritance of humane striving, already done to death." Finally, it means to Steiner, I think, to stand in a deep sense for the whole generation of his peers —these children who did not survive, who left this great tradition bereft of its natural protégés, who make such a haunting absence today in the life of the European mind. I may be overstating the matter, but I don't think so: there is a driving, obsessive quality to Steiner's acquisitiveness, a fever in his point of view which goes beyond curiosity and self-assertion. Here is the high heritage you have decimated, he seems to be saying, as he moves rapidly from Kafka to Hofmannsthal to Broch; here is the linguistic and literary fallout of your lies and terror, as he searches for the poisoned marrow of the German language; here are the deterrents of your humanism, as he raises over and over again the damning fact that

. . . The ultimate of political barbarism grew from the core of Europe. . . . Not only did the general dissemination of literary, cultural values prove no barrier to totalitarianism; but in notable instances the high places of humanistic learning and art actually welcomed and aided

the new terror. . . . We know that some of the men
who devised and administered Auschwitz had been
taught to read Shakespeare or Goethe, and continued to
do so.

Language and Silence is everywhere pervaded by the "radical humanism" of those Central European Jews in whose
name and spirit Steiner takes his stand and does his work.
There is the "particular bias of rational feeling" which informs his manifold account of "The Retreat from the
Word," particularly the temptations of silence that literature
has experienced in the face of the loss of expressive vocabulary produced by a kind of linguistic Gresham's law in which
the debased verbal coin of politics and the mass media is driving out precise and vital speech. Or again, the European-Jew-
ish enlightenment which eagerly took the whole body of
Western culture as its province can be seen in Steiner's bold
foray into recent scholarship on Homer, his command of Bib-
lical scholarship found in his essay on "The Book," his variously informative ways of approaching Shakespeare. Or again,
the ground of humane, civilized values that anchored the far-
flung thought of Marx and Freud, Broch and Kafka, alike—
desperately held, in each case, against the evidence of the inhuman that they themselves uncovered—is also apparent in
Steiner's moral imagination, whether it turns upon the issues
of the *Olympia Reader* or Jean-François Steiner's *Treblinka.*
Or again, the freedom and anxiety of the Jewish outsider, the
need to define himself in alien, if not hostile, circumstances
that gave rise to a vision of creative possibilities and a flair for
dramatic self-characterization found in the "experimental"
work of a Schoenberg, a Karl Kraus, a Walter Benjamin, also
clearly stimulates Steiner to envision a new tradition of prose,
which he names "the Pythagorean genre," and to place himself generally and to perform on the frontiers of contemporary thought and sensibility.

But it remains to say that there is something "artificial"
about this enterprise, as Steiner at one point acknowledges

himself. For, as one might suspect, anything as grand as Steiner's sense of vocation runs the risk of becoming grandiose, any mind as open to the range of cultural portents as his is can begin to appear unduly portentous. At many more points than I can hope to detail here, *Language and Silence* promises more than it delivers, runs through more material than a paragraph, an essay, or a collection of assorted pieces can hope to do justice to. Though his preface asserts, for example, that literary criticism is "no longer a very interesting and responsible exercise" and that his essays are aimed in the direction of a "philosophy of language," I am hard put to see what this "philosophy" is: there are some scattered references to Wittgenstein's and Broch's reflections on the limits of language, a tentative assent to the McLuhan apocalypse of the printed word, an interest in Lévi-Strauss and the work of structural linguistics, most of which bears a curious relation, to say the least, to Steiner's normative judgements about the vitality and morality of language, such as in his well-known essay about the impact of Nazism on German linguistics and literature.

Since Steiner is in fact writing literary criticism and not philosophy, his formulations about "the inhuman," "the authority of silence," and so forth are often prey to a kind of cultural melodrama that he seems to be conducting under the name of "crisis," in which rhetoric often does the work of analysis:

> Has our civilization, by virtue of the inhumanity it has carried out and condoned—we are accomplices to that which leaves us indifferent—forfeited its claims to that indispensable luxury which we call literature? Not forever, not everywhere, but simply in this time and place, as a city besieged forfeits its claims to the freedom of the winds and the cool of evening outside its walls.

To which there is no answer, of course, because there is no question. Even the imagery is imprecise to the point of meaninglessness, and the mentality behind it is merely grandiose and portentous. Of course, one can say that Steiner is writing at the emotional pitch of "a kind of survivor," but I think that he tends to exploit this situation—except when he directly confronts it—and I also think that a survivor of the tradition with which he identifies so proudly should be more firm with himself.

Steiner goes on to remark, "I am not saying that writers should stop writing. . . . I am asking whether they are not writing too much, whether the deluge of print in which we seek our deafened way is not itself a subversion of meaning." I would agree and I would recommend this wisdom back to its author. For, reading through *Language and Silence*, I found myself thinking how much more language there was here than silence. In a really first-rate critical work one is always conscious of a reservoir of silence, of the reserves of intelligence, learning, verbal power, meditation, and individual conviction that lie behind what a T. S. Eliot, Walter Benjamin, or R. P. Blackmur chooses to say. I don't often get that deliberateness or individuality in Steiner; instead there is a kind of busyness and repetitiousness, the writer constantly running through his capital in his pressing need to explain, refer, display. The truth is simply that Steiner writes too much to be very convincing on the subject of silence, whether in its political or literary form. He is too anxious to be both *au courant* and *avant-garde* to make us experience the crisis in letters as a fact of his own feeling and style. I once asked the poet Irving Feldman if writing poetry was hard. "No, the writing is easy," he said. "It's the waiting that's hard." George Steiner has many gifts of mind and heart and he belongs, if anyone of his generation does, to the tradition of "radical humanism" that he describes in this book. But if he is to go as far as his mentors, I think he will need to learn to sit still and to be silent himself.

(1967)

Paul Goodman: The Pursuit of Paradise

In this decade of radical opposition and revision, Paul Goodman looms increasingly as our most exemplary intellectual—that is, the most deeply representative and the most worthy one. This may still come as a surprise to many readers as well as to the hard-headed establishmentarians—the mass-media pundits, academicians, foundation executives, ineffectual advisers to the President—who determine the public status of the writers. Within their network of opinion and influence, whether in the area of letters or the social sciences, Goodman is still taken lightly, if at all ("Oh yes, Paul Goodman. Very interesting. But let's get back to realities"). The university people are somewhat more involved with Goodman because he is more directly threatening to them, a sort of Pied Piper who has caught the ear of the college students and who asks all sorts of embarrassing questions about the education they receive and the lives they are being prepared to lead. But in general Goodman remains a marginal figure, and this is precisely why he is so exemplary. For most of the serious intellectual action today has shifted from the centers of orthodoxy and authority to the margins of liberating doubt and protest. This is true of politics, social thought, religion, education, the arts, where one or another group of libertarians is riding against the powers-that-be and flying the colors of vitality, humaneness, and reason. And it is in these growing fringe groups who oppose the conventional wisdom of social control that Paul Goodman holds his court.

It is hard to characterize this development, since it is less a movement than a mood. The libertarian spirit is most prevalent, or at least most publicized, among the young, but it is evident that the civil-rights movement and the war in Vietnam have fostered the feeling among mature intellectuals that we have arranged our society and our minds badly in America, that we are hung up on a tragically constricted pragmatism that parades as realism. The mounting disbelief in the Johnson Administration provides an immediate ground for this spirit, but it goes well beyond the issues of Vietnam or of Watts, well beyond politics. It is not simply a resurgence of radicalism, since the old distinctions between left and right are themselves being dissolved by the general mood of skepticism toward our institutions and their executives. The anxious question that emerges from it is whether American society, for all its visible affluence and efficiency, is a fit place in which to live—whether, indeed, we are living in a rational society or in an increasingly absurd one. And the writer who best articulates this temper and carries it farthest as a mode of analysis is Paul Goodman.

Goodman has occupied this role since 1960, that fateful year which saw the first major break in the cultural weather of the Eisenhower Age with the campaign and election of Kennedy and the development of the Negro movement. If there was a single book that helped to dispel the prevailing atmosphere of complacency and conformity, it was Goodman's *Growing Up Absurd*. Almost as though on cue, Goodman emerged from two decades of obscurity to appear at the side of the intellectuals, awakening from their long sleep of apathy and error, and to lead them, Virgil-like, through the inferno of "the organized system." The message of *Growing Up Absurd* is that this system is depraved. It pays little attention to "the object, the function, the program, the task, the need" and "immense attention to the role, procedure, prestige, and profit"; the system is therefore indifferent to the "utility, quality, rational productivity, personal freedom, in-

dependent enterprise, human scale, manly vocation, or genuine culture"; and the full weight of this failure to provide
adequate scope and incentive for its human resources falls
upon the young, casting the high-school dropout and the
whiz-kid, the beatnik and the junior executive in the soup
together.

A series of books, essays, and a rather tract-like novel
quickly followed, in which Goodman extended the approach
and insights of *Growing Up Absurd* to public education, university life, institutional structure, specific social and political
offenses, and which blended the utopian imagination of possibilities with a tough, technical grasp of actual conditions.
What he has understood better than anyone else is that the
chief enemy of social change and sanity is what Karl Mannheim has defined as "functional rationality," which is the ideology of technocracy and bureaucracy, one that is so fixated
on the organization of means that it leaves its ends unexam-
ined and thus paralyzes the capacity for rational judgment.
Goodman's utopianism provides a powerful instrument of
what Mannheim calls "substantial rationality," one that
begins with a firm concept of human welfare and then reasons toward means that would make our cities livable, our
schools educational, our vocations meaningful, our politics
relevant to our needs. The main effect of Goodman's work
has been to break through the constraints of the narrow "realism" in which our minds most securely operate, to make a
little space in our heads for the operation of free inquiry, to
hold up a model of society organized for human ends rather
than of humans organized for the ends of social rationalization and control. In so doing, Goodman has provided fresh
motive and material for the doctrines of humanism, a creed
that has been living off its heritage for a long time now, like a
well-bred rentier cultivating his garden in a neighborhood
that has become a slum.

The considerable interest of *Five Years*, a collection of
Goodman's journals from the years 1955 to 1960, stems partly
from its relation to his subsequent career, partly from its re-

markably clear, candid, and complete revelation of a man
through his daily reflections. The learning, the energy, the
conviction required to take on "the organized system" are
graphically displayed in these pages; so, too, is the allegiance
to natural human desires on which Goodman has based his
own life and his utopian models of the true community.
Most of his days and nights during these five years were spent
in loneliness, frustration, even at times in despair. But the
pursuit of "paradise," to use the name of his desire, that
goaded and unstrung him also enabled him to experience
himself directly—in this flesh, this mind, this spirit; he had
little left to repress and so could describe his inner life and his
way of being in the world freely and fully. The result is that
simple, unmistakable, and rare feeling of the man standing
immediately behind his words. Open this book at any point
and you touch a person.

When Goodman began writing down these "thoughts" he
was in his middle forties and his career and his personal life
had both reached rock bottom. He had written many books
and published only a few of them, ranging from Gestalt theory to city planning, and had done original work in fiction,
poetry, and drama. He finished his massive experimental
novel, *The Empire City,* during this perod, finally found a
publisher for it, who then called back the copies of the book a
few weeks after it appeared. In a surge of "patriotic" feeling,
he wrote *Growing Up Absurd* for another publisher, who not
only turned it down because he was advised it would make a
fool of him but also demanded his advance back.

During the fat years of the later 1950's, then, Goodman
had about as hopeful a vocation as a revolutionary at Bell
Telephone Company. Unlike many artists of the modern tradition, he had little use for his alienation, saw nothing of a
calling in his silence, exile, or cunning. "I am continually tormented by not being published," he writes. "I am continually
nagged by my original sin: to be Virgil and manufacture a
meaning for this Empire. But instead I come on like a Cicero
who has never had his day." Moreover, the neglect he

suffered was sadly at odds with his grand, and grandiose, dream of working in a "rational community," of being "aggressive for the general welfare." Except for an occasional university conference and his practice as a lay analyst, he talked mainly to himself, carrying on his incredibly diverse intellectual life—philosophy, religion, semantics, psychiatry, education, social and political theory, music, letters—in the little notebooks that make up this volume.

The rest of the time he prowled for sex: an earnest, pipe-smoking Socrates of the bars and docks and playgrounds of Manhattan, the streets and cafés of Europe. Because he was faded and unhandsome, because he was attracted to rough trade, because he refused to pay, he endured a good deal of fear and rejection, and because he was looking for pupils as well as bedfellows, a good deal of post-sexual *tristesse*. Adversity dogged his tracks in other ways: his daughter fell ill with polio, his long marriage progressively deteriorated, he suffered cruelly from hemorrhoids as well as from the anxiety that his proud intelligence, his sword and his shield, had become unreliable and perverse: ". . . it seems that without the illusion that I am right, great, misunderstood, etc., I do not know how to take the world at all: I have never learned how. Oh God! *can anything be salvaged from all that effort?*" (His italics.)

But all of this dreariness is finally no more than background for the bright figure that steadily forges on through his life—sharp-eyed, meditative, resourceful. For these "five years" of isolation from an audience and of imprisonment in his obsessive drives are merely a tough stretch in the long journey of Paul Goodman, who, like one of Silone's heroes, "comes from far and is going far." Living on the margin for so many years, pursuing so singlemindedly a vision of personal and public liberation, he has the resources of a highly developed solitude and aspiration—patience, independence, inwardness, learning—that will eventually turn his losses to profits, his wounds to the scars, as he is fond of saying, "of healed suffering." No matter how much in the dumps Good-

man may be, a good-looking boy crosses his path, a social absurdity rears its head, a new insight into scientific method or
dramatic form occurs to him, a quirk of his personality reveals
itself, and his quick mind begins to stir, his powers of analysis
and relevant association revive, and his prose runs freshly
again.

At one point Goodman characterizes the American writer,
in contrast to the European, as "a lonely individuality grown
to humanity." This is an apt description of his own life. The
driven and derided figure prowling the waterfront and hand-
ball courts becomes in due time the author of *Growing Up
Absurd*, who stands up for the young and argues their case
against the "rat race." Partly because of his sexual attachments Goodman is in closer touch with the young than most
of us are and more ardent in their behalf: he wants them to
become men—free, self-reliant, potent creatures—while most
of us want them to be well-adjusted, though adjustment to
the "system" breeds neurosis in us all. Or again, the years of
bitter isolation, underemployment, and neglect serve to confirm and deepen Goodman's demand for a community that
meets the real needs of its members and enables them to
serve it. Or again, his struggle to hold on in a dark time provides a kind of tough-minded simplicity that cuts through
much of the existentialist froth about "extreme situations" to
the common plights and responses of contemporary man.

In these and other ways, *Five Years* is a record of both
steadfastness and growth, a testament of the struggle for liberation that Goodman has maintained for a long time now
and that becomes palpably sweetened, as he goes along, by his
uses of adversity. And it is this voice of sweet reason pushing
on against perplexity and despair that makes *Five Years* not
only such a fine book but also a harbinger of Goodman's
place in America today and a demonstration of his right to
it.

(1967)

R. D. Laing: The Uses of Madness

R. D. Laing is a forty-year-old English psychiatrist who has been making a name for himself as an unusually lucid and humane student of schizophrenia, as one of the more articulate exponents of the school of thought known as existential psychoanalysis, and as an imaginative member of the English New Left. More generally, Laing can be said to belong to the small band of intellectuals found in each major culture today who are trying to create a new humanism in the face of the pieties and defeats that have undermined the old; who are searching for a faith in man that can withstand the acids of nihilism that modern experience continually secretes. Like them, Laing is struggling to make a new basis for the unity of body and spirit, mind and heart, that our society seems committed to dismember, and to redraw the lines of sanity in an age that has seen "normal" men destroy nearly a hundred million of their fellow men.

All of this makes him a deviant member of his profession, to say the least: contemporary psychiatry being one of the most conservative, complacent, and narrow of the intellectual professions—and, increasingly, a symptom of the illness of the alienation, to paraphrase Karl Kraus, that it seeks to cure. Except for a few voices here and there (most of them belonging to men trained in Europe, such as Bruno Bettelheim, Erik Erikson, Erich Fromm), the psychiatrists seem content to accept the reality principle as given by society, no matter how pathogenic the realities of our society have become. The enormous influence they wield in the private lives of the educated middle class is only matched by their silent acceptance of a public world that is, quite literally, driving more and more of us crazy in the effort to adjust to it.

Laing's relatively brief career has been marked by a steady expansion of interests from the clinical to the social and by a personal development from the detachment of the analyst to the passionate inwardness of the critic and lately of the prophet. "Detachment" is not quite the right word, though. Laing's first book, *The Divided Self*, is for all of its calm, dispassionate tone, one of the most moving accounts of madness I have ever read as well as the clearest. Its strength derives from Laing's insistence on viewing his schizoid and psychotic patients as persons rather than as cases. He explains their behavior as an effort to preserve their lives in a world that has been made unlivable for them by their early formative relationships—relationships that have bred an anxiety that pervades their existence as thoroughly as coldness pervades the existence of an Eskimo. This state of "ontological insecurity" creates a terrible logic; to preserve his small sense of aliveness, reality, and integrity, the person constructs a "false self" that draws attention and threat away from his "true self" and also enables him to function to the extent that he can in the real world. At the same time, however, this splitting of the person's being progressively worsens the problem that it sought to manage by depriving the "true self" of any sustenance save that of fantasy and by making the functioning of the false self increasingly compulsive and artificial. This basic dilemma spawns a variety of subsidiary ones, and when the torments of the division become intolerable, the schizoid person will decide either to murder his self or abruptly begin to act out his true self despite everything. Either decision is likely to produce a psychosis.

All of which is meant to describe not a "disease" but rather a state of radical privation (and a desperate struggle to cope

with it) that is all too human. Laing beautifully fleshes out
this analysis by descriptions of the character and experiences
of his patients that are to the usual case histories what Ham-
let is to those scholarly disquisitions on his motives. Indeed,
Laing's portraits of "David," "an adolescent Kierkegaard
played by Danny Kaye"; of "Peter," an apparently robust
young man who was at home only with dogs, who lived, as he
put it, "on the fringe of being," and who was "driven by a
terrible sense of honesty to *be* nothing"; of "Marie," a girl
suffering from acute contactlessness who cured herself by going for a week to see *La Strada*—these and others form a
gallery in *The Divided Self* of the radically abused and in-
jured victims of the common life that not only demonstrate
Laing's theories about the integrity of madness but also make
the book a deep literary experience.

In a recent preface to a new edition of *The Divided Self*,
however, Laing expresses a dissatisfaction with the book: "I
was already partially falling into the trap I was seeking to
avoid. I [was] still writing . . . too much about Them and
too little of Us." Much of his intervening work, particularly
that in *Reason and Violence*, which he wrote with David
Cooper and directly under the influence of Sartre, has sought
to relate the sources of individual alienation not only to the
family background but also to the broader social norms that
govern the relations between the individual and others. In his
new book, *The Politics of Experience*, Laing has reached the
extreme position to which many younger intellectuals are being driven today by the manifest brutality and absurdity of
these norms:

> We do not live in a world of unambiguous identities and
> definitions, needs and fears, hopes, disillusions. The tre-
> mendous social realities of our time are ghosts, specters
> of murdered gods and our own humanity returned to
> haunt and destroy us. The Negroes, the Jews, the Reds.
> Them. Only you and I dressed differently. The texture
> of the fabric of these socially shared hallucinations is

what we call reality, and our collusive madness is what we call sanity.

The Politics of Experience thus goes well beyond the Freudian resolution of civilization and its discontents. Laing argues that society is not only sexually and instinctually repressive but also that its steady barrage of pseudo-reality alienates us from our senses and sense, impoverishes and destroys our experience. This "condition of alienation—of being asleep—of being unconscious, of being out of one's mind, is the condition of the normal man. . . . If our experience is destroyed, we have lost our own selves."

The Politics of Experience is both a technical and prophetic exploration of the processes of this destruction: of what we do to each other and to ourselves as alienated beings. There are the defense mechanisms that keep the Other off, that protect us by means of self-mystification from the fear and trembling of what little freedom to be ourselves and to relate positively to others survives. Such mechanisms, as Laing keeps insisting, are not merely personal but trans-personal: in insidiously aggressive ways they distort the Other's experience and turn him into a thing. Similarly, Laing wishes us to realize that the largest sum of these trans-personal alienating mechanisms is the society, the state. How much alienation, for example, is being inflicted at present both on the Vietnamese and on ourselves by those mystified defense mechanisms with which we are "containing Communism"? "in order to rationalize our industrial-military complex," Laing says, "we have to destroy our capacity to see clearly any more what is in front of, and to imagine what is beyond, our noses. Long before a thermonuclear war can come about, we have had to lay waste our own sanity."

Such assertions are, of course, prevalent today. Contemporary politics makes apocalyptics of us all. The question is how much authority Laing's picture of our alienation carries. *The Politics of Experience* suffers from being made up of papers that were originally intended for special audiences, whether those that read psychiatric journals or the *New Left Review*. As a result, the writing tends to be often baldly assertive and elliptical and often lacks the rigorously sustained development of his ideas that one finds in *The Divided Self*. But, more crucially, I think Laing has fallen victim to the kind of literary terrorism that our chronic desperation encourages: what might be called the "signaling through the flames" school of writing. The trouble is that desperation is not enough. We are all desperate. The notions of freedom on which Laing grounds his analysis of man—good existentialist that Laing is—require that we be responsible for the attitude we bring to the experience of fragmentation, contactlessness, violence, that we try to hold together the whole man in ourselves, in all his ambiguities, even as he is being daily torn apart. In a sense we are, as Laing says, "all murderers and prostitutes . . . no matter how normal, moral, or mature we take ourselves to be," just as we are all, to a greater or less degree, schizoid. But we merely begin to mystify ourselves, and to foster further alienation, when we try to substitute these definitions for our experience of being in the world. The ugliness of one feeling does not cancel out the decency of another, just as the dehumanization of children in one household does not mean that pre-psychotics are also being created next door.

The overwhelming problem that all sensitive men face today is to maintain their balance, and not to con themselves by believing, as Laing says he does, that the worst has already happened. Curiously enough, the most convincing pages of *The Politics of Experience* are those devoted to the sanity and spirituality of "madness," rather than those that seem devoted to driving the rest of us out of our "wretched minds." Which is perhaps only to say that Laing writes best when he writes from the integrity of his own experience and eschews the temptation to make a total, vague, and baiting politics of it.

(1967)

A Primer for Survival

Alex Comfort is a remarkable English writer in whom the "two cultures" have come together in a sturdy, companionable, and fertile marriage. A biologist who publishes good fiction and poetry, a specialist in the problems of aging as well as of the erotic literature of India, a planner of a new "technology of the emotions," and an anarchist who writes lyrics for Pete Seeger, Comfort is a genuine man of parts: a C. P. Snow raised to the next power. Now Comfort has brought these parts together in *The Nature of Human Nature,* one of the richest and most sane books that I have come upon in a good long time. Published this past summer in America and followed, as far as I can tell, by virtual silence, Comfort's book deserves to be read by everyone who is seriously interested in the very open question of human survival. Its purpose is both to describe and to minister to the human situation in the name of what Comfort calls "sociality"—the capacity of the human animal, "programmed" into his nature by the evolutionary process, to live in societies without tearing his fellows or himself apart.

Part of the paradox of recent human development is that it has become both more and less human: we no longer hang children for theft; on the other hand, we take out our aggressions by bombing them. Against the background of the carnage of our century (some fifty million killed in World War

II alone) the Enlightenment image of man as "a social animal liable to outbursts of irrational aggression" has given way to the image of "an irrationally aggressive animal liable to outbursts of sociability." Moreover, whether he was an optimist or a pessimist, the eighteenth-century student of man was likely to believe in "higher" and "lower" faculties: man was a rational being, his intellect was the center and governor of his existence. Descartes' "*Cogito, ergo sum*" was more than a principle of epistemology; it summed up the existential position of the Enlightenment. The aggrandizement of reason and the distrust of irrational feelings may have been one reason why the intellectual life of the eighteenth century carried a groundnote of pessimism to the point of morbidity: think of Swift, Pope, or Johnson, for a start. Be that as it may, we have now begun to grasp the truth (though mostly to the extent of being impaled on it) that our animal nature is our basic part and that it is more interested in its creaturely needs than in being reasonable or virtuous. "The paradox still remains," to quote Comfort, "that while our culture traditionally views the life of the senses as 'lower' and antipathetic to the strenuous discomfort required by virtue, the facts all point the other way—to a correlation between the senses and our more benevolent and social face, and between repression and denial of the senses and our more murderous side."

According to Comfort, the axial line from ape to man involves the conversion of sexuality into social behavior. A character in Aldous Huxley's *Point Counter Point* wondered what human society would be like if its females had rutting periods like most of the other mammals. Comfort believes that the development of human life depended upon the transformation of the estrous cycle into more or less continuous sexual receptivity; this was the first step in socializing the reproductive function and creating the rudimentary family unit that is found among the higher primates, such as the gorilla and gibbon, and not among the lower, such as the baboon, where the estrous cycle is still present. By providing an expression of "togetherness," as well as play and sensory pleasure, continuous female receptivity enabled mating rather than merely reproduction and male dominance. The purely biological characteristics that trigger reproduction began to be replaced by habits and conventions, a process of regulation that is completed in all human societies that we know about.

The second major development among the higher primates is the extended period of parental dependence. Comfort conjectures that long before fathers and sons in the "primal horde" could have competed for the same women, as Freud suggested, the "evolutionary demon" pushed forward the sexual feelings and fears of puberty into the earlier phase of psychosexual development, where they cemented the maternal (socializing) relationship; also it postponed the onset of puberty—both physiologically and emotionally—for a period long enough to enable the young to develop within the family matrix. This was accompanied by purely social controls, or taboos, that reinforced the repression of sexual feelings during the latency period.

Comfort's hypothesis throws a powerful light on the regulation of sexuality by social conventions and, conversely, on the erotic and anti-erotic character of our sociality. One consequence of this is the problematic nature of human sexuality; the anxiety bred and sustained by repression, the displacement, diffusion, and deviation of sexual interest from its proper biological objectives, the difficulties and dangers of laying animal nature at the mercy of social controls, some of which are themselves the product of repression. At the same time, the funding of the unconscious with the explosive content of infantile sexuality may have had the further adaptive function, Comfort conjectures, of restructuring our mental processes to provide for conceptual, as distinct from perceptual, thought. By the same token, the "loose" sexual feelings of man have both fertilized other areas of his life and also devastated them. For inside the head of the recondite physicist lies the previous programming of the evolutionary process, large sections of which he shares not only with a present-day Australian aborigine but with Pekin Man. Indeed, the dominance patterns of our primate baboon days are still visible in the Congressional cloakroom and the executive suite, while our nuclear missiles and doomsday machines are the old war gods of the caves newly enshrined in the Pentagon.

We are thus truly strange creatures, capable of virtually controlling the environment and yet subject to a degree of irrationality unknown in any other form of primate life. In Kafkaesque fashion, Comfort describes the mental processes of a modern man in whom, "as it were, directives and messages come to the Head Office from a clandestine department that the staff do not realize is there, with its own logic, its own aims, and the solidified inner attitudes of a child of three."

The middle section of *The Nature of Human Nature* deals with our evolution under the aspects of work and technology, human variability, population and food supply, hazards and enemies. Comfort's intention is not only to fill in the picture of what man and his behavior look like from the perspective of an enlightened biologist, but, more urgently, to point up his thesis that "our intellectual development and technical abilities as a species have outstripped our means of social and emotional expression." The most ominous lag is between food supply and population growth. In Ceylon, for example, malaria has been virtually abolished in the past five years: this has immediately halved the death rate, which means that unless birth control is instituted it will double the birth rate every thirty years. The so-called Great Powers have the resources to introduce workable methods of contraception and to develop new sources of food. Meanwhile, though, their expertise and wealth are allocated mainly to perfecting and distributing man's age-old technique of population control. As Comfort observes: "It requires no social conscience, only the foresight for lack of which the French aristocracy lost their elegant but unemployed heads, to see that . . . our underfed fellow-men will not starve to provide us with two-pound steaks." From the biological perspective, behind the ideological frenzies of China today lies a desperate quest for protein, which our technology is already prepared to produce in abundance from the sea.

Technology has freed man from much backbreaking labor, but again the methods for constructively reemploying him are not yet of much interest to our leaders and planners. Tool-making has also been programmed into human nature, and the denial or perversion of the desire to be employed breeds the destructive behavior recently displayed in such places as Detroit and Newark or the self-destructive behavior of the Madison Avenue executive trying to find still another image of well-being that will keep people smoking cigarettes. Or again, modern society has lengthened the life-span but short-ened its productive years. Hence, we are already creating a generation of the prematurely retired. If you wish to see what this aspect of the future could be like, I recommend a walk along Broadway from 72nd to 96th Streets in New York on a warm Sunday when the walking dead on the benches form block-by-block islands of malaise and pathos.

In sum, we have extended and rationalized human life beyond our present means to sustain it and, increasingly, to endure it without sacrifice of our natures. Comfort's analysis of and remedy for the destructive and self-destructive effects of taking man out of "the tight private social context of the small one-track society" comes to a climax in his final two chapters, the most brilliant in the book. What he wishes us to see and treat before it is too late are the methods of our madness: built in by the love-hate structure of child-rearing, exacerbated by the modern denials and frustrations of our creaturely needs, and powerfully amplified by our modes of social organization and control. Primitive societies appear to have provided better for man's emotional life than ours do. They coped with the unconscious or "dream time" by means of myth and ritual, religion and art, which provided a release of the darker feelings. (Comfort, for example, gives a startling Freudian reading of the Yoruba myth that a man's troubles are sent by the ghost of his grandmother.) Modern society offers the ritual of psychoanalysis; otherwise we are commanded to be mature and go our tight-lipped way. Thus, against the primitive's willingness to feel and admit unpleasant mental sensations, we have the modern executive "who likes to look busy and stressed (to prove his efficiency) but not to look anxious (which implies that he is falling down on the job) and who might be fired if he burst into tears." Our "convention" of desperation is suicide; short of that, our death instinct is transmitted through the social fabric, where it takes over and energizes even our more constructive beliefs and attitudes for irrational ends, such as devastating Vietnam in order to live up to our commitments there and to the cause of freedom, self-determination, and peace.

Short of psychoanalyzing everyone, then, what do we do about the irrationality of man; how can we redirect his built-in capacity for sociality? Comfort's answer follows from his analysis of the genesis of human nature: "the eroticization of experience and society." This is not a novel solution: it is the libertarian extension of Freud that has been adumbrated by other thinkers such as Herbert Marcuse, Norman O. Brown, Paul Goodman, Edgar Z. Friedenberg. It is being enacted these days by young people in Haight-Ashbury and the East Village, where religion in its original archetypal sense, art, work, sexuality, and play—"the materials for the further emotional and social evolution of Man," according to Comfort—are forming a new *Gestalt* of human sociality. From some of its behavior, particularly the use of drugs, Comfort would dissociate himself: he is interested in the discharge of emotion that would enable us to be more rational and realistic rather than in the pursuit of kicks, which he regards as merely the mirror image of the repressions of our Puritanism. But whether in previous theory or present practice, I have not seen the case for erotic libertarianism made with the hard-headed wisdom of Comfort's closing pages.

Like any radical program, particularly one that wishes to enlighten us about human possibilities rather than plan our immediate lives, Comfort's ideas will seem impractical. All right, you may say, go eroticize Queens. But his ideas are not so much programmatic as consequential: this is what follows, he is saying, from what we know of the history of the primates on this planet. This is also what we know if we pay attention to the babbling of the ape and the aborigine in our heads and to the little moments of crisis when we can hear the doomsday machine ticking away inside each of us.

Between the institutional mind and the apocalyptic one— between, let us say, Dean Rusk and Norman Mailer—we flounder from one form of hysteria to the other. But if you're still holding out for sanity, *The Nature of Human Nature* is what you've been looking for.

(1967)

Meyer Liben

Meyer Liben is one of those writers who come, as it were, out of the blue. A businessman who retired early because of illness, he began a second career as a writer when he was in his forties and has waited another ten years for the publication of his first book. Certain advantages have followed from this late start. Liben remains an amateur in spirit, though not in performance: he writes because he likes to write, because it is a natural way of expressing himself, of keeping track of the flow of experience, of situating himself in the world. Though an experimental writer, he has none of the mannered obscurity one associates with the term: in technique, his experiments are rather simple, homey ones —an open conversational form, somewhere between narrative and essay, often punctuated by headings at the transitional points like the subtitles of the old silent movies. (His ruminative fiction somewhat resembles that of Paul Goodman, though Goodman has told me that the indebtedness is his.) It is as though Liben one day dropped in on literature, found that it was a pleasant place to spend his time, and, having passed the age of intimidation, rearranged the furniture just a bit to make himself more comfortable.

The other main advantage of Liben's belated career is that he comes on the scene after his generation has more or less had its say and left the floor to the succeeding one. In his accent as well as in his subject matter, Liben belongs to the marginally middle-class world of the second generation of East European Jewish immigrants. This makes him unfashionable and, at times, a bit dated; but it also makes him fresh and salutary by virtue of his ability to restore a dimension of his generation's character that has been obscured in recent years: the dimension of depth.

The sense of the second-generation Jew one has today may be no more than a stack of tendentious and superficial images, minted from the coin of its present prosperity. Whether created by his apologists, such as Harry Golden, or by his assailants, the second-generation Jew is, at bottom, a pretty gross figure: the compleat bourgeois businessman, still a little anxious, perhaps, but basically at ease in the suburbs. Whether hailed as a hero of individual and group enterprise or bitterly criticized as a materialist and a cop-out, the second generation has suffered a reduction of its experience: the struggle of the 1920's to get out of the ghetto and to get the ghetto out of oneself, the social and political intensities of the Depression years, the trauma of the holocaust—all these have become, in one way or another, merely stages along the route to Great Neck. All the vulgarity belongs to the second generation, all the sensitivity to the third; all the complacency to the second, all the crises to the third. And, recently, all the struggle, spirit, and color to the first. Under the spell of phony nostalgia and devious revenge, as well as of writers such as Singer and Malamud, my generation seems to be cultivating the idea that the only authentic Jews are the impoverished, bizarre, or dead ones.

All of which is a pretty silly state of affairs. The young rebels who like to write novels about the lower East Side with Hasidic overtones did not spring fully armed from the head of the Lubavitcher Rebbe, nor did the supercilious young intellectuals stumble all by themselves on their great tradition of Marx, Freud, Einstein, *et al.* Most of us—whether literary or advertising men, psychiatrists or tax specialists—follow the

common fate, are living out the dreams of the business generation, just as they have lived out the dreams of the immigrant
workers. The aspirations link up all the way back to the
Emancipation, as do the discontents—whether one calls
them "*Angst*" or "aggravation" or "*tsores*."

Under these circumstances, the fiction of Meyer Liben is
particularly illuminating. In his modest way, Liben is a kind
of Sholem Aleichem of the older, middle-class urban Jews,
who expresses the poetry of their interests and sentiments by
remaining faithful to the sources of his own development and
to the continuity of experience linking the old East Harlem
neighborhood, City College, and Greenwich Village; the
family life of the generations; the artisan, the businessman,
and the writer. Here is one of his typical characters, a distrib-
utor of encyclopedias who drives himself hard—"I get a certain pleasure (if not basic) out of buying cheap and selling
dear . . . there's no standing still, you either go ahead or retreat"—but who deeply envies the man in the next office because he makes his living by dreaming up products, is reputed
to have invented the yo-yo and the hula hoop.

> Whether he was indeed the creator of these remarkable
> toys I do not know, but certainly that was the way his
> mind ran—toward the creation of the absolutely simple,
> what answers a universal emotional need, the kind of
> thing that, once on the market, causes people to say:
> "Absolutely obvious. How come I didn't think of it?"
> without realizing how hard the perfection is to come by
> and how hard it is to wed the perfection to the obvious,
> the universal.

Most of the stories in *Justice Hunger* are told in the first
person, and the narrator-hero is usually the same kind of
man, whether he is the graduate student of history in the
novella "Justice Hunger," who is trying to keep his head
above water in the ideological riptide of the Thirties, the
officeworker in "A Note on Chivalry" who rescues an elegant

girl from a sociologist's jargon, or the tireless go-getter in "Ball of Fire" who rediscovers a sweet vein of lassitude in himself through reading *Oblomov*. Liben's imagination is essentially a reflective one: his heroes are generally designed to express his point of view, to speak with his voice, to stand in his shoes. They are sensible fellows, devoted to the work of the world, to the practical opportunities and responsibilities; but they carry in themselves a hunger for romance, whether of action or thought, that secretly opposes the patterns of their compunctions and repressions and wishes to destroy them.

"Position is everything in life," says the narrator of "Justice Hunger," "that much at least I had learned in the poolrooms." His sense of position, however, is characteristically prey to deeper yearnings, like a pool player who is tempted by the fancy billiard shots. In this case, the narrator is an earnest young liberal who is attracted to a girl who glows with the radical convictions of the Thirties, an ex-dancer, a divorcee, a Midwesterner with a Gentile background: in sum, the image of all his desires. He struggles to overcome his temperamental bias for political detachment and objectivity ("I thought of that fine word 'disinterest' and how it was slowly losing its meaning"), his aversion to the temper of the Marxist enclaves, both grandiose and grim (a "loveless cynicism"), as well as his patient sexual timidity ("I should have liked to come closer but did not know how"). The division within between pleasure and realism, passion and prudence, sensitizes his consciousness, makes him a tireless analyst and conversationalist—the verbal flow being his way of bridging the inner split and of connecting to the world, of fighting off "the sense of separation and loss that is forever crowding us." But he remains a man who cannot line himself up for long with the deeper objects of pleasure, for his hunger is basic to his nature, seemingly a state of permanent dissatisfaction that determines his divided view of experience, organizes his sacrifices and compensations, and leaves him standing in his own way.

In story after story, Liben describes this situation with unusual subtlety and poignancy. The speaker in "The Locking Gas-Cap," perhaps his best single story, has been engaged for six years to a girl who is hung up on the image of her father, an adventurous civil engineer who died when she was very young, as well as on the possessive strategies of her mother. The couple own a car together, a sort of surrogate home, over which they delight and worry, "the primary cathexes," as he puts it, "having attached themselves to the secondary phenomena." One day she reports that the gas-cap has been stolen for the fourth time. He judiciously suggests a ride in the car to calm her down; she embraces him ardently ("I must say she seemed unusually aroused by the theft of these accessories from our car"). With a show of masculine competence (or is it timid prudence?) he suggests a locking gas-cap, takes her to a garage, goes through the usual small humiliations of such places (though he has been a salesman of automotive parts, knows the owner, and hopes to show off a bit—always competing, as he feels, with the dead father). But with the new cap in place, her passion suddenly turns sour; she worries about the device (suppose she loses the key), then about her mother's latest depression. Always perceptive, always obliging, he dissipates the tension by suggesting they take her mother to the movies with them that night. It is, as he puts it, "a perfectly stable unhappy situation," the two of them cooperating expertly to maintain a common front against the risks of deliverance, getting in just enough desire to keep their inhibitions lubricated, their regressions in working order.

It all sounds more pat than it is; like the symbol of the gas-cap, the story is both immediately expressive and rich in implications. As with much of Liben's fiction, it encloses a psychoanalytic framework within a sensitive grasp of the variations of individual character, the nuances of the living moment. The girl is overly attached to her parents, but she is still a complex and desirable girl. The narrator's subservience in the name of "understanding" her keeps him standing on a dime, emotionally speaking, but does not rob him of wit, affection, awareness. Liben's heroes may lose out, but they are always more than the usual portraits of the *nebbish*, and there is always more at stake than their weakness, their failure. Most of them are, peculiarly enough, bachelors, though tied to their mothers in the standard Jewish way. But the mother of the narrator in "The Office Next Door" is not the standard devouring monster, nor are his feelings toward her cheaply caricatured in the current fashion. He explains his attraction to the inventor's secretary as follows:

> She looked to be the age of my mother at the time that I was twelve or thirteen. It was then, for reasons I never clearly understood (though I now assume it must have been related to some crisis in the family life), that my mother turned toward me with a love, affection, and, yes, need of an extraordinary intensity. I think she realized that this feeling was too powerful for my own good, too powerful for her own good, but she seemed unable to control herself. I was impressed, flattered, as well as confused by this torrent of affection. Never since has a woman loved me the way my mother loved me for that unforgettable year. . . . She went with me to unlikely places, up to Yankee Stadium, for example, to look at those games, about which she could not have been more ignorant, from both a technical and historical view. There she sat at my side, gazing at this complex choreography, occasionally asking questions, less out of desire for knowledge than to make it appear that she was interested, and so, she thought, adding to my pleasure.
>
> In going out with girls, I have always felt uncomfortable in being with those of my own age or younger and have shied away from those older, though it was to these older girls that I was most strongly drawn.

Much of Liben's temperament is reflected in this passage, one that suggests the source of the basic hunger that he writes about as well as the emotional quality and range with which he invests it. Thus the themes of exile and loss and frustrated deliverance well up naturally in his fiction; so does a tenderness toward the unfulfilled; a highly developed feeling for the fantasies of desire and guilt; and an awareness of the shifting grounds of a relationship, of the buried oceans of feeling that can lie beneath a word or a gesture.

As in Freud, the discontents of Liben's characters are also embedded in their social drives; in this case, those of a generation whose main business in life was to climb the shaky ladder into the middle class. The basic hunger works to keep them hustling after its goods and values, underwrites their prowess in business, stimulates their strong political interests ("we [were] all hungrily reaching out to one another, to create a sense of individual value, a sense of communion"), and supports their striving for culture. Liben's characters are, typically, involved in that great pursuit of what used to be called "refinement" (the courtship in "Justice Hunger" is mainly carried on at lectures, recitals, foreign movies; the hero of "Ball of Fire" sits up at night in a hotel room in St. Louis meditating on *Oblomov*; a secretary in "Solomon's Wisdom" uses the time when her boss is out of the office to write poetry).

What rings most true throughout *Justice Hunger* is a certain wry tone—both commonsensical and cultivated, a quiet blend of irony, curiosity, and patience—which expresses the ethos of the second generation. It is a tone that is beginning to fade into history, though one still hears it, *mutatis mutandis*, in the poetry of Charles Reznikoff or the essays of Milton Himmelfarb. One hopes that in the years to come Liben will write the novel that captures the temperament and experience of his generation in the same definitive way that Abraham Cahan did for the preceding one in *The Rise of David Levinsky*. But in the meantime there is *Justice Hunger*. It is an uneven collection of his stories, a couple of which bear the marks of his apprenticeship, just as the long title story is allowed to spread out rather thinly in places. But it is a unique, important, and lovely book, one that I especially commend to those members of my own generation who are looking for their actual roots.

(1967)

"Remember Those Tissues They Wrapped the Fruit In . . . ?"

About fifteen years ago Herbert Gold, a relatively unknown writer in his middle twenties, published a remarkable story in *Hudson Review*. Titled "The Heart of the Artichoke," it dealt with the struggle between an immigrant grocer in a Cleveland suburb and his rebellious son. The hard-driving, hard-headed father wants the boy to help out in the store on Saturdays, in order to learn the business and the value of a dollar; the son wants to be free to run with his gang, to pursue sybaritic little Patty Donahue and all that she represents. On the one side, the Jewish family ethos of effort and solidarity; on the other, the allure of the confident Gentiles and their greener lawns. At the time, the theme was nothing new: the wages of acculturation, the conflict between the father's dreams and the son's, being a familiar one in American-Jewish writing. What was new, or at least rare, in 1951 was the color and bounce of the language, the full range of feeling that enabled Gold to do justice to the father's vitality as well as the son's sensitivity, and the subtlety of vision which located in the particular poignancies of this generational conflict the age-old imperatives that drive a son to wrestle with his father.

With few noticeable changes, Herbert Gold has incorporated "The Heart of the Artichoke" into *Fathers*, "a novel in the form of a memoir" which follows the long road from

Kamenets-Podolsk, where the father began, to San Francisco, where the son now lives, and which charts the continuities of character and fortune that underlie their seemingly divergent careers. Other key sections of the book are also made up from previously published fiction such as "Aristotle and the Hired Thugs" and "One Sunday Morning at the Russian Bath." In fairness to Gold's claim that "this is a book I have been writing all my life," I see nothing wrong with his procedure. Nonetheless, it does have consequences. One is that the book is written in different styles: the early swinging one and a later one that is much more controlled and direct. Another consequence is that *Fathers* inevitably creates a sense of *déjà vu* for the reader who is familiar with this part of his previous work. Finally, the lack of a developing power in the book, the randomness permitted by the weakness of the form, of set pieces being tacked together, place a heavy burden on the material itself. And what this burden points up, at least to this reader, is that "Jewish" material has begun to wear thin, even in the hands of the inventive writers, that the swinging style is no longer so fresh as it once was, and that the pangs and elations of the Jewish slant have become as predictable as those of the Southern writers a decade ago.

Indeed the innovations of Gold and Malamud and particularly of Bellow (*Augie March* being the *Huckleberry Finn* of this literature, the one book from which it emerged) are so widely imitated today that it is difficult to keep a book like *Fathers* separate from the competition. Each publishing season now brings half-a-dozen more or less sophisticated novels devoted to the wild heartlands of Jewish family life, to stabs into the dark of the immigrant history, or to the perplexities of acculturation. As the books proliferate, so do the stock characters, situations, and themes: the typical presented often enough loses its individual edge and fades into stereotype. The mother in Gold's book, for example, who runs each family meal as though a famine were imminent, "serving even when there was nothing to serve," who complains of her "waricose" veins and her son's lack of "consideration," who is convinced that at fourteen he has made up his mind to marry a *shiksa*, and so on and so forth: she may still be sociology but she's not news. The bachelor uncle who can't somehow get started in the new world, the aunt who begins virtually every sentence with "My Irwin," the young cousin who saves up for his future operations: one has the feeling he has been here many times before even when he hasn't. Similarly, the effort to retell the sketchy family tales of Cossacks and wonder-working rabbis, to invoke the lost world of the East European communities by means of guesswork and improvisation, has become increasingly superficial, increasingly silly: "It was also a religion of medals, magic and charms. Jews raved and sang; Jews rolled in the woods in public ecstasies. They conquered the miseries of the police and a murderous peasantry by rocking and rolling." It is painfully ironic that fifteen years farther along, Gold's presumably final effort to come to grips with his background, to capture the pattern of its meaning and the substance of his birthright, should be partly swamped by the wave of "Jewish" fiction that some of its parts have helped to foster. But passages such as the above make me feel that there is some justice in this fate as well.

What continues to run deep and hence fresh in *Fathers* is Gold's feeling for his father. Under the spell of his interest, affection, and pride, Gold seizes upon every expression, mannerism, material detail of this coarse and canny man to create a character who is as bright and sturdy on the page as he is in life. Sam Gold, in his sheepskin coat, the silvery claw of his crate hammer protruding, his gold tooth flashing the talisman of his purpose and power—is one of the few natural heroes of modern American writing as well as the most solid portrait of the greenhorn businessman since Abraham Cahan wrote *The Rise of David Levinsky*. Along with showing what love can do for characterization, the treatment of Sam Gold also indicates what a personal urgency of purpose can do for structure and meaning. His relation to his father matters to

Gold and it is virtually all that makes this book matter—provides its significance, makes it cohere.

The earlier sections which deal with Sam Gold's escape from Russia, his struggle to get started in New York and then in Ohio, like the later sections which follow the author out of the family and into his own world, are often pretty thin in content, provisional in statement. But the middle of the book, where the relation between father and son engages, is solidly joined and rich in implication. For the actual daily being of his father, not those vague family tales, is the soil from which Gold springs. In his father's hands, horny from labor but sensitive to the touch of produce and money, he finds the image of his vocation as a novelist; similarly, his father's temperament, that of the patient, industrious shopkeeper but also that of the inveterate poker player, the eventual real-estate speculator, provides the model of his own way of taking and making the world. From his father's treatment of an anti-Semitic bully (he has him beaten up—but within reason) Gold learns about prudence and justice; from his father's pleasures in the Russian baths he takes his cue of how to inhabit his own body; from the memory of his father's griefs he knows his own sources of sorrow.

But the rest of *Fathers* is not redeemed by this potent conjunction of memory and desire. What one gets, often enough, is the kind of tarted-up nostalgia that provides one of the staples of Jewish fiction. Now, nostalgia is a very trickly literary emotion: it reactivates the past, but it also sentimentalizes it, gives it an unearned increment of significance merely because it was once possessed. Moreover, lacking emotional validity, nostalgia tends to feed on itself and turn perverse: much of the rage for camp that has been afflicting the culture is a systematic perversion of childhood. Be that as it may, nostalgia has a particular attraction for many Jewish writers: some of them, like Gold or Bruce Jay Friedman or Wallace Markfield or Irwin Faust, seem to possess virtually total recall of their adolescent years, as though there were still

some secret meaning that resides in the image of Buster
Brown shoes, or Edward G. Robinson's snarl, or Ralston's
checkerboard package.

This preoccupation with the past is in marked contrast, as
Gold observes, with his father's virtual indifference to it. "I
don't look back," says Sam Gold. "What should I see? My
shadow. . . . You take care of the shadows. Your department." Unlike other minorities, who came from a country of
their own, the immigrant Jews from East Europe tended to
make a clean break with the past, to forget it as quickly and
completely as possible. In this respect, they resemble Negroes, in whom cultural amnesia is even more the better part
of sanity. At the same time, though, the Jews are the people
of memory, if any group is, and so while the immigrant generation says "Forget," the later one answers "Remember."
Perhaps, too, the close ties of Jewish family life and, in my
own generation, the anxious but vivid background years of
the Depression and of World War II all help to encourage
this widespread appeal and use of nostalgia. So too, of course,
do the cold comforts of the present.

Be that as it may, I think that the vogue of Jewish fiction,
with its heavy component of an outgrown and overworked
past, has begun to be as much of a drag on talent as it is a glut
on the market. Perhaps it's time to be up and doing again, to
carry the search for roots and continuity into the present
where it merges with the common plight of old and young,
Gentiles and Jews alike. I don't want to discourage anyone,
but, as *Fathers* makes clear, the evocation of local Jewish
color has no more claim to intrinsic interest than any other
material; only the passions of art can save it now from artificiality, triteness, and irrelevance.

(1967)

The American Nightmare

I looked forward to reading this first novel by William Mathes, *Minotaur, Minotaur* . . . , from having seen a few of his reviews and a number of his unpublished stories. In them, Mathes came across as a young writer with very visible qualities of heart and strong-mindedness rather than merely a "persona," as they say in the literary journals. He also seemed free of the usual cant of the young writer who tries to put down the society before he has even seriously begun to take it on. A former biology student rather than an English major, Mathes had a steady power of observation, a directness of expression, a tone that was both manly and sensitive. All of this was promising.

But all of this has also left me somewhat disappointed and disconcerted by his novel. *Minotaur, Minotaur* . . . is not a book that one can dismiss; it has passages of the genuine purpose and perception that I expected to find; yet its over-all effect is thin, literary, derivative. Partly this may be due to Mathes' inexperience in sustaining a narrative, but it is also due to a bind that he has been led into by his choice of material and by his approach to it. Since this bind is common in the contemporary novel, particularly as practiced by the better younger writers, I would like to try to say something about it.

As with the typical serious novel today, *Minotaur, Mino-*

taur . . . is a study of alienation as seen through the lens of a mixed style—half realistic, half fantasy. Now, alienation may well be an inescapable subject. This is not because we are all necessarily divided men, all of us having lost a grasp of our creaturely nature, but because the man who is intact, whose purposes in the world make immediate sense, is felt to stand outside of everything that characterizes the present point in history. Thus, though most novelists lead relatively integrated lives (otherwise they would not have the stability or stamina to saw away at the long middle of a book), they gravitate toward characters who embody in a radical way the conditions of emptiness and dissociation that are felt to be the product of the vast dismaying changes that are sweeping over society, accelerating the separation of the human from the natural, splitting most persons from the sources and norms of their experience, ranging from the personal and local to the abstract and planetary levels. Over these splits is spread a layer of material comfort and manipulative pseudo-experience: the correlative of the vacuous and anxious inner world being the merchandised and denatured character of the social environment. When the chairman of the board, or something, of U.S. Steel urges students to become conformists because conformity aids free enterprise—what novelist can afford to look the other way?

The trouble, though, is that alienation has become as banal a theme as that of togetherness. Indeed, much of its triteness is owing to the fact that its "data" are often less the result of accurate and imaginative observation than of the proliferation of merely counter images to the myths of conformity; its negations are as reductive and facile as the affirmations of the ladies' magazines. This is the trap, I'm afraid, that Mathes has led himself into.

Bert Lepton, his main figure, is in many respects the standard suburban vegetable, California-style, who is saved from rotting away by the onslaught of a psychotic episode. He happens to be a dentist, but he might be anything that would allow him to own a home and a swimming pool, and except for a couple of bizarre episodes during his service days, he has no past, just as he has no present apart from his *Angst*. Everything about his life is cut away to reveal the more nakedly his symptoms of malaise, paranoia, and regression: his primary source of pleasure is immersing himself for long periods in his pool; his one achievement was to build a small aquarium in which he swam with the fishes, feeling himself to be a god; his one vice is peeping through a partition while his assistant changes into her uniform. His wife is the standard suburban mannikin whose main interest in life is psychoanalysis and whose one claim to individuality is that, having formerly been an airline stewardess, she is sexually aroused only on airplanes. His children are the standard suburban monsters who regard having a swimming pool as "gauche" and otherwise aren't worth anyone's attention. There is also the dental assistant, the standard depraved cheerleader type, and there is Bert's one friend, a local Chinese hi-fi specialist pretending to be a mandarin. All in all, another gallery of one-dimensional caricatures of contemporary humanity, touched off by a snideness that is on much the same level, though at the opposite extreme, as the drippy facetiousness of those ads for the Cosmopolitan Girl.

What saves *Minotaur, Minotaur* . . . from its black platitudes is that it eventually comes in touch with the ambiguous, complex substance of a truth. This truth is that madness may be more than disease; it may be one of the remaining modes of experience that enable us to relate to the remnants of our interior life, to begin to rejoin what society dismembers. Pursued by a paranoid hallucination of an "evil one" who is all devouring mouth (a psychotic development of his womb fixation), Bert hides out in the hills above the Golden Gate Bridge, where he rapidly deteriorates into an animal-like state and nearly dies. Rescued from his lair and committed to a mental hospital, he retreats further into a catatonic security which he calls his "cave." A sympathetic psychiatrist manages to draw him partly out of it, but his encounter with the terror and grief of his self-destruction must run its own course; and Bert returns to the world only after he has fled from his treatment, saved himself from drowning, lived again in a state of nature and finally killed a bear in mortal combat—the bear being a final projection of the "evil one."

Mathes attempts to structure and broaden the implications of this experience by giving it a mythological base of reference *à la Ulysses*: Bert is a latter-day version of Theseus, his heroism scaled down and adjusted to our age of anxiety; his "cave" is the Labyrinth of the Minotaur; the Minotaur is the Evil One, Dr. Adriane, his therapist, stands for Ariadne and her ball of twine, and so forth. But the strength of the vision here has very little to do with these literary parallels and is deflected, in part, by their demands. What Mathes does get across very well is the profoundly ambiguous landscape of psychosis and the harrowingly paradoxical intentions that lead a man to enter the heart of his darkness. There is a passage, for example, in which Bert explores his "cave" and there encounters three corpses—each an aspect of the death of his self which he has been enacting—that deserves a place with the best psychological writing of our time. And, in general, Mathes' ability to identify the process of Bert's madness as a natural act—to do so not as a construct but as a fusion of incident, character, scene: that is, as art—enables *Minotaur, Minotaur* . . . , for all of its cartoon-like quality, to emerge on the far side of reality, to grasp the primordial truths that still join the human to nature.

In keeping with the apocalyptic school of writing to which Mathes gives partial allegiance, the definition of daily social reality is filled out by several bizarre fantasies, the principal one being the development of an apparatus that supplies a total environment to the children housed within it—half learning machine, half womb—and even automatically eliminates any deviates from its norms. This kind of "wild" fantasy is much applauded today: it appeals to the social dropout in all of us and to the facile belief that the more extreme we imagine the future to be, the more discernible the social forces of the present become. But Bert's dilemma is that he exists in the world-as-it-is; to impair the force of this involvement by travestying it is to simplify the character of his breakdown and to rob it of actual relevance. Or, to take a positive example, it is the deadly accurate portrait of the Upper West Side of New York and of the money culture which it represents that, in good part, makes Saul Bellow's *Seize the Day* so much more powerful a study of the ground of alienation between the individual and society, between the "True self" and the "pretender" one.

The moral, I imagine, is that man is a social animal after all, and when this dimension of his experience is scanted, reduced, and negated, the description of character becomes thin and incomplete. The revulsion that many writers today feel toward society breeds its own air of unreality and creates myths and fantasies of the American Nightmare that are as facile and sentimental as those of the American Dream.

(1967)

William Burroughs: The Algebra of Need

William Burroughs wrote *The Ticket That Exploded* after *Naked Lunch* and as a sequel to it: "a mathematical extension of the Algebra of Need beyond the junk virus." It is only now being published in revised form in America, having been preceded by *The Nova Express* and *The Soft Machine*. If you have struggled through either of the latter, you are likely to find *The Ticket* to be more of the same "cut-up" account of the Nova Mob, the Nova Police, and the perversions of the future. Being an earlier version, however, as well as a less extreme experiment in pastiche, collage, and electronic writing, about which Burroughs has added a number of passages of commentary, *The Ticket* provides a somewhat clearer sense of what Burroughs is doing in this series of "blue" science-fiction novels.

The basis of Burroughs' fiction from *Naked Lunch* forward has been his depiction of the endemic lusts of body and mind which prey on men, hook them, and turn them into beasts: the pushers as well as the pushed. His model of this condition is, of course, drug addiction: the junky being the creature of total need and hence of total vulnerability. He is controlled both biologically and socially—both by the insatiable demands of his body and by the ruthless economy of the drug market. As Burroughs puts it: "Junk is the ideal product . . . the ultimate merchandise. . . . The junk merchant does not sell his product to the consumer, he sells the consumer to the product. He does not improve and simplify his merchandise. He degrades and simplifies the client."

Burroughs' experience of this combination of physical and social control, through fifteen years in the cracks and gutters of society, has enabled him to envision a general state of being which in earlier ages was known and felt as Hell. In *Naked Lunch* he develops a series of brilliant improvisations, or "bits," in which the more fiendish tendencies that possess men and society are raised to the same power of "total need" as the drug addict's. In these sketches, impersonations, and fantasies, Burroughs acts out an Inferno where everyone is turned on, each in his own way; sex addicts, violence addicts, money addicts, power addicts, and so forth. The result is a species of gallows humor—obscene, ghastly, and timely—of bodily abuse and spiritual death.

Much of Burroughs' manner derives from the caustic mentality and idiom of the carny, the con-man, the vaudeville hoofer. Though it wanders across continents, *Naked Lunch* is firmly rooted in the dark side of the American imagination, where the figure of the cracker-barrel hustler has had a complex and vivid career. Burroughs' rural sheriffs, county clerks, and doctors, for example, recall the frontier comedy of Twain, T. B. Thorpe, George Harris, among others. They produced a wild humor, raw and crafty, based on the bodily functions, deformations, and torments. Burroughs brings it up to date, thickens it with other idioms, but it is essentially the voice of the native American underground. There is Dr. Benway's tale of the carny ventriloquist, for example, who taught his bowels to talk:

> . . . After a while the ass started talking on its own. He would go in without anything prepared and his ass would ad-lib and toss the gags back at him every time.
>
> Then it developed sort of teeth-like raspy in-curving hooks and started eating. He thought this was cute at first and built an act around it, but the asshole would eat

its way through his pants and start talking on the street, shouting out it wanted equal rights. It would get drunk, too, and have crying jags nobody loved it and it wanted to be kissed same as any other mouth. Finally it talked all the time day and night, you could hear him for blocks screaming at it to shut up, and beating it with his fist, and sticking candles up it, but nothing did any good and the ass said to him: "It's you who will shut up in the end. Not me. Because we don't need you around here any more. I can talk and eat *and* shit."

This is also, of course, a brilliant fantasy of anality. Burroughs' grasp of the "Algebra of Need" and the power of his imagination often carry his comedy far into the buried recesses of the psyche. The only other contemporary artist I know of who has been able to spring repressions in this virtually total way and hold up for inspection the maniacal impulses on which all of us sit, some better than others, was Lenny Bruce. It is more than a coincidence that they were both drug addicts, both conversant with the far reaches of fantasy and with the baleful knowledge of how desperate and diabolical men are under the right conditions. Moreover, the addict's special view of the smug inhumanity of society— for example, the fact that some addictions such as nicotine and alcohol are national pastimes while others are criminal offenses—and his natural animus against the authorities and citizens who thrive within the society provide an aggressive energy and razor edge to their insight. The fact that they are both comedians is also much to the point, for humor is a powerful instrument in mediating the incongruities of the psyche, in giving a structure and power to the dull gibberish that makes up most of the actual content inside our heads. Most of us have had the experience of striking a vein of comic fantasy that goes on and on, cuts deeper and deeper, knits up more and more threads of experience. Burroughs, like Bruce, has the gift—I'd say genius—to do so almost constantly.

Often in *Naked Lunch* Burroughs' imagination of depravity goes so far out that the human fades into the animal and the upturned, crawling, horrific visions of the unfed junky come into view. Thus, at one point, he writes of "Mugwumps" and "Reptiles":

Mugwumps have no liver and nourish themselves exclusively on sweets. Thin, purple-blue lips cover a razor-sharp beak of black bone with which they frequently tear each other to shreds in fights over clients. These creatures secrete an addicting fluid from their erect penises which prolongs life by slowing metabolism. . . . Addicts of Mugwump fluid are known as Reptiles. . . . A fan of green cartilage covered with hollow, erectile hairs through which the Reptiles absorb the fluid sprouts from behind each ear. The fans, which move from time to time touched by invisible currents, serve also some form of communication known only to Reptiles.

In his more recent books Burroughs has been transmuting the addict vision more persistently in this way. *The Nova Express*, *The Soft Machine*, and now *The Ticket That Exploded* all make use of the same futuristic locale as a framework for inventing surrealistic images of virulent life that obeys the laws of the "Algebra of Need." For example, there are the "heavy metal" addicts from Uranus (junkies), the "flesh addicts" (homosexuals) from Venus, the hot Crabmen (police), and so forth. At the same time, the pushers, con artists, and other reprobates from *Naked Lunch* have been brought together as the Nova Mob, which runs the planet by controlling the mass media—as well as the other channels of addiction—which they use to infect the citizenry with a "word virus" that sustains and exacerbates group conflicts. And in each novel the Mob is defeated and disbanded by the Nova Police led by Inspector Lee (a reformed addict who is one of Burroughs' surrogates in *Naked Lunch*) along with underground partisans that attack and dismantle the word and image machinery of the "control addicts."

This fable and the commentary about it form a thin thread of continuity through what is becoming the virtually trackless landscape of Burroughs' imagination, which he presents in these books as a kind of dream movie going on in his mind. Just as this "film" is edited to conform to the associative, non-logical imagery of dream, so the sound track is often "cut-up" and mixed together. Thus, his fantasies of the future often mingle with and dissolve into his memories of the past; monologues, dialogues, and commentary fade in and out; while certain figures and obsessive themes—masturbation and sodomy; hanging, mutilation, and cannibalism; parasitism and plasmic transformations; brainwashing and electronic consciousness, and so forth—loom up and fall away in the maze and haze of the language:

> Naked boy on association line—I stay near right now—be shifted harsh at this time of day—The levanto dances between mutual erections fading in hand—trail my Summer afternoons . . . My number is K9—I am a Biologic from frayed jacket sitting out in lawn chairs with the St. Louis suburb—not looking around—taking away—arab drum music in the suburban air—

Some of the sections, to be sure, are a good deal more clear and straightforward than this; and some of the versions of "cut-up," such as the mingling of popular-song titles and lyrics in a hilarious and gruesome parody of sentimental "*love*," are very effective. Moreover, as one goes back over such passages, they become more intelligible and at times beautiful. But though Burroughs has broken up the syntactical logic of English in order to renovate and heighten its expressiveness, and to rescue it—and us—from the debased and insidious uses to which it is put—one finds that the method often lands him in merely a different kind of banality. The associations that invest the images with significance and tie them together in some kind of meaning derive from habits of thought and feeling that Burroughs feels free to indulge, and perhaps has to indulge to keep track of himself. Thus, what is gained in language is lost in content. The result is often arresting fragments of scenes, characters, thoughts that never develop and merely repeat the same circuit of consciousness —a kind of brilliant merry-go-round of Burroughs' psyche.

Still Burroughs is such a good writer, his imagination works in such original as well as compulsive ways, that one can only reserve judgment about the eventual outcome of these experiments. Moreover, for all of his acting out of impulse and cutting up of phrases he is a deadly serious man. If he has one foot in the garish, corrosive sensibility of the addict, the carny, the lower depths of show biz, the other is anchored in a moral austerity that is almost Puritanical. However curious or perverse it may seem, the modern writer he most makes me think of is T. S. Eliot, whose language and themes pervade Burroughs' later work far more than those of any other author and whose own experiments in pastiche and collage such as *The Waste Land* are a major resource of the modern tradition which Burroughs is attempting to extend. It is worth noting that both Burroughs and Eliot grew up in the Protestant, genteel class in St. Louis. (In his essay "St. Louis Return," published in the *Paris Review*, Burroughs recalls a friend whose "mother had been to dancing school with Tommy Eliot," and he, characteristically, goes on to muse: "His socks wouldn't stay up. His hands were clammy. I will show you fear in dancing school.") Both writers carry in their bones that strain of Puritan refinement that characterized the WASP elite in America and that often went hand-in-hand with the salty imagination of the hinterland to produce a certain dry but charged wit. For all of his sordid, gray years as an addict, there is still in Burroughs a very visible core of the aristocrat. Conrad Knickerbocker in his *Paris Review* interview with Burroughs—a fine and indispensable one—describes him as follows:

He wore a gray lightweight Brooks Brothers suit with vest, a blue-striped shirt from Gibraltar cut in the English style, and a deep blue tie with small white polka

dots. His manner was . . . didactic or forensic. He
might have been a senior partner in a private bank. . . .
A friend of the interviewer, spotting him across the
lobby, thought he was a British diplomat.

The description could serve for Eliot, whose Anglican appearance became so complete in later life that one easily for-
gets how conversant he was with the wild side of life in a
work like "Sweeney Agonistes." In a way, Burroughs is a sort
of Eliot turned inside out: what Edmund Wilson sees as the
buried "rascal," the canny impersonator in Eliot carried to
the fore in Burroughs, while Eliot's surface of the man of
spiritual austerity is driven deep in Burroughs' nature. But
the vision of the modern world as a wasteland, a gray, ugly
soulless place where everything is permitted, is finally the
same. Here is a passage by Burroughs, taken from his St.
Louis essay and put in poetic form:

> Acres of rusting car bodies
> Streams crusted with yesterday's sewage
> American flag over an empty field
> Wilson Stomps Cars—City of Xenia Disposal
> South Hills, a vast rubbish heap
> Where are the people?
> What in the name of Christ goes on here?
> Church of Christ . . . crooked crosses in winter stubble.

I know that it seems odd to compare a writer to Lenny
Bruce and T. S. Eliot in one and the same review. But such
are the extremes of experience from which the writing of
William Burroughs seems to me to derive and to draw its
energies. He is one of the small group of American novelists
today who are both vital and complex, and though his last
three books seem to me to reach a brilliantly lit dead end,
they also may prove to possess the kind of genuine innovation
that keeps fiction alive and the literary enterprise going.

(1967)

Paul Bowles: The Desert Within

Paul Bowles is known mainly for two books
—*The Sheltering Sky* and *The Delicate Prey*—both of which
appeared in the early years after World War II and immediately established him as one of the best of the new crop of
writers. Trained as a composer and influenced by the French
symbolists and surrealists, Bowles came on the scene as a fully
developed artist who was looking to revive the modernist
movement. This movement had noticeably declined in America during the political and social fervors of the 1930's and
during the gigantic public effort of World War II; but in the
years immediately thereafter, the negations of the avant-garde
imagination, and its master theme of alienation began to find
a fertile ground in the moral wastelands left by the war.

Though the public mood during the late Forties was robust, sanguine, expansive, full of the sense of new and
heightened possibilities, the literature of this period reflected
a profound unease and dismay about the human situation.
While the suburbs began to boom and the universities to
hum with the citizens of a brave new era, the mood of the
literature turned bitterly grim, if not horrific. The younger
American writers coming on the scene—Bowles, Eudora
Welty, Carson McCullers, Tennessee Williams, Saul Bellow,
Truman Capote, Vance Bourjaily, William Styron, Norman
Mailer, James Baldwin, Ralph Ellison, *et al.*—were specialists

in loneliness, anxiety, hatred, and terror, while the older writers who mattered most—such as Hemingway, Faulkner, Eliot, Nathanael West—were the prophets of the broken moral order. In short, it was the writers—again "the antennae of the race," in Pound's phrase—who detected the nihilistic malaise left by the destructive energies of World War II and that the nuclear age and the cold war were to keep active and poisonous. Looking back today from the vantage point of our horrible adventure in Vietnam, one of the more salient legacies of the mentality of "massive retaliation," one can see how accurate these detections were, how ominous the prophecies, say, of *The Naked and the Dead* are proving to be.

Of the writers who devoted themselves to negation and despair, Bowles was probably the most subtle as well as the most uncompromising. The stories in *A Delicate Prey* with their lucid, quiet evocation of mood and motive leading to revelations of scarifying depravity were often so powerful that they made the nihilism of the early Hemingway seem like a pleasant beery melancholy. The title story, for example, deserves to live forever in the annals of human cunning and cruelty: a tale of a desert bandit and tribal fanatic who wins the confidence of three brothers traveling in a caravan, murders the two older ones after conning them into a hunt, and then, intoxicated with hashish ("carried along on its hot fumes, a man can escape very far from the world of meaning"), wounds, mutilates, rapes, and finally, after many hours, kills the youngest brother. The emotional current of the story is provided by the boy's innocence, which leads him to distrust his suspicions of the Moungari's treachery; distracted by the lusts and self-consciousness of youth, he is the human equivalent of the desert gazelles, the "delicate prey" that were to be hunted down. The tale concludes with the detection of the murderer, whom the police turn over to the tribesmen of the three brothers. They calmly bury him up to his neck in the desert sands "to wait through the cold hours for the sun that would bring first warmth, then heat, thirst, fire, visions. The next night he did not know where he was, did not feel the cold. The wind blew dust along the ground and into his mouth as he sang."

Virtually all of the stories in A *Delicate Prey* take place in a primitive setting, usually either Central America or North Africa. The jungle and more notably the desert, the place where "all philosophical systems collapse," as a French colonial officer puts it, have provided Bowles with a natural background for narratives that are intended to crack open the standard models of reality and morality and to reveal the demonic sources of human conduct. The destructive element in which Bowles immerses his tight-laced and empty pilgrims from the modern world takes many forms: there is the incredible brutality of the Reguiba bandits, who quickly reduce an anthropologist, led to them by a spiteful native guide, to a state of catatonic terror in which he functions as a kind of tribal pet; but there is also the encompassing languor of a Caribbean island into which a retired professor sinks so far that he sends his teen-age son away to a life of sybaritic perversion rather than be disturbed by his scandalous behavior.

Though most of these stories in A *Delicate Prey* still make one feel they were written with a razor, so deftly and chillingly do they cut to the bone, there was clearly more to Bowles than the desire to shock, dismay, and terrorize. "Pastor Dowe at Tacate," for example, is a profoundly ironic comment on the white man's burden, a kind of *Heart of Darkness* in miniature, in which a prim missionary finds himself sliding from Christian rationality into atavism, until he finally is faced with the necessity of taking an eight-year-old girl for his wife and literally runs away in terror from the Indian village.

The abysses and furies of the human psyche; the fragile, provisional nature of the civilized instincts; the lure of the primitive and the inhuman; the sadness of deracinated people; the underground warfare of marriage and friendship; the lonely divisions between desire and behavior, between

having and holding, between one motive and the next; the
modern world's contagions of *Angst*, dread, deadness: all
these strains of the existentialist vision are dramatically presented in Bowles's earlier work and come to a classic statement in his novel *The Sheltering Sky*, one of the most beautifully written novels of the past twenty years and one of the
most shattering.

Bowles was not the philosopher that Sartre or Camus were,
but he was an existentialist to his fingertips, and beside the
emotional concreteness of *The Sheltering Sky*, books like
Nausea, *The Age of Reason*, and *The Stranger* seem vague,
arbitrary, imaginatively barren. Bowles's novel is a study of
two American travelers, Kit and Port Moresby, and of the
subtle processes between and within them that carry each to
a destructive self-fulfillment in the North African desert. The
epigraph of the book is Eduard Mallea's observation that
"Each man's destiny is personal only insofar as it may happen
to resemble what is already in his memory," the point of
which is richly developed in the unfolding of Port's isolate
values, his yearning to exist outside of the human community, to experience the mysteries of nothingness, which has
brought him to the desert and which culminates in a series of
terrible voyages into the beyond that he makes during the
final stages of a fatal attack of typhoid fever. His wife, who is
afflicted by a sense of dread that wars with her considerable
intelligence, finally achieves the utter submissiveness she
craves by falling into the hands of a young Arab merchant
and undergoing a sexual enslavement that eventually drives
her into madness. These parallel lines of fate, of two people
consumed by accidents that minister to their deepest wishes,
are drawn with a fineness and density of specification that
makes the novel anything but schematic. Bowles has much
the same feeling for the delicate tangibilities of character that
D. H. Lawrence did and much the same powerful ability to
establish the atmosphere of physical reality that reveals and
conditions behavior: the squalid, sagging accouterments of

colonialism in a desert hotel; the fragments of mystery in a
street wind at dusk that carries "the smell of lilies, drains, and
hashish smoke"; the piles of garbage in a broken-down patio
amid which lie naked, scrofulous infants and pink dogs, their
hairless, raw skin "indecently exposed to the kisses of the flies
and the sun"; and preeminently the desert itself, with its
spectacular negation of everything human except for the arid,
howling void within.

In retrospect, *The Sheltering Sky* stands as the climax of
Bowles's literary career: the book into which he put his
strongest image of life and his deepest knowledge about it.
This image and knowledge admit of little expansion. For if,
as Port says, contemplating the only book he might have
written, the one absolute truth for him is that "the difference
between something and nothing is nothing" and that the
only interest is "in all the complicated processes that make it
possible to get that result," then the novelist is doomed to
rework the algebra of nihilism until he grows weary of the
problem. Indeed, this has been one of the burdens of modernism, and the literary landscape of the twentieth century is
littered with the abandoned careers of writers who ran into
the sands of the desert within and found themselves unable
to go on.

Be that as it may, Bowles's fiction since *The Sheltering Sky*
has been infrequent and uneven. His most recent novel, *Up
Above the World*, is a sort of psychological thriller; visually
effective, as always, but thin in characterization and theme,
its craft seems more appropriate to a good movie than a
novel. *The Time of Friendship* brings together his first collection of stories in more than twenty years. Most of them are
effective, but only one seems to break fresh ground. This is
the long title story, in which Bowles abandons his relatively
static view of primitivism, and moves beyond his somewhat
fatigued fascination with its mysteries and perversities, to
write about post-colonial Algeria.

"The Time of Friendship" is a surprisingly poignant ac-

count of the deepening relationship between Fräulein Windling, a Swiss schoolteacher who lives part of each year in a
desert village, and an adolescent Arab boy. The teacher is not
one of Bowles's world-besotted travelers, nor is the desert any
longer the burning, silent center of negative truth to which
she makes her confused and final way. She is a sensible, resourceful spinster, and the oasis village is a place where
people live from day to day and make do with the earth,
grass, palmwood, and animal skins that comprise their economy. As for herself, the desert is a healthy environment
which strengthens her "resistance" to the civilized world's
slow stain and each year puts her "in touch with life again."
She is enamored of the ancient ways of the village and regards the rebellion going on in the north as part of the modern "virus of discontent," from which she hopes the village
will be spared. Slimane, the Arab she comes to befriend, is
not a cunning demon who will eventually betray or rape her,
but rather a simple, soulful boy who is devoted to her. Several
years pass, during which their only conflict is whether Christ
was a Moslem; stymied by his obduracy on this one issue, she
tactfully resolves to teach him something about Christianity
by building a *crèche* for Christmas. But, to her dismay, she
finds him eating the figures intricately made of chocolate,
raisins, and nuts when she briefly leaves him alone with the
crèche. Slimane is impassive about his offense—he had gone
without dinner—and his mentor comes to realize that he was
right to do so. "This is the desert. . . . Here food is not an
adornment; it is meant to be eaten." As for her Christian
zeal, "It had been too much head and high ideals, she reflected, and not enough heart." The next day the French official in the village orders her to leave Algeria because of the
war. Slimane accompanies her to the town where she will
take the train to the coast. The trip to Colomb-Bechar is her
chance to say goodbye to him; but she discovers that it is his
chance to leave the oasis, live in a city, and fight against the
French. While she was packing, Fräulein Windling had got-

ten a splinter under her nail; the story ends with her thinking of Slimane's fate, while her wound throbs away.

The story is as complex in the telling as any Bowles has written; what is so strange and moving is its sympathy. What it portends for his future work, I don't profess to know. But it's interesting to find him writing a tender story which at the same time broadens his grasp of life. The "difference between something and nothing" depends on what you feel. Fräulein Windling's splinter was only a speck of wood until it penetrated her being.

(1967)

Interpreting Susan Sontag

It gets harder and harder to see Susan Sontag through the smoke of opinion that smolders away now on all sides of her work. *Against Interpretation*, her collection of essays and reviews, produced much more heat, as they say, than light: almost every reviewer seemed compelled to stand up and be counted as to whether Miss Sontag was a cultural hero or villain, the lovely, brave Minerva of a genuine new underground/*avant-garde* or the glib bootlegger of the latest wave of French modernism, East Village Pop, and other modes of the higher unseriousness. Like the celebrity that Miss Sontag appears to court with her left hand and disclaim with her right, her critical stance somehow managed to be both matter-of-fact and outrageous: a tone that gets under the skin in much the same way that those dust-jacket photographs of her—poised, striking, vaguely sinister—either seduce or repel. The result was that the ideas there were in *Against Interpretation* went mostly by the board. Now, along comes *Death Kit*, her second novel, to much the same apparent effect: so far, the book has been either wildly touted as the second coming of the modern novel or taken as firm evidence that Miss Sontag has little or no talent for fiction at all. Rather than let *Death Kit* drive us to the wall of such ultimate and exaggerated claims, it might be well to try to understand what the book is intended to do—indeed, to interpret it: a procedure it requires virtually every inch of the way.

Not only requires—despite Miss Sontag's theories about interpretation—but also deserves. I think that *Death Kit* is an unusually interesting novel in its own right as well as a clear advance over her first one, *The Benefactor*. For one thing, it's alive. *The Benefactor* had next to no vitality in it: it was all literature, and could have been taken for a parody of the post-expressionist novel of moral exhaustion and exquisite nerves were it not so exhausted and nervous itself. *Death Kit* is worth taking seriously because it is searching, charged, meant. Though its subject, like that of *The Benefactor*, is self-perception—or, better, perceiving—its qualities are much more like those in Miss Sontag's better essays: those in which she succeeds in being both intelligent and audacious, instead of just one or the other. There is a great deal of creative bravura in *Death Kit*, Miss Sontag having struck a vein of invention which has produced an overflow of imaginative commentary on the interior life and also some genuine art. In the end, *Death Kit* doesn't dare or feel as much as it should as art and hence provides too much in the way of a talkative analysis of her hero's unconscious progress into death and too little *formal* demonstration, to use one of her favorite terms, of his slow extinction. But I'd much rather see Miss Sontag being carried away by her own invention than trudging drearily after the old *avant-garde* novel like a lady English professor looking for signals in Paris.

The "story" in *Death Kit* should be well enough known by this time for me not to have to rehearse it here. What may still need pointing up is Miss Sontag's device and design, at least as I read the novel. Put briefly, the novel is precisely what the title says it is: the material that Dalton Harron, "Diddy," carries into death with him and assembles in death. He does not go to Buffalo: his "business trip" is the business of completing his death, following his successful suicide attempt at the beginning of the novel. He does not twice murder Incardona, the railway worker: he twice reenacts the murder of himself. He does not fall in love with and live with Hester: he invents and invests her with those qualities that express his desire, powerful but doomed, to be "reborn." In sum, the action takes place in the conscious and subconscious mind of a dead man: quite literally, in his after-life. This is the basic conception of the book and its major source of power.

Since the book has been badly misjudged because badly understood, it seems best to clear up its supposed obscurity, which has generally been taken as pretentious obscurantism. Obviously, Miss Sontag does not want to give the game away: the point of *Death Kit* being that Diddy's after-life is mainly a continuation, raised to a second power of purpose and perception, of the life he had lived. The tone, atmosphere, quality of his life-in-death are intended to resemble, though in a purer and more potent form, the death-in-life of this former decent, well-behaved Madison Avenue type WASP, the typical unsolid citizen of our day who, "not really alive," merely "inhabited" his life. That is to say, Diddy alive or Diddy dead merely makes a distinction, not a difference.

Faced with this point to make—as art, not as another banal statement of modern deadness—Miss Sontag perforce has to write her novel in a double-speaking way. Thus Diddy, still alive, is compared to a "failed amphibian." In the passages that open the novel, Miss Sontag describes his malaise as a contamination of the existence he has inhabited, a dissolution of the dense amniotic-like fluid that has been his element or "medium": "the soft interconnected tissuelike days are unstrung. The watery plenum is dehydrated, and what protrudes are jagged, inhuman units. The medium steadily evaporates; the teeming interlocked plenitude is drained of its sustenance. Dies."

Diddy's actual death is similarly and properly equivocal: "Diddy's guts dried out with humiliation; in three days he was discharged from the hospital minus twenty pounds of substance. . . . Knowing one has a life induces the temptation to give it up. One is dead. Therefore, one wants to die.

Equally, one wants to be born." Diddy's after-life, though described with more or less naturalistic, everyday details and probabilities, is everywhere pervaded by an underlying feeling and vision of mortality. This comes to a climax, of course, in the final journey from the tunnel where he kills Incardona once and for all and enters the charnelhouse which contains his final "inventory of the world." But this merely makes explicit what has all along been variously and intricately suggested. Certain items are fairly obvious: his hotel room that is likened to a coffin, the company car to a hearse. Even a dilapidated train station quickly takes on the character and import of Diddy's situation:

> Diddy can't help marking the steady deterioration of the surfaces and furniture of this station. . . . Not only mere negligence is at work here, surely. A question of policy or principle. Only a matter of time before the wrecker's ball gets around to undoing this generous space. . . . But isn't there a good deal to be said for keeping a doomed place clean and in decent repair? Especially since nemesis is proving to be somewhat dilatory in paying its anticipated call.

Miss Sontag is not being merely arch, arbitrary, "literary" in her symbolic rendition of Diddy's journey between life and death. Though she has ended by putting on her literal-minded readers, her analysis of Diddy's progress into his new realm proceeds along fairly obvious Freudian lines, as well as the more arcane ones of the European phenomenologists, notably Bachelard. Whether one regards *Death Kit* as the content of Diddy's final coma (there is some basis for this reading, though I don't think it adds up) or as a supernatural account of his after-life, the basic strategy of the book remains the same: the strategy of the unconscious in fantasies and dreams. Miss Sontag, indeed, comes very close to giving the game away at one point. Diddy has taken Hester away from the hospital to live with him and finds that his morbid guilt about murdering Incardona is gone. "He can't imagine ever, in Hester's company, being frightened of Incardona. . . . Because he no longer has to think only, or even mainly, of himself. Hester is here, interposed between Diddy and himself. Unable to see. Refusing to acknowledge the doubling of the self in dreams."

Just as the spatial phenomena of Diddy's "world" are usually informed and colored by his concerns and feelings, so is the divided self that has undone him bodied forth sharply in the figures of Incardona and Hester. Incardona, the surly, devious, lascivious worker that he twice murders, is an image of the dreary workman in himself, of his baffled masculinity, his repressed animal nature. A more benign, because earlier, version of Diddy's instinctual life is the Wolf-boy, a fantasy of its fugitive and fearful privations that he had tried to exorcise in a college novel. Incardona arises from a further and more complete splitting off of the animal in Diddy, a more pernicious stage of repression that Miss Sontag at the outset likens to the "monstrous malfunctioning" of a generator in the basement of a house, one that has "gone amok" and sends forth a "torrent of refuse that climbs up into Diddy's life, . . . befouling Diddy's world and rendering it unusable. Uninhabitable." The brutal Incardona, smashing away at the barrier in the tunnel that has stalled the train, is Diddy pushing against the limits of his character and finally aiming his baffled fear, rage, and dismay back at himself. (Diddy reenacts his self-destruction as a self-defense, but when it comes to suicide, it probably doesn't matter very much, emotionally speaking, which way the gun is pointing.)

If Incardona is Diddy's death-wish, Hester, of course, is the opposite. She is a much more complicated and unconventional figure than Incardona since she functions as an aspect of the theme of perception (which generally overloads the novel with extraneous detail), as well as Diddy's life force, feminine nature, and self-idealization. With all of these tags of significance clinging to her, the blind Hester moves less adeptly in the dark of Diddy's "world" than Miss Sontag says she does. As a character she is spectral—inadvertently so, I suspect, unlike, say, Incardona's wife—and as a psychological embodiment she is abstract, unlike, say, Hester's aunt, a subtly wrought version of the housekeeper who raised Diddy. But if Hester seems more her author's creature than Diddy's, and if she makes him seem more androgynous than Miss Sontag apparently intended him to be, still Hester serves well enough to carry out the elaborate and beautifully integrated pattern of Diddy's dreamwork, which, through his affair with her, both extends and reiterates the meaning of his life-in-death, death-in-life.

As with dreams, *Death Kit* is situated in the borderlands of consciousness where art and psychology cross. The intense formalism of the novel—each detail held in place by the pattern, each event shaped by the underlying logic of Diddy's intentions—is not only another demonstration of Miss Sontag's faith in the hegemony of form but also a heuristic method of mapping the interior life. One of the reasons that psychoanalysis is an art is that the unconscious is an artist—an endlessly cunning metaphysical poet that transmutes feelings into images, disparities into structures. Thus, to the extent that one is in touch with himself, life can be said to follow art—indeed, to be art. At the same time, the realities of this life are deeply at odds with what we say and do as socialized beings: the poetry of our nights being a muted or screaming protest against the dissimulating "sensible" prose of our days. Or, as Miss Sontag puts it:

When Joan [Diddy's wife] left, Diddy became wiser. . . . He hadn't been watching the wrong play for thirty years. But he'd been watching it without understanding the theory behind its staging—assuming naturalism of script and staging. In retrospect, a naive error. The script is intricate, and charged with obscure references; and the presentation concocted by the director, set designer, and lighting technicians is fanciful and stylized.

Though *Death Kit* is an autonomous work that generates its own terms, much of it is anticipated by Miss Sontag's recent essays on style as well as her studies of "formalism" in contemporary French thought and art, especially the cinema. Like the artists of the *nouvelle vague*, Miss Sontag holds, to use her phrase, "a dedicated agnosticism about reality itself," and *Death Kit* is a *demonstration*, as she would say, of the unreliability of our practical reason (a view that has been borne out, I'm afraid, by most of the reviews it has received). By the same token, all the usual trappings of the realistic novel (the literary form most attuned to practical "reason" and hence Miss Sontag's aesthetic *bête noire*) are not so much ignored as subverted, tilted, turned inside out—both to bring out their inner lie and to facilitate what Miss Sontag would call the purely formal exploration of the structure of Diddy's "kit." Thus the conventional third-person point of view abruptly shifts to the first person plural, the author's commentary fades in and out of Diddy's meditations, and the over-all tone is highly stylized to provide the mixture of intimacy and detachment, pathos and coldness, that Miss Sontag admires so much in the films of Resnais, Godard, and Bresson. Indeed, her description of the "formula" of the new French formalists—"coldness enclosing and subduing an immense pathos"—is a precise definition of the method and mood of *Death Kit.*

No doubt many readers by now will have found *Death Kit* to be a teasingly ambiguous puzzle, and perhaps among those who have solved it there will be some who agree with me that it is all too cold a pathos. I followed Diddy's progress with fascination but without ever quite believing in him: like Hester, he is too much an object of predication, too little a distinct and distinctive man, an experiencing subject of his own plight. As a result, my attention was often deflected from experiencing the book to interpreting it, unlike, say, Tolstoy's *The Death of Ivan Ilyitch*, a study of deadness which to feel is to understand and vice versa. Except for the two scenes in the tunnel and the trip through the house of the dead at the end, *Death Kit* lacks impact; its narrative writing is competent as well as intricate, but Diddy's journey doesn't stay in the mind, stick to the bones. It is more figure than carpet, so that one will hang it on the wall to admire rather than put it on the floor to live with. It is miles beyond the *longueurs* and artificiality of *The Benefactor*, yet still an essentially analytic, technique-ridden work of art. But a work of art nonetheless: bold, complex, coherent in its own purpose, resolutely faithful to its own vision of "life."

(1967)

The Busy Hand of Burgess

Anthony Burgess isn't Irish, but he could be. He writes with the lilt, and a good deal of the blarney, and the roving eye for earthy detail. As it happens, Burgess is a lower-middle-class Catholic from Manchester, which is already two thirds of being Irish, and his garrulousness takes him almost the rest of the way. Like Wilde, Shaw, Yeats, Synge, O'Casey, Joyce, O'Connor, Behan, he is a nonstop talker with temperament to burn, and whose language is rinsed clean of literary detritus. He has also been playing the Irish role on the English literary scene, which is to pepper and stir the pot: to be amusing about the things London takes seriously, such as status, and serious about what London finds amusing, such as sin.

The Irish note is also owing to Burgess' feeling for Joyce, about whom he has written a long commentary (*Re Joyce*) as well as an an abridgment of *Finnegans Wake*. Joyce has been the lion in the modern novelist's path, but Burgess, whom nothing much intimidates, meets him eye to eye: a fellow musician (Burgess was trained as a composer), a linguist, a renegade Catholic, a cultural aristocrat from the back streets and pubs of a hard city. He shares Joyce's true sense of the pith and pitch of the spoken language, his uncommon touch for the common life of a man, a family, a community, that creates a thick social atmosphere in which characters move and breathe, rather than just a background against which they stand. Finally, there are strong affinities in point of view: a sympathetic attitude toward men, tempered by the Catholic awareness of human presumption, and emerging as comedy.

Joyce's talents and vision, however, were poured into four books and little else. Burgess' spill over in all directions, sprawning creations rather than nurturing them. Since he started writing seriously in the late Fifties, he has produced eleven novels, as well as enough literary journalism to keep another writer fully employed. I wonder what makes Burgess run. Perhaps it's money. A good English writer still has to hack out a living under conditions that few American writers have any longer to accept. But there is also a performer in Burgess who obviously likes to stand up and have his say, to try his hand at this and that. He has written a novel of Shakespeare's love life in fine Elizabethan prose and a portrait of a future juvenile delinquent, sometime around 1984, in a slang that brilliantly assimilates Russian and English. He has produced a spy novel with the dark, Jansenist overtones of Graham Greene and an anti-utopian fantasy on population control and atavism that takes off from Huxley's *Brave New World* and *Ape and Essence*. His fiction has toured Russia and the Third World, suburban Manchester and Soho. He can describe anything, animate the most farfetched material. He is one of those writers who seem almost cursed by their facility. His last novel, *Tremor of Intent*, begins with a fine, grave wit, heads off into James Bond land, and then slyly circles home to its "eschatological" theme. Only *A Clockwork Orange* and *A Right to an Answer* seem fully written. The rest are full of splendid mimicry and improvisation and froth, as though Burgess were some sort of cross between Joyce and Peter Sellers.

If anything, his new novel, *Enderby*, bears out sharply this difference between the artist's hand and the entertainer's. The first half, published separately in England as *Inside*

Mr. Enderby, is Burgess at his very best: a magically brewed chronicle of small beer about a minor poet who is lured out into the world by a fashionable lady editor. Enderby is another of Burgess' marital victims and his plight is another illustration of Burgess' master theme: the settled weight of habit and custom, both personal and social, and the danger of disturbing them. Existence is a complex and uncertain thing, and anything that has gone on long enough, whether a life, a marriage, a society, has worked out its own equilibrium, however imbalanced it may appear to be. The greatest sin is against stability. In writing *Inside Enderby*, Burgess manages to achieve his own stability; instead of just doing something, he stands there and fixes the terms of his hero's destiny firmly and deeply. Both the humor and sadness of the novel are sustained in a low, intimate key, and the prose, page after page, has the quiet rightness of a gifted novelist who is talking less to an audience than with himself.

Inside Enderby begins with a dream in which posterity visits: not the towering unborn who visit major poets, but a giggling group of teen-agers led by their English teacher. As the teacher reverently rattles on, the children poke and pry; a volume of Enderby's poems is knocked over and out fall some photographs: "What, Charles, are they doing? The man and woman in the picture? They are minding their own business, that's what they're doing. . . . Fellation, if you must know, is the technical term." Nor is Enderby in repose quite like a monument. Tubby, balding, toothless, dyspeptic, and flatulent, he visibly and audibly belongs to the "world of eating and dying." The poet's flat in a seaside roominghouse provides a similar view of his earthly bourne, somewhere between frugality and squalor. In one small room, furnished with his landlady's Victorian shards, he eats and sleeps; in an even smaller one, he cooks up the scraps of this and that which sustain him; in the third and smallest of all, he performs his other bodily functions, including those of his art. Here is Enderby's kingdom: a small desk, a heater to warm his legs, a bathtub that serves as filing cabinet and wastebasket, a throne where the divine afflatus can mingle comfortably with the other chronic winds that blow through Enderby, where the passions of the mind and the flesh can be happily coordinated and safely discharged. Besides, as Enderby puts it, the "poet is time's cleanser and cathartizer." Besides, there are other reasons.

In one of Burgess' busier novels, the bathroom fixation would be another picturesque detail. In Enderby it functions as the core of a meticulously assembled portrait of a man who is both a mess and an artist. We all know one thing or another about the psycho-sexual implications of art, but Burgess' Enderby is a rich, concrete revelation of the physiological, emotional, and social phenomena that parallel or intertwine in the daily life of this poetry-secreting organism. Words or gas: it's all become one to Enderby's system: an inadvertent, imperative pressure. At the moment of receiving an award from an insufferable publisher and poetaster, Enderby finds himself blurting out a sneering rejection that is as uncontrollable and embarrassing as the rude criticism that his innards have been making of the lunch. Or again, Enderby on his morning round of the seashore and pubs winds up with a hare—a present from 'arry the cook, his one friend—and a few scraps of experience—the squawking of the gulls, a Lesbian's raucous laughter—which almost simultaneously become a stew and a poem. His emotional patterns have become as simplified as his digestive ones: the Lesbian's laughter is followed by a "very clear thin voice" that begins whispering lines of verse as though at his ear, but then the Lesbian begins singing some atrocious pop hit, and the other voice ceases:

Walking home quickly he tried to call back the rhythm, but it had gone. The fragments ceased to be live limbs of some mystical body that promised to reveal itself wholly. Dead as the hare, meaningless onomatopoeia; a silly jingle: *widow, shadow, meadow*. The big rhythms of the nearing tide, the winter sea-wind, the melancholy gulls. A gust shattered and dispersed the emerging form of the poem. Oh, well. Of the million poems that beckoned, like coquettish girls, from the bushes, how very few could be caught.

Enderby's inner life is characterized by these two female voices he has heard in the pub. In the vulgar laughter and song lurks the abiding presence of his dead stepmother, an obscenely obese and slovenly woman full of Catholic xenophobia and superstition, and with her own digestive problems that she shared with the world; the other voice is that of his muse, an exquisitely feminine young coquette that he has fashioned from his desire for his own mother, who died young. The traumatic event of his life was the night when his stepmother, frightened by thunder, climbed into his bed and, in his own terror, the adolescent Enderby locked himself in the bathroom, from which, emotionally speaking, he has never emerged. Impotent since his stepmother's death, Enderby has been left with her money and with many of her attitudes and ways, and amid his own domestic squalor, his passivity, his physical aches and rumbles, he senses his stepmother boring further within him as he advances into middle age.

The world outside Enderby is also mostly his stepmother writ large: a fearful, disorderly, disruptive place. He keeps his contacts minimal—a few rounds in a pub frequented by senior citizens who are too old and ill to do him harm, a drink with 'arry, his main provisioner, a walk on the beach to feed the birds. Still, no man is an island, etc. A jealous neighbor harasses him, his landlady raises his rent and forces him to move. Then, against his better judgment, he leaves his lair and goes up to London to receive the poetry award. There he meets Rawcliffe, a corrupt "defrocked" poet, and Vesta Bainbridge, a shining and glamorous editor of a woman's magazine. Widowed from one famous man, a racing-car driver, she sees possibilities beneath Enderby's scruffy obscurity, and in a moment of domestic crisis—too complicated and hilarious to describe here—Enderby succumbs. They live together chastely, marry, go off to Rome, and there Vesta Bainbridge, always a hearty eater for one so dainty, begins to belch, pick at the wax in her ears, cling to him in a thunderstorm, and lure him back toward the Church.

Enderby's narrow self-sufficiency falls apart. Vesta has his income—"His stepmother had given and his stepmother had, in a youthful, well-spoken, dove-soft, spring-smelling, highly improbable disguise, taken away again." Rawcliffe steals his long poem on original sin, the Minotaur as Christ, and turns it into a science-fiction film. Doubly betrayed, Enderby tries to resume his old life, but his Muse has left him. Everything fails, including an attempt at suicide—death being, as he discovers at the very last moment, only his stepmother again. He passes into the Big-Brotherly hands of Dr. Wapenshaw, who convinces him that poetry has merely been his way of prolonging adolescence. On a note more sad even than the poignant description of Enderby's decline, *Inside Enderby* ends with the defunct poet transformed into the future bartender Hogg, his mother's maiden name: the star of the rehabilitation center's quiz team, a "good trier," a man who marches in step.

All of which is beautifully written, masterfully woven. For all its strange changes, the air of immediate reality never dwindles, nothing farfetched intrudes. Each stage is subtly anticipated and yet comes as a revelation. Like his poems, Enderby is a creature of continuity and chance, of the probabilities of conditioning and the mystery of choice. This is characterization that begins in sound psychology and ends as art.

Unfortunately, there is the second half of the novel, *Outside Mr. Enderby*, which Burgess appears to have reserved for the ham in himself. Playing Enderby-Hogg for laughs, he has abandoned his proleptic method, impatiently unpinned chance from continuity, and created mostly a romp for his fantasy. Early on, Enderby-Hogg witnesses the attempted assassination of the pop singer and poet Yod Crewesy, managed by Vesta Bainbridge, who has passed him some of Enderby's old poems. The gun is thrust into our hero's hands, and he and Burgess are off to the races: Spain and Tangiers, Enderby hiding out as an Arab beggar, a surrealist café complete with William Burroughs, an unconsummated affair with a lady astronomer (Enderby leaps off her to scribble a poem), and an unconsummated fling with his flesh-and-blood Muse. Finally, Burgess stops long enough to deal with the slow death of Enderby's enemy, Rawcliffe, and the prose has a real occasion to rise to. Otherwise, *Outside Enderby* is mostly bravura. On the other hand, if you like black humor . . .

Yes, I know, realism is dating fast, as well as being out of phase with our unreal world in which, as in *Outside Enderby*, anything can happen. *Anything can happen.* Just think! . . . If only Kafka had known. It looks now like it will take us years of John Cage, Godard, Burroughs, *et al.*, to absorb it. In the meantime there is *Inside Enderby*, with its fine insistence on making connections, on keeping its feet on the ground, on revitalizing the art of fiction instead of greasing the skids.

(1968)

The Young Camus

When the Greenwich Village Independent Democrats decided to support Humphrey after all, a spokesman dignified their retreat by quoting . . . guess who? " 'In this absurd world, the only thing one can do is make choices.' Hubert Humphrey is not my choice. But . . ." One hardly needs Camus for that kind of reasoning. But if he speaks now from the grave, as he does virtually every day, it is usually in this way: to confer some sort of nobility on other men's positions or prose. His reputation seems more and more honorific; his work has been carved up into quotations—a kind of *Bartlett's* of liberal piety, which now only awaits an edition. During their famous fight, Sartre said that Camus carried a "portable pedestal." This was partly true, just as it is partly true to say that Sartre has carried a portable barricade: a committed writer needs something to mount; the best ones stand upon the image of their self-esteem. But if unduly cruel, Sartre's remark has proved prophetic. If it is hard to think about Camus any more, it is partly because one has lost sight of the writer inside the statue.

A good way to begin seeing Camus himself again is by reading a new collection of his prose titled *Lyrical and Critical Essays*. The "lyrical" part contains his first two books—*L'Envers et l'endroit* (*The Wrong Side and the Right Side*) and

Noces (*Nuptials*)—which he wrote in his middle twenties after a recurrence of tuberculosis, and which are often so bleak or ardent in feeling, despite their diffuseness, that they immediately begin to reveal the human clay beneath the bronze. Written at times in imitation of the self-commemorative poetic meditation which is virtually a genre of French prose ("If it is true that the only paradises are those we have lost, I know what name to give the tender and inhuman something that dwells in me today"), *The Wrong Side* and *Nuptials* also show a hard hand inside the stylish glove. The essay that begins on the above note ends on this one:

> But I must break this too limp and easy curve [of the absurd]. I need my lucidity. . . . It's men who complicate things. Don't let them tell us any stories. Don't let them say about the man condemned to death: "He is going to pay his debt to society," But: "They're going to chop his head off." It may seem like nothing. But it does make a little difference. There are some people who prefer to look their destiny straight in the eye.

The last statement is no mere gesture. At twenty-four, Camus' "destiny" was staring coldly back at him, and even his elegant paradoxes were bitterly true. Not much has been written about Camus' youth, but he appears to have been one of those vital, able, manly kids who somehow manage to raise themselves in the slums. His father had died in World War I; his mother supported him by working as a maid. His revolts began early. From his family's poverty and sadness he escaped to the Algerian beaches, whose sunlight and surf, as he claimed, molded his spirit. A talented swimmer and boxer, he was also the goalkeeper on a crack soccer team by the time he was fifteen. Despite his family's illiteracy, he was a star pupil, moving from scholarship to scholarship until he became the protégé of the philosopher and stylist Jean Grenier. When he was seventeen he came down with tuberculosis and rebelled against that too: he completed his course in philosophy, married at twenty and also became the lightweight champion of Algiers. But at twenty-three his tuberculosis recurred. This harsh confrontation of so much vitality and apparent fatality lies directly behind the life-death dialectic that forms the theme of these first two books.

From the start, as throughout his career, Camus felt more lucidly than he reasoned. His ideas were the home truths of his experience, linked less by logic than by their emotional fit and weighed by their existential consequences. "I have never seen anyone die," as he put it, "for the ontological argument." Just as his theme of the absurd came directly from his life, so did its resolution—the conquering indifference in which he had been raised. His emotions had been shaped by his mother's detachment and solitude as surely as his physical élan was nurtured by the climate and mores of Algiers. He writes of her as weak-minded and inarticulate. She apparently had been brainwashed by her own mother, who raised Camus and who liked to make him say, in company, that he loved his grandmother more than his mother. Loving his mother so passionately and hopelessly ("she has never hugged or kissed [me], for she wouldn't know how"), Camus always felt himself to be enclosed within her isolation and indifference. In the 1957 preface to *The Wrong Side*, he writes that his real work will begin only when he has rewritten this first book and placed at its center "the admirable silence of a mother and one man's effort to rediscover a justice or a love to match this silence."

All of which gives a seriousness and poignancy to these youthful meditations on the divided aspect of being. His first essay, "Irony," presents three sharp descriptions of the "horrible and dirty adventure of dying," as he later puts it: a moribund, clinging old woman whom her daughter and boyfriend desert to go to the movies, leaving her in the darkness that is "her only hope" and with the "God she loves so poorly"; an old café chatterer who realizes that the end has come because there is no one left in the world who wants to listen to him; and, finally, Camus' grandmother, who is rudely overtaken by the death whose imminence she has been feigning. Her death redeems nothing; the only thing about it that moves him is the radiance of the winter afternoon on which she is buried, whose serene and remote sky points up the sordid negations he has been describing.

Throughout *The Wrong Side*, Camus continues to think against the grain of sentiment, to station himself in the "steady breeze blowing in from the dark horizon of his future" that his Meurseult discovers only as his life is ending. Struggling for an affirmation that is completely free of hope, he views himself as the uprooted stranger he discovers during a week of utter solitude in Prague, climaxed by a man dying alone in an adjacent room in his hotel, and during a week in Italy, whose warm, bare countryside revives his love of life and connects it to his despair. Nothing of his daily existence in Algiers is allowed to intrude, for he wishes to strip himself of the familiar and secure, of the little acquiescences and illusions on which he, like other men, study and work and marry, on which humanity gets by. Thus, he is drawn to the inhuman: his mother's "animal silence," the depraved gleam in the eyes of a cat that has been eating the litter she could not feed, the moment at the bottom of a night of fever when the world "has melted away, taking with it the illusion that life begins each morning." In the inhuman he finds both his terror and his peace: the majestic indifference of the earth supplements his mother's "lesson" as the model for his own point of stillness between no and yes, between the wrong side of the world and the right. "The great courage is still to stare as squarely at the light as at death." His strength lies in his power of acceptance: not of death but of responsibility for the attitude in which he approaches it, for the whole individual who exists until the trauma tears him apart.

Despite this strength, despite the moments of joy that sustain it, *The Wrong Side* is a bleak book, as lonely in the writing as in the subject. Its disjunctions of mood and image are more convincing than the rhetoric that connects them: Camus' voice grows confident only when it becomes ironic. In the year or two between its composition and that of *Nuptials,* his health revived, his unfortunate first marriage was dissolved, and he experienced an "overwhelming sense of life." The two books are as different as day and night. He no longer views the sun from the pit of despair or through the bars of estrangement. Rather than as a condemned man, he writes as a celebrant of his marriage with nature, of the "simple agreement," as he says elsewhere, "between the earth and the foot," and of his companionship with the Mediterranean "race born in the sun and the sea, alive and spirited." Written at a pitch of sensuousness, two of the essays, "Nuptials at Tipasa" and "The Wind at Djemila," contain the most imaginative prose that Camus was ever to write, as rich as D. H. Lawrence's in *Sea and Sardinia.* Even such statements as "the loving understanding between the earth and the man delivered from the human" are justified by the intensity of the communicated experience that embodies them. Thus, he writes of the beach at Tipasa, the wild scent of absinthe and roses, pine and cypress, the taste of peaches, the consummation of the skin with the sunlight and water, the "joy that descends from sky to sea." Coming from the sea, he throws himself down among the plants and inhales their scent. "I am fulfilling a truth which is the sun's and which will also be my death's." At Djemila the stone ruins of a Roman colony, the heavy, unbroken silence, and the tearing desert wind slowly evoke his sense of man's nakedness and vanity, which annihilates the mind "so that the truth which is its very denial may be born."

In "Summer in Algiers" Camus for the first time places the terms of his dialectic in a social context. He describes his city under its aspect of carnality: a city enamored of the body and its intense, violent, and brief pleasures, where the haste to live borders on the extravagant, where "a man has played all his cards by the time he is thirty." Under the spell of his own hedonism, Camus even views the absence of culture in Algiers as an augury of its future greatness and creativity. Here the dull brain neither perplexes nor retards: here people live without the usual hopes, myths, or consolations. In the lush Algerian landscape, ravished by the sun, he realizes that "only one thing is more tragic than suffering, and that is the life of a happy man." In a review of *Nausea*, written about this time, Camus faults Sartre for failing to realize that the true source of the absurd is that which exalts life rather than impugns it. "Without beauty, love, or danger it would be almost easy to live."

The concluding essay in *Nuptials*, "The Desert," applies the cult of the carnal to art. In Florence he discovers that the Tuscan masters are not concerned with the flickering play of consciousness but with the essential expression of a face; "the shape of its bones and the warmth of its blood. What they have expelled from these faces molded for eternity is the curse of the mind: at the price of hope. For the body knows nothing of hope," etc. The work of art, like the unmediated life, is a stripping down to truth: the Franciscan monks of Fiesole who live among flowers and meditate over human skulls, the sun worshippers on the beaches of Algiers, even the incest and rapacity of the Italy of the Borgias, all testify to the same "fierce and soulless grandeur," the same "resolve to live" that Piero della Francesca places on the face of his risen Christ. Full living and expressing begin with beauty and lead past the far side of morality to a point of awareness at which "the heart is closed" and the mind "feeds on nothingness." It is in this "desert," the one that Rimbaud found in Abyssinia, that the healing springs of indifference begin to flow.

On this pure nihilistic note, *Nuptials* ends. As the rest of the essays in this volume demonstrate, it is as far as Camus was to go. He had reached the limits of his essentially positive nature: the point at which the inhuman demands more of man's creaturely existence than it can provide and the will of a Caligula begins its experiments. The essays in *Summer*, spanning the next fifteen years, represent a retreat from these demonic paradoxes. Dionysus gives way to Prometheus, nature to culture, the inhuman to the unjust, death to the death camps. The prejudice against mind becomes a prejudice in its favor: the mitigable suffering of men, the plague of violence that has overtaken Europe, desperately require it. Like Tarrou, the traveler who makes his sacrifice and stays in Oran during the plague, Camus found in the Resistance and in his work for the newspaper *Combat* an allegiance to the party of humanity that ended his long estrangement and redirected his temperament as an opponent of nihilism: the vocation on which he, like Gide, eventually based his pride in being a man. Thus the noble savagery of Algiers is displaced by the rationality, moderation, and "tragic optimism" of classical Greece as the center of the "Mediterranean culture" Camus brought north with him to Paris. Finally, his literary criticism, like his prose itself, grows progressively more austere and conservative; as though everything since Greek philosophy and drama represented to him either inspired imitations of their circumspect, measured approach to the great themes of human destiny, or else a falling away, the final collapse being the cult of personality and improvisation found in the writing of his time.

The civic stance and burdened tone of the later Camus, the excessive *mésure*, the clear loss of sensuousness are paralleled in his criticism. He rejects the perversities of modernism: "if the words 'justice,' 'goodness,' 'beauty,' have no meaning, then the world becomes absurd and men can tear each other to pieces." Language is not meant to express what is most personal in men but what is most strictly impersonal and closest to their common experience. If the novel is to revive, if it is ever again to present men in "their flesh and their duration," it will need to recall itself to this "higher banality." Similarly, the freedom of the artist, like that of the political rebel, lies in his recognition of limits. The secret of a

Stendhal or a Proust or, for that matter, a Sade is not originality but fidelity: an obstinate hewing to "a certain tone, a certain constancy of soul, and a human and literary knowledge of sacrifice."

We are back again with the familiar, public Camus. But we will be in much better touch with him if we keep in mind the young, solitary explorer of "the desert," who was no stranger, after all, to the author of *The Stranger*, *The Fall*, or the stories in *Exile and the Kingdom*. His final rebellion, against the power of the inhuman, began with his own character, and from it he acquired his own "knowledge of sacrifice." Or, as he wrote in the later preface to *The Wrong Side*: "In order to be created, a work of art must first of all make use of the dark forces of the soul. But not without channeling them, surrounding them with dikes, so that the water in them rises. Perhaps my dikes are still too high today. From this, the occasional stiffness. . . ."

(1968)

Autobiography as Art

We seem to be in the middle of a literary age in which the autobiographical impulse is as catching as a virus. In recent months there have been, for example, *The Double Helix*, *Making It*, *North Toward Home*, *Stop-Time*, and *The Armies of the Night*, books of varying purposes and qualities but whose lines of inquiry rely heavily on self-documentation. Meanwhile the contemporary novel has been taking on more and more subjective cargo as the realism of character and place gives way to the spontaneities of improvisation and fantasy, and contact with the world flows mainly across the arc of the novelist's obsessions.

Why there should be this sudden traffic in the revelations and imagery of the self is anybody's guess. Mine is that the faith in common, objective experience, in what one might call certified public reality, has reached an all-time low. This has opened the way to the belief that the only truths worth communicating about human affairs are those perceived in a personal, even idiosyncratic way, the more subjective the point of view, the more unconditioned and therefore valid the report.

Regularly conned as we all are by the agents and media of public reality, which is already difficult enough to grasp as it is, it is not surprising that writers should fall back on sincerity as the ground of truth. Autobiography gives direction to the enterprise, and witnessing, in both senses of the word, confession, and other modes of individual testimony are brought to bear. Directly behind cant, writers seem to be saying, lies the honest truth. Although such writing develops its own cant, a ready esteem for the offensive and daring, the aberrant and perverse, no one loses readers on that count since it then ministers to the kind of psychic voyeurism which, thanks to pop psychiatry, we confuse with insight.

In any event, the result of all this coming clean in print has been a mixed bag of edification and entertainment that would take the rest of this review just to begin to sort out. But, in brief, it has sprung and given new scope to comic talent such as Philip Roth's and has fostered a firm, clear note of contemporary pathos in a writer like Frank Conroy. It has beckoned Mailer on to create an immense checkerboard of perceptions and distractions in his account of the Pentagon demonstration. Carefully restrained, it can produce the pleasantly personal cultural journalism of *North Toward Home*, and, recklessly pursued, it can lead to the tendentious and purblind self-caricature of *Making It*. If there is any immediate moral to be drawn, it is that candor does not necessarily provide instant honesty or relevance. An exhilaration to one writer, it fosters doublemindedness, as Kierkegaard would say, in a second, and is clearly a burden to a third. And, like garlic, a little goes a long way, a truth that former ages, less preoccupied with candor and more with inwardness, were willing to accept, without appreciable loss to their knowledge of human nature. This was not just a matter of good taste and an unwillingness of readers to forgo their dignity in being addressed, a right that many have abandoned to keep up with literary fashions. Besides all that, candor is a very tricky motive: the product of malaise, as much as anything else, it is particularly vulnerable to the mutterings of those two conspirators of the ego, guilt and vanity, that establish the "line" we hand ourselves and others. As such, candor requires a great deal of the complexity and effort of art to support its claims to truth.

All of which is prologue to my admiration for V. S. Pritchett's A *Cab at the Door*, the best 250-odd pages of autobiographical writing that I know of by a living author. What makes it so good is that Pritchett is, first of all, a master of the natural, direct style. As with Thoreau or Shaw, open any page and you are immediately in touch with the man. Or, as Pritchett has said of E. M. Forster, when he begins to speak the machine stops.

A *Cab at the Door* is written with plenty of candor, but it is also written with something even better, which is artistic tact. Reversing the customary procedure in contemporary autobiography, Pritchett places at the center of his memoir a solid and deliciously detailed commentary on lower-middleclass English life in the first two decades of the century, based on his family, educational, and early business experience; meanwhile he modestly lays around the rim the account of his own troubled development as a person and of his inchoate intentions as an artist.

The effect is a beautifully sustained priority of interests in which the depiction of concrete social conditions and forces, of manners and mores, stands by itself as a portrait of an age and a class, while serving as the ground that outlines the formation of his character. This not only places the emphasis where most readers would wish to see it—on the way things were rather than how they felt, on the individual life seen less through its accidents than as common experience—but also enables Pritchett, both as writer and as subject, to exist naturally and unselfconsciously among his interests and feelings. The result is a splendid montage of persons and places fixed in their individual being, casting their representative light, and suggesting the evolving personality of the author through his relations to them. By this kind of artistic strategy, mediating deftly between figure and ground, an autobiography turns into a life.

In his criticism, no less than in his fiction or travel writing,

Pritchett's great gift has been for characterization, the over-flow of relevant, vivid, surprising detail that actualizes a person, a place, a book. Pritchett among the hallowed dead of literature is like Odysseus in Hades: a little of the blood of his critical vitality, and even as spectral a figure as Samuel Richardson immediately begins to speak again and have his being. Still, one is unprepared for the dramatic sketches of the Pritchett family and the full, dominant portrait of his father. Moreover, if Pritchett brings to his autobiography the gifts and aims of a social novelist, he also belonged to a family that seems especially designed for this enterprise: a veritable treasure trove of individual types. Thanks to the adventurism of his father, whose field of wild oats was commerce—"one of nature's salesmen," as Pritchett delicately puts it, "he was even more one of nature's buyers"—the family lived in a good many different places and circumstances, one step ahead of its creditors. And since the boy was regularly being farmed out to relatives, he led a more picaresque youth than David Copperfield.

His formative influences began with the austerities of the north and the laxities of the south.

> On my mother's side they were all pagans, and she a rootless London pagan, a fog worshiper, brought up on the folklore of the North London streets; on my father's side they were harsh, lonely, God-ridden sea or country people who had been settled along the Yorkshire coasts or among its moors and fells for hundreds of years. There is enough in the differences between North and South to explain the battles and uncertainties of a lifetime.

So it proved, at least in the first twenty years recounted in *A Cab at the Door*. Family crises sent him frequently into his paternal grandfather's household. A man who had pulled himself out of poverty with one mighty lunge from the army and bricklaying into the ministry, he "looked like a sergeant-major who did not drink." His guides were Carlyle and Ruskin as well as the Gospel; a somewhat mellowed authoritarian by Pritchett's time, he urged his iron aspirations on his grandson, and whatever will to learning and self-improvement and independence Pritchett was to live out began with the influence of this solitary and hardheaded Dissenter. There was also his great-uncle Arthur, a cabinetmaker in York, who had literally taught himself to read with Burton's *Anatomy of Melancholy* and had made himself into an amateur naturalist and antiquarian. From these two resolute figures and their industrious households, one gets a feeling for the powerful religious and economic forces that had created mobility at long last in the working class and enabled it to make its first significant inroads into English culture.

Still, there was a long way to go, and Pritchett speaks of his grandfather as being like an immigrant, so strange to him was his place in the middle class. Exhausted by his early climb and devitalized by the vocation that had enabled it, he was eventually dominated by his fastidious and stuffy wife and by his own dream of status. Pritchett's father inherited the dream and the fastidiousness; in full flight from the rigidity and repressiveness of the minister's household, he became a premature gentleman, addicted to fashions and comforts that his exaggerated sense of opportunity and his superficial resourcefulness never quite earned for him and that had to be purchased at his family's expense. A softheaded businessman, a fantasist, his mobility was mostly circular, now tilting upward toward respectability, now downward into sordidness. His religious upbringing led him into various denominations, which he tried on for style, and eventually his obstinacy, expansiveness, and self-righteousness found an abiding stay in the teachings of Mary Baker Eddy, the "other woman" in his life. His relation with his wife, as Pritchett puts it, was "like a marriage of the rich and the poor." A sly, imaginative ex-shopgirl, she vaguely followed with her four children in the turbulent wake of her husband's career, wryly singing to herself "At Trinity Church I met me doom."

Needless to say, Pritchett grew up with deeply ambivalent feelings toward this flashy and unreliable father who still dominated his family in good Victorian fashion ("Until 1918," Pritchett remarks, "England was a club of energetic and determined parricides"). Early on, he can only helplessly accept his father's nutty glory: "We have no desire to see things like the pantomime or Peter Pan; other children see such shows, but we prefer to send Father there on our behalf; it will be one more chapter of his fantastic life." He wears cut-down striped morning trousers to another one of his slum schools, imbibes his father's myopic view of reality, even takes for a time to Christian Science. "No one else had (I was sure) our dark adventures. We were a race apart, abnormal but proud of our stripes, longing for the normality we saw around us."

But eventually he found he had his own singularities to cultivate. The first good teacher he encountered led him directly into literature and painting, a deviation which his father, hot for emulation, met with open contempt and secret jealousy. So began Pritchett's long struggle to work himself free of his father's ego, from commerce and religion, from the family mania for "getting on." Visits to his more stable and enlightened relatives helped. So did his busy life in the streets and schools of London and environs, a boy's first line of escape from a neurotic home.

His family settles for a time in Dulwich, Ruskin's neighborhood, and this patron saint of lower-class aspirations beckons him on. The great novelists also begin to offer him some solid ground. One day, in the peace and quiet of the countryside, a sense of purpose forms: "Money would have nothing to do with it. . . . The important thing was to be alone . . . and always walking and moving away." Prescient but still sad. He remarks on his poor performance in school, on his being "self-burdened," on "the dirty cunning and flightiness of my priggish nature"—that is to say, on being his father's son and suffering from two generations of the Non-conformist vertigo. That he will grow up to be V. S. Pritchett is less surprising at this point than the fact that he is growing up at all.

Yet his brother, who adored his father and therefore remained suitably dull, springs to life once he leaves home and returns from France a success in business. Such is the resilience and toughness of the human stuff. After four years spent in the relative sanity of the leather trade—here the book rises to the most sustained and luminous level of social observation—Pritchett is ready at nineteen to begin his own life in France. His father puts him on the boat train, still self-importantly fussing over him, the elder Pritchett's portly, almost sumptuous manner the mark of the dreamlike appetite that had seduced his own father and perverted himself. Exhausted by their anxieties, hatreds, conflicts, Pritchett has little to say to him; they watch two Italians, father and son, passionately embracing each other.

It is a moment of pure revelation: the profits and losses of the family's long climb into the middle class registered by the contrast. In his modest, unsentimental way, Pritchett quickly passes on to other matters and feelings, but this detail in its setting leaves behind for the reader, as does the memoir as a whole, a very clear sense of the difference between writing as self-display and writing that enables the self, through the tactics and tact of art, to arrive at its meanings.

(1968)

Holden Caulfield at Columbia

The Strawberry Statement is a journal by a sophomore at Columbia who was caught up in the events of last spring and, as they say, "radicalized." The title comes from a remark by one of the deans that a university is not a democracy, and that students' opinions on such matters as the Institute for Defense Analyses and the Morningside gym have about as much significance as their telling him they like strawberries. So, as one of the unruly plebeians of this modern Rome, James Simon Kunen sets about filling the authorities in on what he likes ("trees . . . wiliness in a good cause . . . nice policemen") and dislikes ("Texas . . . calling people consumers . . . racism, poverty, and war") and goes on to record "the little things I've done and thought" during the rebellion and for a few months thereafter. The early sections, dealing with the rebellion, were published in *New York* and the *Atlantic*, where they received a good deal of attention. Far from being a scrawny, sneering nihilist, Kunen showed himself to be a sort of mod version of the boy-next-door, a well-coordinated Holden Caulfield who has gone to Andover, rows on the varsity crew, has a lingering fondness for "that old fascist" Walt Disney, and worries a lot about looting and damage while occupying President Kirk's office.

Then, presumably, along came an editor hot for a book on the generation gap that even parents would read. Though

unimpressed by the opportunity ("this youth-cult scene is a
disservice to everyone," he says at the start), Kunen went on
filling up his spiral notebook while he hung around Columbia and the Movement for the rest of the summer, fell in
love, went on the Merv Griffin show, hitchhiked home to
Massachusetts, and drove up to Canada with his girl to look
into the draft-resister scene, which he did for about ten minutes. When the spirit moved him, he also interviewed Archi-
bald Cox, or Mark Rudd, or the program director of
WABC to find out why he wants to use his "50,000 watt
pump to pour such crap into the already polluted air." Finally, he added a few deflating remarks on the big, obliga-
tory issues—sex, drugs, and violence—and pocketed "the
coin" he tells us he has been desultorily pursuing. "The best,
truest way to read this book would be to rip it up and throw
the scraps all over the house. Then, later, when you come
across a piece read it, or don't read it, depending on how you
feel. . . . Above all don't spend much time reading it because I didn't spend too much time writing it."

All of which may seem like a pose—hip bravura—but it's
not; though it is a style, an audacity that wants to be firm
and clear. Kunen writes in a natural, articulate way that
conveys confidence in his own voice and attitudes, and little
else. Like most children of the educated middle class, he has
grown up expecting to be listened to, and though he is
ironic about his narcissism—"this ego-blast" of a book—he
is not inhibited by it. This keeps his writing directly personal
rather than pretentious—the vice of more intimidated generations—and makes him worth listening to. His language
is terse, his thoughts fragmentary and tentative, both keyed
to the immediacy of the here and now. Like Hemingway's,
the main function of his sensibility is to screen out the crap;
a practice he probably owes to growing up with TV:

Just heard that Walt Disney died . . . "and the world
mourns." It doesn't really, but it at least notices, which

is certainly some tribute. That would have been a comfort to Walt, as he lay dying. Of course, if he just dropped dead, then it wouldn't have been a comfort to him.

This matter-of-factness makes Kunen's tone seem representative and reliable. So does his account of himself. Before the April uprising at Columbia, his main experience with the left, as he says, was rowing port on the varsity crew. At the same time, the entries in his journal disclose that he was suffering from the malaise that is said to be common among the better students in the more high-powered schools. He has the lively mind, the gift of integrating all manner of information, of the born student, but by the end of his sophomore year still seems to be without a clue as to his proper direction. Though constantly rummaging through his thoughts to fill out his book, he almost never mentions a teacher or course he has had at Columbia, or instances any sense of connection with its fabled intellectual life. The most he can say is that "there is no mainstream of Columbia life. Columbia is a lot of meandering rivulets up which the students struggle, vainly attempting to spawn." The pressure to find a vocation, to "make something of yourself"—as we used to say, as I still say, haplessly, to my own semi-adolescents— doesn't appear to operate at all on Kunen and his friends, nor does the competition for grades, scholarships, admission to professional schools that went along with it.

Like poverty, affluence has its lessons to teach, however fatuous they may make us feel. Unless he has a strong economic motive, a felt sense of necessity, a college education doesn't make that much sense to a bright nineteen-year-old. Why should it? He has already been sitting in classrooms for fourteen years. Moreover, his energies and interests are focused on the life-problem of entering manhood, for which he needs the actual world, not an artificial one carved up into fields of study and presided over by distracted specialists.

Further, as *The Strawberry Statement* tells us, the privileges of Columbia students are sad and guilty, protecting them from an absurd and evil war which the rest of their generation must fight, sealing them off from an America of racism and poverty which begins two blocks away, and associating them with an institution that profits from war, racism, and poverty. The first impact that SDS had on Kunen appears to have been when Mark Rudd walked out of Columbia's memorial service to Dr. King, which, Kunen agrees, was "obscenely hypocritical" in view of the school's employment, real-estate, and research practices.

During his first two years of college, Kunen's main intellectual activity appears to have been an elaborate dormitory fantasy of an "alternate world-structure," in which the issues of existence are sharply defined and "the legions of evil bother to attack us." By the beginning of his sophomore year, he is indulging in small, private acts of violence, while waiting for a mythical letter that will tell him where he's at. Though living in New York adds to his sense of contactlessness, his correspondents at other schools are in the same uneasy boat, adrift on the dull estuary of campus life, exchanging letters which are full of collegiate chatter but whose secret message is: "still holding out."

All of which may be hard to take seriously, particularly if your go-getting days began before or during college. But Kunen's malaise is as real as the rest of him, and it helps explain why, when the buildings began to be occupied, he was one of those who entered and stayed. He more or less drifted into the initial protests, mainly in order to make some friends, but once inside Low Library and occupying Kirk's office, he is suddenly full of energy, purpose, resourcefulness. He stands watch, runs messages, hustles in food, participates in the discussions that decided virtually every step that was taken. Along with another student he takes apart a Xerox and fixes it so they can copy documents. As he says, "I'll do anything to feel like I'm doing something." Through most of the occupation he attends crew practice and even rows the final race of the season, then hurries back to his revolutionary post. He has his lows as well as highs—wondering at one point if the Paris Commune was so boring at times, or whether Lenin was so concerned about the breast size of his cohorts. He keeps insisting to himself that he is not one of the "sheep." Under some New Left graffiti he chalks, "I'm sorry about defacing the wall, but babies are being burned and men are dying, and this university is at fault quite directly."

The "jocks," the police, and the Columbia administration all play a part in strengthening Kunen's association with the rebels, but the main ground of his radicalism, once activated, is the war. As the rest of *The Strawberry Statement* indicates, Vietnam is never more than a thought away in his mind. When he hears that Bobby Kennedy has been shot, his immediate reaction is that "this is no novelty, you know, because people get shot every day, and bombed and burned and blown up. But no one cares about that." If he sees people coming out of church in a Boston suburb, he wonders which of them will be going to the office the next day "to work on maximizing kill-densities." His preoccupation with "Them" or "the Biggies" is typically fleshed out by his memory of the military brass gazing down at the demonstrators from the roof of the Pentagon, or by the vacant yet obdurate words of President Johnson:

> Doesn't he know anything? Do statistics hide the truth and keep him from feeling? When I see statistics I practically throw up, I can never forget. It's in me that my friends every day hear gunfire and see others fall and hate the enemy. But when they see the ground spin up at them and feel the wetness of their own blood, whom do you think they hate then?

As his journal moves along, Kunen loses much of his initial despair. He attributes this to his growing anger, which the Columbia uprising and repression helped to set free and to focus. He seizes on a remark that the university has instituted its own pacification program, for the behavior of the Kirk administration indicates to him the hollow and blindly coercive authority that makes a mockery of our claims in Vietnam. He becomes attentive to the little ways that the multiversity, the warfare state, and the consumer economy fit together. He delivers enraged speeches on militarism and racism to his journal. He considers the possibility of becoming a "pro-revolutionary," though he seems unable to find anyone in the New Left that he agrees with. He no longer gets his hair cut before going home: long hair is the "peace Thing," and he wants to be identifiable.

He finds it works the other way as well. He goes to Fenway Park, where the year before the Red Sox had climbed from last place to first, winning the pennant in the final game of the season. And, poignantly enough, that baseball team still stands in his mind as the only real embodiment of his values: "happiness, enthusiasm, courage. . . . Because of them I could talk to anybody at all and share something and be together and understand. . . . They were something people would open to you for." But now his long hair and his Columbia T-shirt make him feel out of place and resented. He ponders the change in himself—or, rather, the complication. Watching baseball and rooting for your team is a good thing: "people doing something they like and enjoying themselves and not hurting anybody . . . is being free and happy just a little and it's very opposite to fighting wars." On the other hand, caring too much about such problems as Yastrzemski's slump makes you forget about other things: "the starvation and death which must be stopped before Yaz's next home run can truly be cause for joy."

As of last summer, when the journal ends, Kunen had put his final shred of allegiance to the System on Senator McCarthy. Where he's "at" now, I don't know: though probably still with the people who flash V's rather than flags. The latter practice disturbs him—"It's a real down to get bad vibrations from your flag"—for he has strong feelings of patriotism, though for another America than the one that surrounds him:

> There used to be a dream in America . . . America was going to be different . . . free and good. Of course, they blew it right away. As soon as the Puritans came over they set up religious laws. But at least they clung to the dream. Until now. Now no one hopes for America to be different. I guess it was the dream that ruined the dream. People thought the U.S.A. (a great-sounding, nice, informal name) was special so we could do anything and it's okay. . . . I wish people would wake up and dream again.

Along with a country he can respect, he wants a community in which the brief brotherhood he felt with other Red Sox fans is a permanent possibility. It would be hard to find a better example of the natural outcropping of anarchist sentiment among the young than *The Strawberry Statement*. It permeates Kunen's growing hostility to all forms of reification and manipulation, to everything "mass" that denatures and dehumanizes the social bond; by the same token, it permeates his bias in favor of the self-regulating cooperative, the comradely instincts that he found springing up in himself and his fellows in the brief commune of Low Library. I doubt if Kunen has read a page of Kropotkin or, for that matter, Paul Goodman; but if he gets over the idea that "the book writers are not where it's at," he should read them because they are where he's at. On the whole, his independence of spirit does him honor, but I hope that he, like many of the best of his generation, won't allow it to impoverish his understanding.

(1969)

Saul Bellow: The Lines of Resistance

One afternoon a few years ago I was returning to New York from a lecture I had given. The subject was recent Jewish writing: Bellow, Malamud, Roth: aspiration, suffering, spiritual discovery, and so forth. My audience had risen to the "theme," as suburban Jewish ladies will, and, rocked along by the Long Island Railroad, I was still bemused and touched by the mood of idealism I had induced. The soft facts of life are not to be discounted, I thought; otherwise why has man developed sentiments? It's only a matter of refining them, of educating the impulses to be good and true. The other solitary passengers in the car, I imagined, carried the same "counsels of the heart" that I had been talking about and that were stirring in my own. Then, moved to place more of the world within my transforming awareness, I looked out the window.

There were the outskirts of Queens. It was about four of a winter afternoon, the sky about thirty feet up, the flats looking like a testing ground for biological warfare, the horizon smoking away. Then the train passed a town: impacted files of bungalows and long slabs of brick two-families, a huddle of gas stations around an intersection, an all-purpose shopping center, then the wasteland again. What had been swamp twenty-five years ago was now a community, but everything conveyed a sense of the grimness of things, as though only the tenacity of the inhabitants kept such places from sinking back into the landfill of ashes and garbage. All of it seemed terribly remote to my vision and obdurate in its own: its aspirations were expressed by the TV antennas, its values were "property" and "Blue Book." Queens was the social contract writ large, and, placed against it, any better scheme of life seemed evanescent. Go tell it to the owners of those brick two-families, shouldered together like a team making a goal-line stand, protecting those few feet of lawn in the back. "The counsels of the heart"? My own heart sank. And who was I to say they were wrong—the millions of them? So they would never read Saul Bellow. . . .

All of which came back to me as I was reading *Mosby's Memoirs*, a new collection of Bellow's stories. Hot for uplift, I had apparently missed the basis. Not that Bellow isn't a humanist but that he is also a realist: his fiction begins about the point where my little shock of recognition left off: the resistance, density, intractability of normal life. This is why his imagination is so strong. It has to be: it encompasses and lifts the full weight of a man's existence. This, in turn, is why his characters are so real: Joseph, Leventhal, Wilhelm, Henderson, Herzog, whose principle might be, "I am burdened, therefore I am." In "A Father-to-Be" a young research chemist rides the subway to dine with his expensive Jewish princess of a girlfriend and finds himself studying with disgust a smug middle-aged man in a stylish overcoat and blue suede shoes: the very prototype, Rogin realizes with horror, of what their prospective son would be like in forty years:

> What a vision of existence it gave him. Man's personal aims were nothing, illusion. The life force occupied each of us in turn in its progress toward its own fulfillment, trampling on our individual humanity, using us for its own ends like mere dinosaurs or bees, exploiting love heartlessly, making us engage in the social process, labor, struggle for money, and submit to the law of pressure, the universal law of layers, superimposition.

The beginning is Schopenhauer, the ending is pure Bellow. The law of pressure, layers, superimposition: that is how he builds up figure and ground, so that Rogin's ride on the IRT on a Sunday night becomes as effortful and portentous as a bad dream.

As most of these stories indicate, Bellow has an extraordinary ability to enter directly into the mixed conditions of a particular life or experience and conduct the reader toward a general truth embedded in it. Three of the six stories—and they are the three that matter most; they may well be masterpieces—mine the ore of common life: a mismatched old woman in the Utah desert trying to hold on to her house and independence; a white intellectual trying to deliver relief checks in the Black Belt; the rise and strife of an immigrant Jewish family. But each of them is far from commonplace. Against the dullness, stupidity, hopelessness of Hattie's struggle in the Utah desert, against the terrific vacuousness and gloom of the Chicago ghetto during the Depression, against the stridency and acquisitiveness of the Braun family, a steady and searching pressure of consciousness is exerted, encompassing and at the same time animating, preserving things both in their literalness and multivalence. In "Looking for Mr. Green," George Grebe searches in one of the Negro tenements:

> He began to climb to the third floor. Pieces of plaster ground under his feet; strips of brass tape from which the carpeting had been torn away marked old boundaries at the sides. In the passage, the cold reached him worse than in the street; it touched him to the quick. The hall toilets ran like springs. . . . Then he struck a match in the gloom and searched for names and numbers among the writings and scribbles on the walls. He saw WHOODY-DOODY GO TO JESUS, and zigzags, caricatures, sexual scrawls, and curses. So the sealed rooms of pyramids were also decorated, and the caves of

human dawn. The information on the card was, TUL-
LIVER GREEN—APT. 3D. There were no names, however,
and no numbers.

Along with the clarity of observation, an imaginative idea is
working through this material like yeast in dough, and eventually it will make the story rise, as the passage itself does, to
indicate something of the inner truth of our human relationships and to restate it in action. The decay of the tenement,
the regression to the primitive cave-like conditions of shelter, the atavistic markings, the gloom, the anonymity stand at
one extreme; the ex-classicist Grebe and his address-cards and
checks at the other. The social nexus between them has collapsed, revealing in a particularly naked form what Grebe's
erudite boss refers to as "the fallen world of appearances."
This is the terrain that Grebe must cross, full of fantasy and
tension, for the "faltering of organization [has] set free a
huge energy, an escaped, unattached, unregulated power
from the giant raw place." At the beginning of the story,
Grebe feels he might as well be looking for Mr. Green in the
jungle, but—as he comes to realize, and this makes him
press on in his search—the adversity of appearances is an aspect of the general fate in a city like Chicago, where neighborhoods such as this one rise and fall into ruin every fifty
years. Amid so much flux, what then abides?

> Objects once so new, so concrete, that it could [not]
> have occurred to anyone they stood for other things, had
> crumbled. Therefore, reflected Grebe, the secret of them
> was out. It was that they stood for themselves by agree-
> ment, and were natural and not unnatural by agreement,
> and when the things themselves collapsed the agreement
> became visible.

As one of his other clients helps him see, this "agreement" is
a function of human trust—and need: "the need that keeps
so many vast thousands in position." The reality system is no

different, finally, from the money system. When Grebe finally finds Mr. Green's address, he is met by a naked, drunken, obscene, angry woman who refuses to identify herself. But having learned what he has learned, Grebe gives her the check: she stands for Mr. Green and Grebe has to trust too.

This metaphysics of the human tie, as Grebe scornfully reminds himself, is pretty remote to the immediate conditions in this jungle of blight between Cottage Grove and Ashland. In the face of such misery, he can only mark the honest direction of his imagination—the question of whether "there is *something* that is dismal and permanently ugly" in the human covenant—and press on to deliver his very real check. As Norman Podhoretz points out in a concise and trenchant reading of the novels up to *Herzog* (in *Doings and Undoings*), Bellow's social and political bias has been pretty much the neo-conservative one, with which Podhoretz associates his pessimism, his refusal to arraign the institutions that produce his characters' malaise, his damming up and deflection of rage, and his tendency to end his dark novels on an upbeat note: recently, that of love. The detection of this bias is accurate but to ask Bellow to drop it and to adopt a more radical one is to ask him to turn his art, and the ideas and emotions that support it, upside down. What Bellow knows before he knows anything else—knows in his bones—is the settled weight and ambiguity of existence, both inner and outer. It is precisely from this feeling for the accumulation of circumstance, contingency, error, conflict, paradox, anomaly, *as an individual experiences it*, that he derives his amazing descriptive power—a power, incidentally, that makes *Seize the Day* the best criticism of the money culture, as it affects the middle class, that I know of. To open his art to meliorative politics would be to rob it of its specific gravity and to place Bellow outside his own sense of the perdurable and the changing from which he draws his clues to the "axial lines" of a life and its place in the scheme of things. He is at heart an essentialist: man and his nature are absolutes and what is most true is what most preserves a man in his emotions and duration and kind. To the "law of layers, superimposition," Bellow has no solution: but the mastering emotion he prescribes and through which he conducts his protagonists is clearly not love, as Podhoretz says, but grief: the active kind, that lifts some of the burden of mismanagement off the spirit and allows it to breathe.

Take Hattie Simmons Wagoner, a "city woman," still proud of her Philadelphia connections, her china, linen, engraved stationery, who has been eking out an existence for twenty years at Sego Desert Lake, with the local Indians and Mexicans, the dudes from the nearby ranch, the six white residents. Mistress of a long-departed cowboy, companion and servant to another old divorcee, whose house she has inherited, Hattie is a "character": a "cheerful, plugging, absent," and hard-drinking old woman of seventy-two, who keeps her canned goods on her library shelves and more than anything else wants "to be thought of as a rough, experienced woman of the West." One day, driving drunk and fast as usual, she stalls her car on a railroad crossing, and while it is being towed off, her arm is broken. She tries to go on against the odds, which include a record of dependency, fantasy, procrastination, dispersion, but the pain and impairment from her injury have brought on senility and the harsh, testing way of life in the desert has become too much for her. Yet she is unable to leave her house and its belated satisfaction, unable to live with her stuffy brother, unable to accept old age and death. Like her car, she is stalled at the crossing. Her plight whips her through the gamut of emotions—rage, resentment, regret, grief—and forces her toward the belated recognition of the borrowed, jerry-built structure of her life: "I was never one single thing anyway. . . . Never my own. I was only loaned to myself." Wanting to make at least the final gesture of responsibility, to sign her unbalanced account with a flourish of pride, she sits down to make her will and give away her house. But soon drunk again, her mind staggering from one unsatisfactory beneficiary to the next, she once more assails what she knows to be sensible and proper, and leaves her house to herself.

Now, to draw a moral (the retributions of sloth and illusion) or to extract a social meaning (the neglect of the aged) is to lose the immediacy and life-meaning of Hattie's batty and poignant will to live, of the intricately related processes by which she succors as well as defeats herself. It is also to dislodge the figure from the ground—Bellow's beautifully rendered mixture of the pseudo-frontier and the exigent desert community where the reality principle still rules. Finally, it is to denature his art, whose power derives from his grasp of the primary emotions and essential issues of a life and which culminates, like Tolstoy's, in an image of the necessary, of the way things are.

Finally, there is "The Old System," Bellow's most recent story and a high point in his career. An immigrant Jewish family chronicle, it is written with an authority of observation and insight that enables its forty-odd pages to outstrip almost all the fiction that has come to burden this subject. One lazy Saturday, the traditional day of rest and re-entry, Dr. Braun, a ranking geneticist, finds himself meditating on his two cousins from upstate New York, Isaac and Tina Braun, the one "born to be a man in the direct Old Testament sense," who trusted the old system of the patriarchs and became a millionaire, the other, a harsh, obese, rapacious woman who trusted nothing, hated her brother's success, and eventually forced him to bring $20,000 when she was dying of cancer in order to be reconciled with her. Now they are both dead. What did all that energy and effort and emotional tumult signify? Dr. Braun reviews the circumstance and events, looking for the patterns of causation, the general human implications "within the peculiar system of light, movement, contact, and perishing in which he tried to find stability." Heredity and nurture, cultural transmission, ego psychology, recent social history, even astronomy offer their perspectives, framing his idea that these two hostages he has given to death represented "Necessary existence." But the main point that is revealed about their respective lives is the emotional core: deep, solid, old-fashioned in Isaac; volatile, manipulative, modern in Tina.

"Oh, these Jews—these Jews! Their feelings, their hearts. He often wanted nothing more than to stop all this." But whether direct or devious, natural or undergoing the modern perversions, quietly spinning a destiny or making a circus out of dying, emotions are what Dr. Braun, having grieved, in his fashion, for his cousins and buried them again, finds himself left with: messy, uncertain data alongside the molecular processes, yet humanity's vague clue to "why life, why death," and its possible link to "the great begetting spasm billions of years ago" that cast the stars outward. As the cold-eyed but bitterly moved scientist puts it to himself: "Material details were of the greatest importance. But still the largest strokes were made by the spirit. Had to be."

(1969)

Philip Roth: A Personal View

One day in the fall of 1957, I was sitting in a course on Henry James at the University of Chicago. The semester had just begun, and there were a few new faces: one that I had been noticing belonged to a handsome, well-groomed young man who stood out in the lean and bedraggled midst of us veteran graduate students as though he had strayed into class from the business school. The text for the day was *Daisy Miller*, and toward the end of the hour, one of the other students began to run away with the discussion, expounding one of those symbolic religious interpretations of the story that were in fashion at the time everywhere but at Chicago. Eventually the instructor asked me what I thought of this reading, and in the rhetoric I had learned from my mentors among the Chicago critics, I said that it was idiotic. I was immediately seconded by the debonair young man, who, in a very precise and concrete way, began to point out how such a reading turned the purpose and technique of the story inside out. Like two strangers in a pickup basketball game who discover they can work together, we passed the argument back and forth for a minute or two, running up the score of common sense. It was one of those fine moments of communication that don't occur every day in graduate English courses, and after class we met, shook hands, and exchanged names. His was Philip Roth.

So began a relationship. Since we were leading complicated, busy, and quite different private lives, our paths didn't
cross that much. But almost each time they did, a connection
was made and the current flowed. Though I was five years
older than Roth, we were rather alike in temperament—aggressive, aloof, moody, and, as graduate students go, worldly.
We also had a number of things in common that turned us on
to each other. We were from roughly the same background—
the practical, coarse, emotionally extravagant life of the Jewish middle class—as well as from neighboring cities in northern New Jersey. So there was an easy, immediate intimacy of a
more or less common upbringing—Hebrew schools and
YMHA's, the boardinghouses and boardwalks of Belmar and
Bradley Beach, the Empire Burlesque House in Newark; the
days and ways of possessive Jewish mothers and harassed Jewish fathers; the pantheons of our adolescence where Hank
Greenberg, John Garfield, Norman Corwin, and Longy
Zwillman, the outstanding racketeer in Essex County, were
enshrined; and so many other "Jewish" artifacts, experiences,
nuances of feeling and attitude, about which we found ourselves to be about equally nostalgic and contemptuous, hilarious and burdened. At the same time, we were both involved
in the similar journey from the halfway house of semi-accul-
turation, whose household deity was neither Sholom Aleichem nor Lionel Trilling but someone like Jack Benny, into
the realm of literature and culture. In our revolt against the
exotic but intransigent materialism of our first-generation
bourgeois parents, we were not in school to learn how to earn
a living but to become civilized. Hence our shared interest in
James. And, finally, we both thought of ourselves as writers
who were biding their time in the graduate seminars we took
and the freshman composition courses we gave. Hence our
quick hostility toward any fancy, academic uses of James.

All of which meant that we were also somewhat wary of
each other. Since each of us served as an objectification of the
other's sense of position and purpose, we spent a lot of time

secretly taking each other's measure, comparing and contrasting. Also I had more or less stopped writing, except for term papers, while Roth was writing all the time and was getting published. One of his stories had even been anthologized in a Martha Foley collection; two others had just been bought by *Esquire*; and he was also doing movie reviews for the *New Republic*. After a quarter or so Roth dropped out of graduate school in order to concentrate on his fiction; meanwhile I slowly forged on through the second year of the Ph.D. program. To our other roles came to be added those of the creative writer and the critic, respectively.

During this year I read several of the stories in manuscript that were to appear two years later in *Goodbye, Columbus*. Raised as I had been, so to speak, on the short-story-as-a-work-of-art, the cool, terse epiphanies of the Joyce of *Dubliners*, the Flaubert of *Un Coeur simple*, of Katherine Mansfield and Hemingway, I didn't at first know how to respond to a story in which the narrator says:

> Though I am very fond of desserts, especially fruit, I chose not to have any. I wanted, this hot night, to avoid the conversation that revolved around my choosing fresh fruit over canned fruit, or canned fruit over fresh fruit; whichever I preferred. Aunt Gladys always had an abundance of the other jamming her refrigerator like stolen diamonds. "He wants canned peaches. I have a refrigerator full of grapes I have to get rid of. . . ." Life was a throwing off for poor Aunt Gladys, her greatest joys were taking out the garbage, emptying her pantry, and making threadbare bundles for what she still referred to as the Poor Jews in Palestine. I only hope she dies with an empty refrigerator, otherwise she'll ruin eternity for everyone else, what with her Velveeta turning green, and her navel oranges growing fuzzy jackets down below.

But my resistance quickly toppled like tenpins. It was like sitting down in a movie house and suddenly seeing there on the screen a film about the block on which I had grown up: the details of place, character, incident all intimately familiar and yet new, or at least never appreciated before for their color and interest. This story of Neil Klugman and Brenda Patimkin was so simple, direct, and evident that it couldn't be "art," and yet I knew that art did advance in just this way: a sudden sweeping aside of outmoded complexities for the sake of a fresh view of experience, often so natural a view and so common an experience that one wondered why writers hadn't been seeing and doing this all along. The informal tone of the prose, as relaxed as conversation, yet terse and fleet and right on the button; the homely images of "stolen diamonds," of the Velveeta, and the oranges, that make the passage glow. Such writing rang bells that not even the Jewish writers had touched; it wasn't Malamud, it wasn't even Saul Bellow: the "literary" fuzz of, say, *Augie March* had been blown away, and the actualities of the life behind it came forth in their natural grain and color, heightened by the sense of discovery.

Such writing is much more familiar today than it was ten years ago: indeed, it has become one of the staples of contemporary fiction. But at the time the only other writer who seemed to be so effortlessly and accurately in touch with his material was Salinger. For a year or so after reading *Catcher in the Rye*, I hadn't been able to walk through Central Park without looking around for Holden and Phoebe Caulfield, and now here was this young semblable of mine who dragged me off for a good corned-beef sandwich or who gave me a push when my car wouldn't start, and who, somehow, was doing for the much less promising poetry of Newark, New Jersey, what the famous Salinger was doing for that of Central Park West. Moreover, if Roth's fiction had something of Salinger's wit and charm, the winning mixture of youthful idealism and cynicism, the air of immediate reality, it was also made of tougher stuff, both in the kind of life it described and in the intentions it embodied. Salinger's taste for experience, like that of his characters, was a very delicate one; Roth's appetite was much heartier, his tone more aggressive, his moral sense both broader and more decisive.

What fascinated me most about stories like "Goodbye, Columbus," "The Conversion of the Jews," and "Defender of the Faith" was the firm, clear way they articulated the inner situation we sensed in each other but either took for granted or indicated covertly—by a reference to Isabelle Archer as a *shiksa*, or by a takeoff on the bulldozing glottals of our father's speech, as we walked away from our literature or linguistics course. In such ways we signaled our self-ironic implication in things Jewish, but Roth's stories dealt directly with the much touchier material of one's efforts to extricate himself, to achieve a mobility that would do justice to his individuality. Social mobility was the least of it. This was the burden of "Goodbye, Columbus," where Neil Klugman's efforts early in the story to latch and hold on to the little wings of Brenda Patimkin's shoulderblades and let them carry him up "those lousy hundred and eight feet that make summer nights so much cooler in Short Hills than they are in Newark" soon take on the much more interesting, and representative, struggle to have her on his own terms, terms that lie well beyond money, comfort, security, status, and have to do with his sexual rights and ultimately his uncertain emotional and moral identity. At the end of the story, Neil stands in front of the Lamont Library and at first wants to hurl a rock through the glass front; but his rage at Brenda, at the things she had been given and has sacrificed him for, soon turns into his curiosity about the young man who stares back at him in the mirrored reflection and who "had turned pursuit and clutching into love, and then turned it inside out again . . . had turned winning into losing and losing—who knows—into winning. . . ."

Neil's prickly and problematic sense of himself, his resistance to the idea of being a bright Jewish boy with an eye for the main chance, for making sure, an idea that was no stran-

ger to other desires—well, this was not simply fiction to me.
Nor was the Patimkin package, where horse shows and Big
Ten basketball and classy backhands still came wrapped in
Jewish conformity and ethnocentricity. In story after story
there was an individual trying to work free of the ties and
claims of the community. There was Ozzie in "The Conversion of the Jews," who would not have God hedged in by
the hostility of Judaism to Christianity; there was Sergeant
Marx in "Defender of the Faith," who finally refused to
hand over any more of his sense of fairness and responsibility
to the seductive appeals of Jewish solidarity; or, on the other
hand, there was Eli Peck, who refused to close the book of
Jewish history to be more at ease with his landsmen in Suburbia. Or there was even poor Epstein, who managed to pry
apart the iron repressions of Jewish family life to claim some
final gratifications for himself. Or there was my special favorite, a very early story called "You Can't Tell a Man by the
Song He Sings," in which a nice Jewish boy learns from two
Italians—a juvenile delinquent and an ex-radical guidance
teacher—that some dignities have to be won against the rules
and regulations of upward mobility.

Such themes were as evocative to me as a visit from my
mother, but I knew that I couldn't write the stories that embodied them in the way that Roth had. It was not just a
matter of talent but of the intricate kind of acceptance that
joins one's talent to his experience so that he can communicate directly. Though Roth clearly was no less critical of his
background than I was, he had not tried to abandon it, and
hence had not allowed it to become simply a deadness inside
him: the residual feelings, mostly those of anxiety, still intact
but without their living context. That is to say, he wrote fiction as he was, while I had come to write as a kind of fantasist
of literature who regarded almost all of my actual experience
in the world as unworthy of art. A common mistake, particularly in the overliterary age of the late Forties and Fifties, but
a decisive one. So if I envied Roth his gifts, I envied even

more his honesty, his lack of fastidiousness, his refusal to write stories that labored for a form so fine that almost any naturalness would violate it. The gross affluences and energies of the Patimkins, the crudities of Albie Pelagutti and Duke Scarpa, even the whining and wheedling of Sheldon Grossbart turned him on rather than put him off. Once, I remember, I balked. There is a scene in "Epstein" where his wife discovers his rash that they both believe is venereal, and an ugly and not very funny description follows of their fight in the nude. "Why all the *schmutz?*" I asked him. "The story is the *schmutz,*" he snapped back.

Our relationship had its other ups and downs. After he dropped out of graduate school, Roth went on teaching in the college, an impressive post to me, if not to him (he was to give it up after a year and head for New York). And since he was publishing his work and looked to be making good use of his bachelor years, he seemed, at least on the surface (which was where my envy led me to look), to have the world by the tail. On the other hand, the world in those days seemed, at least on the surface, to have me by the tail. I was taking three courses at Chicago and teaching four at Indiana University Calumet Center, a glum building around which lay the oil refineries and steel mills to which most of my students returned from our discussions of Plato and Dante. On my salary of $3000 a year it was not easy to support my wife and two small boys. But, having wasted a number of years after college, I felt that I was getting somewhere. My students were challenging, to say the least, and some of the charm of scholarship had unexpectedly begun to descend upon me. Still the fact remained that Roth was visibly well off and I was visibly not, and it made certain differences. At one point I borrowed some money from him, which made us both uncomfortable until it was paid back. One evening he and his date, my wife and I, went to hear a lecture by Saul Bellow—our literary idol —and afterward went out for a beer. His girlfriend, though, ordered a scotch, and into the discussion of what Bellow had said and could have said there intruded an awkward moment at each round of drinks. Or there was a party he came to at my place to celebrate the arrival of bock beer (our version of the rites of spring). As I've suggested, Roth and I shared our past and our opinions much more than we shared our present lives. When we met, it was almost always at his place. My apartment, over in the Negro section, with its Salvation Army decor and its harassed domesticity, seemed both to touch him and make him nervous. I remember him sitting on the edge of a couch, over which I had just nailed an old shag rug to cover the holes, waiting like a social worker while my wife got our oldest son through his nightly asthma. Then the other guests arrived, the beer flowed, and we turned on with our favorite stimulant—Jewish jokes and caustic family anecdotes—dispensed principally by Roth, whose fantastic mimicry and wit soon had us rolling in our chairs.

That evening came back to mind a few years later when I was reading Roth's first novel, *Letting Go*, which is set mainly in Hyde Park and which deals with the ethos of the graduate-student/young-instructor situation during the Fifties: the "Age of Compassion," as Gabe Wallach, the protagonist, aptly puts it. The story mainly follows Wallach's involvement with Paul and Libby Herz, a needy young couple (money is only the beginning of it), and with Martha Reagenhart, a voluptuous and tough-minded girl who has two children to support and who is looking for some support herself. Attracted both by Libby's frailty and by Martha's strength, and unable to make much contact with the surly Herz, Wallach, an attractive bachelor in comfortable circumstances, spends much of the novel sitting on the edge of his scruples, worrying whether too much or too little is being asked of him, a dilemma he shares with Herz, whose moral self-consciousness takes over whenever the point of view shifts to his side of the story. All of this reckoning of the wages of conscience is accompanied by cool, satirical observation, more successfully of the Jewish background of Gabe and

Paul than of their professional life, which Roth used mostly
to even a few scores. The best writing in the book came in
the scenes in a Detroit boardinghouse when Herz's effort to
push Libby through an abortion gets tangled up with the
schemes of the retired shyster, Levy, to "help" the pathetic
Korngold extract money from his son and to move the cases
of underwear that Korngold hoards in his room, waiting for
the market to improve.

Like a good many other citizens of Hyde Park, my wife and
I furnished a trait here, an anecdote there, but the material
was more thoroughly fictionalized in our case than in some
others. What Roth was mainly drawing on, I felt, was a certain depressiveness that had been in the air: the result of
those long Chicago winters, the longueurs of graduate school
and composition courses, the financial strains, the disillusion-
ment with the university (this was the period in which the
Hutchins experiments were being dismantled and the administration was waging a reign of respectability in all areas), and
the concomitant dullness of the society-at-large, which had
reached the bottom of the Eisenhower era. But mostly this
depressiveness was caused by the self-inflicted burdens of private life, which in this age of conformity often seemed to
serve for politics, art, and the other avenues of youthful experience and experiment. One of the principal occupations in
Hyde Park seemed to be difficult marriages: almost everyone
I knew was locked into one. This penchant for early marriage
and child-rearing, or for only slightly less strenuous affairs,
tended to fill the vacuum of commitment for sophisticated
but not especially stable young couples and fostered a rather
pretentious moralism of duty, sacrifice, home therapy, experiment with domestic roles—often each other's—working
things out, saving each other. It was a time when the deferred
gratifications of graduate school and the climb to tenure and
the problems of premature adjustment seemed the warranty
of "seriousness" and "responsibility": those solemn pass-
words of a generation that practiced a Freudian/Jamesian

concern about motives, pondered E. M. Forster's "only connect," and subscribed to Lionel Trilling's "moral realism" and "tragic sense of life." In contrast to today, everyone tried to act as though he were thirty.

Some of this Roth had caught and placed at the center of *Letting Go.* As the title suggests, the novel is a study of entangling attachments, beginning with Gabe's effort to release himself from his widowed father's possessiveness and ending with his frantic effort to complete, and thereby end, his intervention in the life of the Herzes, through helping them to adopt a child. In between, a host of characters push and pull, smother and neglect each other, usually under the guise of solicitude or obligation. At one point Wallach puts it for himself, Herz, and most of the others: "I knew it was not from my students or my colleagues or my publications, but from my private life, my secret life, that I would extract whatever joy—or whatever misery—would be mine." By "private life" he means relationships and their underlying *Realpolitik* of need, dependency, and control.

It was evident that *Letting Go* represented a major effort to move forward from *Goodbye, Columbus.* The theme of communal coerciveness and individual rights that dominates most of the stories had been opened out to deal with the more subtle perversions of loyalty and duty and creaturely feeling that flow through the ties of family, marriage, friendship. A very Jamesian theme: *The Portrait of a Lady* figures almost immediately in *Letting Go,* as a reference point for its interest in benevolent power plays. Also, in bringing his fiction more up to date with the circumstances and issues of his life, Roth had tried for a more chastened, Jamesian tone. The early chapters have some of the circumspect pace and restrained wit of the Master: well-mannered passages of nuance and implication, the main characters carefully observed, the theme tucked neatly away in the movement of action, thought, and dialogue. The book sails gracefully along for about 150 pages or so. Then it begins to turn as gray and bitter as the Chicago winter and, in time, as endless.

What went wrong? As I have indicated, the Hyde Park we had known had not been an especially chipper place, and there was plenty of reason to deal with it in terms of its grim domesticity. Still, Roth had laid it on and laid it on. If Gabe and Martha have the Herzes for dinner, the mutual strains will be as heavy as a bad Ph.D. oral, and afterward Gabe and Martha will fight about who paid for what. If Paul's passion for Libby revives at a party, it will cool before they can get around the corner. If some children are encountered at a playground with their grandmother, it is because their mother has just tried to flush herself down a toilet bowl at Billings Hospital. In this morbid world, sibling rivalry leads to homicide, intermarriage to being abandoned by both the Catholic and Jewish families, adoption proceedings to a nervous breakdown. Not even a stencil can get typed without fear and trembling.

All of which added up, I felt, not only to an exaggeration of the conditions but to an error of vision. I wondered if this *error* might have something to do with the surface view we had of each other's lives: his apparent fortune, my apparent misfortunes: clearly the germ, at least, of the Wallach-Herz relationship. As I was subsequently to realize, my view of him that year was full of misapprehensions: behind the scenery of ease and success he had been making his payments to adversity: a slipped disc, for one thing; a tense and complicated affair, some aspects of which were to figure in Gabe's relationship with Martha. On the other hand, behind the scenery of adversity in a life like mine, there were positive purposes and compensations that he had not taken into account, and that made the struggle of those years tolerable and possibly significant. Though Wallach is a scholar and Herz a novelist, they might as well be campus watchmen for all the interest they have in their work, in ideas, even in their careers. While this ministers to the central concerns of the novel, it deprives both of them of force and resistance, for, stripped of any aggressive claim on the world, they have little to do but hang around their women and guiltily talk about "working it out" —the true title of the novel. The only character who has any beans is Martha, which is partly owing to the fact that, having two children to support and raise, her life intentions are to some degree objective. Otherwise there are only the obsessive, devouring relationships and the malaise they breed: Libby perpetually waiting to be laid, Paul reminding her to put on her scarf, Gabe consumed by his sense of his obligations and his distrust of it, Martha demanding that payment be made for satisfactions given. From such characters, little natural dynamic can develop, and Roth can only forge on and on in his relentlessly bleak way: now analytic, now satirical, now melodramatic—giving Libby an adopted baby, Paul a religious turn, Martha a dull, dependable husband, and Gabe a wild adventure in Gary with the extortion-minded husband of the girl who bore the baby—none of it especially convincing, none of it quite able to lift up and justify the burden of the pessimism.

In his essay on "Some of the Talent in the Room" Norman Mailer wagered that the depressiveness of *Letting Go* had to do with Roth's "working out an obsession." This seemed to me a shrewd observation, though who in these days of obsessive fiction would 'scape hanging. In *Letting Go* the obsession is with the power of women along with a male queasiness about it that keeps both Herz and Wallach implicated, endlessly looking for moral means to cope with their emotional vulnerability. As Wallach, for example, remarks at one point:

There must be some weakness in men, I thought (in Paul and myself, I later thought) that Libby wormed her way into. Of course I had no business distrusting her because of *my* weakness—and yet women have a certain historical advantage (all those years of being downtrodden and innocent and sexually compromised) which at times can turn even the most faithful of us against them. I turned slightly at that moment myself, and was repelled by the sex toward which at bottom I have a considerable attachment.

This sort of observation hardly leads to insight or movement. It merely maintains an ambivalence by shunting the anger involved off on some courtly, literary track and letting the historical situation of women screen the personal guilt, the deep characterological misery that keeps men like Herz and Wallach in place and wide open. As the novel wears on, the anger if not guilt is more and more acknowledged in Wallach's case, as his priggishness is worn down by Martha and some of his true feelings begin to emerge. Still, the problem of coping with Libby and Martha, posited in moral terms that make it insoluble, nags away at the two men and their author. What they can't "let go" of is guilt, and it drags the book down with them.

When *Letting Go* came out, I was working at *Commentary*, a job that had come my way as the result of an essay that the *TLS* had asked me to write on Roth's recommendation. Since he hadn't liked the essay at first and since I was as touchy as Paul Herz proved to be about such matters as gratitude and pride, there had been a falling out. In New York, however, the relationship resumed, and with fewer of the disparities and diffidences that had made it tense and illusionary. As time went on, there were also reasons to level with each other: we were both separated, both in analysis, both in a state of flux. So we would get together, now and then, for dinner, and talk about problems and changes. One evening I dropped by his new place on East Tenth Street to borrow a book. It was bigger and much better furnished than mine, and he wanted me to know—screw the guilt—he intended to be comfortable here and to sink some new roots. But, for all that, the place looked as bare and provisional as mine: we might as well have both been living in tents, neither of us

bachelors so much as husbands *manqué*. A portable type-
writer was sitting on the dining-room table, and a lot of
manuscript pages were spread around it.

"What's that?" I asked.

"It's a novel." He looked at it without much pleasure.
"I've written it once, and now I'm writing it again."

It was strange to realize that he, too, got hung up. I had
always assumed that he was like Chekhov, who said that he
wrote "as easily as a bird sings."

Perhaps he noticed my silly smile. "You know something?"
he said. "There's not a single Jew in it." He went on about
the strangeness of imagining, really imagining, a family that
was not a Jewish family, that was what it was by virtue of its
own conditioning and conditions, just as the Jews were, but
which were not just those of "the others"—the Gentiles.
Something like that—though he put it, as always, more concretely—acting out, with that gift of mimicry that was always
on tap, the speech and the slant of some small-town citizen of
middle America.

The novel, of course, turned out to be *When She Was
Good*, two years, and several more revisions, later. It was easy
to see why the book had been a trial for Roth to write. Liberty
Center is so far from his line of territory that everything had
to be played by ear, so to speak. The town hardly exists as a
place, as something seen in its physical actuality; it is rather
the spirit of the American Protestant ethic circa 1948, whose
people and mores, interests and values, emerge from the impersonation of idiom and tone: Liberty Center as it might
have been presented not by Sinclair Lewis but by Ruth
Draper. In order to bring this off, Roth had had to put aside
his wit, color, and élan, keep his satirical tendency tightly in
check, and write the novel in a language of scrupulous banality. This impersonality was far removed from the display of
temperament that animated "Goodbye, Columbus" as the
life of the bitchy heroine, Lucy Nelson, so meager and so
arduous, is from that of the bitchy Brenda Patimkin.

Yet, for all the improvisation and guesswork, the surface of *When She Was Good* is solid and real, and though true to the dullness of Liberty Center's days and ways, it is beautifully constructed to take on momentum and direction and to hit its target with shattering impact, like some bland-looking object in the sky that turns out to be a guided missile. As in *Letting Go*, the theme is the wages of possessiveness and self-righteousness, but as embodied by and embedded in Lucy Nelson's raging, ball-breaking ego, it takes on a focus and power that had dissolved in the miasmic male earnestness of the previous novel. There is no false gallantry or temporizing about Lucy. Any ambivalence has been burned away, and Roth presents her and her will to power dead-to-rights. Because of this sureness of feeling, he can also present her in the round—terrible when crossed but touching in her aspirations and inexperience, her baffled need for a fathering trust, the victim as well as the avenger of her grandfather's wishy-washy Good Samaritanism, of her parasitic father's disgrace and her mother's passivity, of the family's stalled drive for respectability, and, eventually, of her husband's arrested adolescence. But from the moments early in the novel when Lucy turns in her drunken father to the police and then bars his way back into the family, the blind force of her aggression, screened by her faith in duty and responsibility and in her moral superiority, begins to charge the novel and to shape her destiny. She is unable to break off her romance with Roy Bassart until she has him safely installed in photography school and thereby ends up pregnant. She refuses the abortion she herself sought when it is offered by her father and when she learns that her mother had had one. She enters into a shotgun marriage with Roy, whom she has come to despise, with herself holding the gun. At each turn of her fate, skillfully paired with another and better alternative, it is Lucy's master emotion—her rage against her father—that directs her choice as surely as Nemesis. And some years later, when her father writes home from the jail he has landed in and thereby pulls her mother away from marriage to a man Lucy can finally respect, she turns it all against Roy in a climactic outburst of verbal castration, and then lets loose the furies of self-righteousness that drive her to madness and death. Like her grandfather's demented sister who had to be sent back to the state hospital because she followed Lucy to school and created a public nuisance, Lucy has been unable to understand "the most basic fact of human life, the fact that I am me and you are you."

In telling Lucy's story as circumspectly as he could, Roth has placed it within a context of cultural factors. Her grandfather had come to Liberty Center to escape from the brutality of the northern frontier, and the town stands in his mind, as it comes to stand in the reader's, as the image of his desire: "not to be rich, not to be famous, not to be mighty, not even to be happy, but to be civilized." Though Lucy rejects the tepid Protestantism on which Willard stands fast, she worships at the same shrine of propriety, which is the true religion of Liberty Center, and whose arbiters are the women. If men like her father and her husband founder in the complexities of society, it is the women who are supposed to straighten them out. They are the socializing agents, and the town's football stars and combat heroes, its reprobates and solid citizens, alike bow to their sway. When the high-school principal says to Roy and Lucy, "So this is the young lady I hear is keeping our old alum in line these days," he is referring to the community norm which Lucy will carry to an extreme.

Still, the cult of Momism in Liberty Center hardly added up to a pressing contemporary note, and the novel tended to be dismissed by most of the influential reviewers as slight, inauthentic, retrograde, or otherwise unworthy of Roth's talents. Coupled with the mixed reception of *Letting Go*, his reputation was slipping. Moreover, as much as I liked *When She Was Good*, it was further evidence that he was locked into this preoccupation with female power which was carrying his fiction into strange and relatively arid terrain. I knew that he had been writing plays in the last few years and had spent a lot of time watching the improvisations of the Second City Group—another part of our Chicago days that had accompanied us to New York—and I wondered if his own theatricality would lead him in that direction. But we seldom saw each other during this time. I was editing *Book Week* during the long newspaper strike, hadn't written anything for a year, and was going through a crisis or two of my own, and if we met at a party or something, we exchanged a word or two and looked around for more cheerful company. I remember thinking that we had both come a long way since Chicago —much of it out to sea.

A few months after *When She Was Good*, Roth published a sketch in *Esquire*. It was a memoir of a Jewish boyhood, this time told to an analyst, and written with some of his former verve and forthrightness. Even so, it ventured little beyond a vein that had been pretty well worked by now: the beleaguered provider who can't even hold a bat right; the shatteringly attentive mother; the neglected, unhappy sister; the narrator, who is the star of every grade and the messiah of the household. In short, the typical second-generation Jewish family; and after all the writers who had been wrestling with it in the past decade or two—Herbert Gold, Wallace Markfield, Bruce Jay Friedman, Arnold Wesker, Mordecai Richler, Irwin Faust, Roth himself, to name only a few—Roth's latest revelations were hardly news. Nor did a psychoanalytic setting seem necessary to elicit the facts of Jack Portnoy's constipation or Sophie's use of a breadknife to make little Alex eat. After five years of reading manuscripts at *Commentary*, such stuff was coming out of my ears. Perhaps Roth was only taking a small writer's vacation from the labor that had gone into his last novel or returning to the scene of his early success for a quick score. I hoped so.

But soon after came "Whacking Off" in *Partisan Review*: hysterical, raw, full of what Jews call self-hatred; excessive in all respects; and so funny that I had three laughing fits before I had gone five pages. All of a sudden, from out of the blue and the past, the comedian of those Chicago sessions of nostalgia, revenge, and general purgation had landed right in the middle of his own fiction, as Alex Portnoy, the thirteen-year-old sex maniac.

Jumping up from the dinner table, I tragically clutch my belly—diarrhea! I cry, I have been stricken with diarrhea! —and once behind the locked bathroom door, slip over my head a pair of underpants that I have stolen from my sister's dresser and carry rolled in a handkerchief in my pocket. So galvanic is the effect of cotton panties against my mouth—so galvanic is the *word* "panties"—that the trajectory of my ejaculation reaches startling new heights: leaving my joint like a rocket it makes right for the light bulb overhead, where to my wonderment and horror, it hits and hangs. Wildly in the first moment I cover my head, expecting an explosion of glass, a burst of flames—disaster, you see, is never far from my mind. Then quietly as I can I climb the radiator and remove the sizzling gob with a wad of toilet paper. I begin a scrupulous search of the shower curtain, the tub, the tile floor, the four toothbrushes—God forbid!—and just as I am about to unlock the door, imagining I have covered my tracks, my heart lurches at the sight of what is hanging like snot to the toe of my shoe. I am the Raskolnikov of jerking off—the sticky evidence is everywhere! Is it on my cuffs too? In my *hair?* my *ear?* All this I wonder even as I come back to the kitchen table, scowling and cranky, to grumble self-righteously at my father when he opens his mouth full of red jello and says, "I don't understand what you have to lock the door about. That to me is beyond comprehension. What is this, a home or a Grand Central station?" ". . . privacy . . . a human being . . . around here *never,*" I reply, then push aside my dessert to scream "I don't feel well—*will everybody leave me alone?*"

And so on. A few minutes later Alex is back in his kingdom, doubled over his flying fist, his sister's bra stretched before him, while his parents stand outside:

"Alex, I want an answer from you. Did you eat French fries after school? Is that why you're sick like this?

"Nuhhh, nuhhh."

"Alex, are you in pain? Do you want me to call the doctor? Are you in pain, or aren't you? I want to know exactly where it hurts. *Answer me.*"

"Yuhh, yuhhh—"

"Alex, I don't want you to flush the toilet," says my mother sternly. "I want to see what you've done in there. I don't like the sound of this at all."

"And me," says my father, touched as he always was by my accomplishments—as much awe as envy—"I haven't moved my bowels in a week." . . .

This was new, all right, at least in American fiction—and, like the discovery of fresh material in *Goodbye, Columbus*, right in front of everyone's eyes. Particularly, I suppose, guess, of the "Jewish" writers' with all that heavily funded Oedipal energy and curiosity to be worked off in adolescence—and beyond. And having used his comic sense to carry him past the shame that surrounds the subject of masturbation, and to enter it more fully than I can suggest here, Roth appeared to gain great dividends of emotional candor and wit in dealing with the other matters in "Whacking Off." The first sketch maintained a distance of wry description between Portnoy and his parents, but here his feelings—rage, tenderness, contempt, despair, and so on—bring everything up close and fully alive. And aided by the hard-working comedy team of Jack and Sophie Portnoy, the familiar counters of Jewish anxiety (eating hamburgers and french fries outside the home leads directly to a colostomy; polio is never more than a sore throat away; study an instrument, you never know; take shorthand in school, look what it did for Billy Rose; don't oppose your father, he may be suffering from a brain tumor) become almost as hilarious as Alex's solo flights of passion. Against the enveloping cloud of their fear and possessiveness, his guilt, and their mutual hysteria, still unremitting twenty years later, Alex has only his sarcasm and, expressive phrase, private parts. He summons the memories of his love as well as of his hate for them, but this only opens up his sense of his vulnerability and, from that, of his maddening typicality:

> Doctor Spielvogel, this is my life, my only life, and I'm living it in the middle of a Jewish joke! I am the son in the Jewish joke—*only it ain't no joke!* Please, who crippled us like this? Who made us so morbid and hysterical and weak? . . . Is this the Jewish suffering I used to hear so much about? Is this what has come down to me from the pogroms and the persecutions? Oh my secrets, my shame, my palpitations, my flushes, my sweats! . . . Bless me with manhood! Make me brave, make me strong! Make me *whole!* Enough being a nice Jewish boy, publicly pleasing my parents while privately pulling my putz! Enough!

But Portnoy had only begun to come clean. Once having fully entered his "Modern Museum of Gripes and Grievances," there was no stopping him. Or Roth. Having discovered that Portnoy's sexual feelings and his "Jewish" feelings were just around the corner from each other and that both were so rich in loot, he pressed on like a man who has found a stream full of gold—and running right into it, another one. Moreover, the psychoanalytic setting had given him now the freedom and energy of language to sluice out the material: the natural internal monologue of comedy and pain in which the id speaks to the ego and vice versa, while the superego goes on with its kibitzing. At the same time, Portnoy could be punched out of the analytic framework like a figure enclosed in cardboard and perform in his true role and vocation, which is that of a great stand-up comic. Further, those nagging concerns with close relationships, with male guilt and female maneuvering, from his two novels could now be grasped by the roots of Portnoy's experience of them and could be presented, not as standard realistic fare, but in a mode that was right up-to-date. If the background of *Portnoy's Complaint* is a classical Freudian one, the foreground is the contemporary, winging art and humor of improvisation and release, perhaps most notably that of Lenny Bruce.

In short, lots of things had come together and they had turned Roth loose. The rest of *Portnoy* was written in the same way—as series of "takes"—the next two of which were published in *New American Review*, the periodical which I was now editing. It may be no more than editorial bias speaking here, but I think these are the two richest sections of the book. "The Jewish Blues" is a sort of "coming of age in Newark, New Jersey," beginning with the erotic phenomena of the Portnoy household and carrying through the dual issue of Alex's adolescence: maleness and rebellion. On the one hand, there are those early years of attentively following Sophie Portnoy through her guided tour of her activities and attitudes, climaxed by a memory of one afternoon when, the housework all done "with his cute little assistance," Alex, "punchy with delight" watches his shapely mother draw on her stockings, while she croons to him "Who does Mommy love more than anything in the whole wide world?" (a passage that deserves to live forever in the annals of the Oedipal Complex). On the other hand—"Thank God," breathes Portnoy—there are the visits with his father to the local bathhouse, the world of Jewish male animal nature, "a place without *goyim* and women [where] I lose touch instantaneously with that ass-licking little boy who runs home after school with his A's in his hand. . . ." On the one hand, there is the synagogue, another version of the dismal constraints and clutchiness of home; on the other, there is center field, where anything that comes your way is yours and where

Alex, in his masterful imitation of Duke Snider, knows exactly how to conduct himself, standing out there "as loose and as easy, as happy as I will ever be. . . ." This is beautiful material: so exact in its details, so right in its feeling. And, finally, there is the story of his cousin Heshie, the muscular track star, who was mad about Alice Dembrowsky, the leggy drum majorette of Weequahic High, and whose disgraceful romance with this daughter of a Polish janitor finally has to be ended by his father, who informs Alice that Heshie has an incurable blood disease that prevents him from marrying and that must be kept secret from him. After his Samson-like rage is spent, Heshie submits to his father, and subsequently goes into the Army and is killed in action. But Alex adds his cause to his other manifold grounds of revolt, rises to heights of denunciation in the anti-Bar Mitzvah speech he delivers to Spielvogel ("instead of wailing for he-who has turned his back on the saga of *his people*, weep for your pathetic selves, why don't you, sucking and sucking on that sour grape of a religion"); but then is reminded by his sister of "the six million" and ends pretty much where he began.

Still circling back upon other scenes from his throbbing youth, as though the next burst of anger or grief or hysterical joking will allow him finally to touch bottom, Portnoy forges on into his past and his psyche, turning increasingly to his relations with the mysterious creatures called "shiksas" as his life moves on and the present hang-ups emerge. His occupation is that of Assistant Commissioner of Human Opportunity in the Lindsay Administration, but his preoccupations are always with that one thing his mother didn't give him back when he was four years old, and all of his sweet young Wasps, for all of their sociological interest, turn out to be only an extension of the fantasies of curiosity and self-excitement and shame that drove Alex on in the bathroom. Even "the Monkey," the glamorous fashion model and fellow sex maniac, the walking version of his adolescent dream of "Thereal McCoy," provides mostly more grist for the relentless mill of his narcissism and masochism. All of which Portnoy is perfectly aware of, he is the hippest analysand since Freud himself; but it still doesn't help him to give up the maddeningly seductive voice inside his head that goes on calling "Big Boy." And so, laughing and anguishing and analyzing away, he goes down the road to his breakdown, which sets in when he comes to Israel and finds that he is impotent.

I could go on writing about *Portnoy*, but it would be mostly amplification of the points I've made. It's a marvelously entertaining book and one that mines a narrow but central vein more deeply than it has ever been done before. You don't have to be Jewish to be vastly amused and touched and instructed by *Portnoy's Complaint*, though it helps. Also you don't have to know Philip Roth to appreciate the personal triumph that it represents, though that helps too.

(1969)

Index

Theodore Solotaroff

Theodore Solotaroff was born in 1928 in Elizabeth, New Jersey, and grew up there. He was educated at the University of Michigan and the University of Chicago, where he also taught. He has been an associate editor of *Commentary* and the editor of *Book Week*. In 1967 he founded *New American Review*, the paperback literary journal published by New American Library. His essays and reviews have appeared in the *New Republic*, the *Atlantic Monthly*, the London *Times Literary Supplement*, and other periodicals. He is the editor of *An Age of Enormity*, a posthumous collection of essays by Isaac Rosenfeld, and of *Writers and Issues*, a collection of topical essays of the Sixties.